PRESENTED TO:

WAYNE SAUNDERS

FROM:

_____

DATE:

_____

BILLY GRAHAM

PEACE
for Each Day

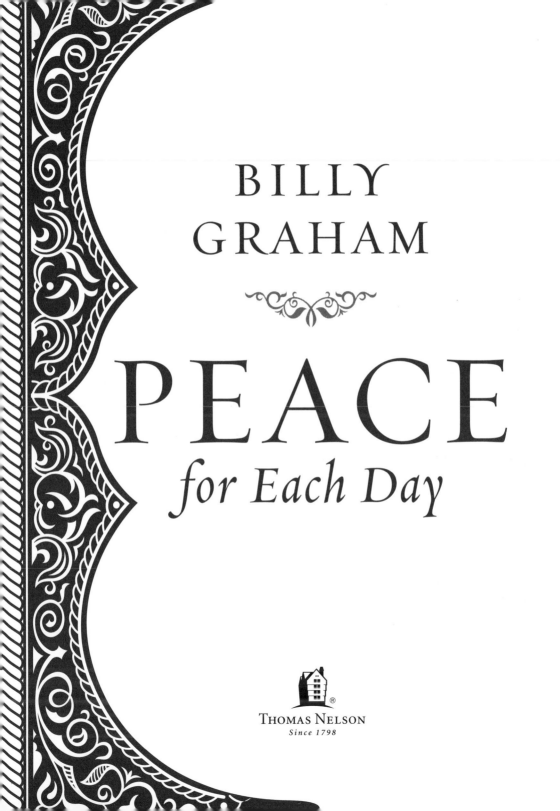

THOMAS NELSON
Since 1798

Published in Nashville, Tennessee, by Thomas Nelson. Thomas Nelson is a registered trademark of HarperCollins Christian Publishing, Inc.

Thomas Nelson titles may be purchased in bulk for educational, business, fund-raising, or sales promotional use. For information, please email SpecialMarkets@ThomasNelson.com.

ISBN: 978-1-4002-2411-1
ISBN: 978-1-4002-2452-4 (audio)
ISBN: 978-1-4002-2447-0 (eBook)

Printed in India

20 21 22 23 24 RPI 10 9 8 7 6 5 4 3 2 1

January

A NEW RESOLUTION

"Consider your ways . . . and build the temple."
HAGGAI 1:7–8

People by nature build, tear down, and rebuild. We build our hopes, get disappointed, and then search for renewed hope. That is why we are fond of New Year's resolutions. They are very popular in our culture today, though most are seldom kept. We get busy; we forget; we fail. Making resolutions, though, at least forces us into a moment of honesty about our need to change.

The Bible tells us to examine ourselves before the Lord. When we do this with sincerity, the Lord reveals where we fall short. This turns us back to God and helps us realize that we are incapable of living lives pleasing to Him apart from His help day by day, hour by hour.

Have you taken inventory lately? Have you considered where you stand with God? As you begin this new year, return to the Lord and consider Him—the One who gives you everything. Consider your ways and build on His foundation. "And in this place," the Lord says, "I will bring peace" (Haggai 2:9 NLT).

What is one area you are seeking God's help this year?

_____

_____

PREPARING FOR THE FUTURE

Having been built on the foundation of the apostles and prophets,
Jesus Christ Himself being the chief cornerstone.

EPHESIANS 2:20

I t's easy to focus only on physical well-being or emotional happiness as we prepare for the future. It is not necessarily wrong to be concerned about some of these things. But is this all it takes to prepare?

The answer is no; even the securest financial plan and the finest health care aren't enough to hold us steady when the challenges come. Will a full bank account satisfy you when disability takes away your freedom or death robs you of someone you love? Will robust health shield you against the storms of loneliness or grief? We need a solid foundation beneath our lives—a foundation that will give us strength and stability no matter what happens. And the time to build it is now.

God does not want us to drift aimlessly through life, desperately seeking happiness and security and peace—but never finding them. Nor does He want us to build our lives on an unstable or impermanent foundation. God has already provided the foundation we need!

What is one step you can take today to build your foundation on God?

THE GIFT OF PRAYER

Be anxious for nothing, but in everything by prayer and supplication, with
thanksgiving, let your requests be made known to God; and the peace
of God . . . will guard your hearts and minds through Christ Jesus.
PHILIPPIANS 4:6–7

P rayer is one of our greatest privileges as God's children. Think of it: the God of the universe wants us to bring every concern to Him! I have never met anyone who spent time in daily prayer, studied God's Word regularly, and was strong in faith who was ever discouraged for very long.

Does God always answer our prayers the way we wish? No, not necessarily—nor has He promised to do so. He sees the whole picture, but we don't. Sometimes He says "No" or "Not now." But God has promised to hear us when we pray and to answer our prayers in His time and in His way (1 John 5:14).

Prayer isn't just asking for things we want. Prayer is really a place where you meet God in genuine conversation. True prayer includes thanking and praising Him for who He is and all He does.

No matter how dark and hopeless a situation may seem, never stop praying. We cannot afford to be too busy to pray.

How can you readjust your schedule to spend time praying today?

_____

_____

THE GIFT OF SERVICE

*As each one has received a gift, minister it to one another,
as good stewards of the manifold grace of God.*

1 PETER 4:10

Just as our bodies need exercise to be strong physically, our faith needs exercise if we are to be strong spiritually.

It has often been noted that several rivers flow into the Dead Sea, but no river flows from it. That's why its water has become so saturated with minerals over the centuries that nothing is able to live in it. Without any outlet it indeed has become a "dead" sea. The same is true with us. If we keep faith to ourselves, if we never allow it to flow through us to enrich others, and if it has no outlet, then we will find ourselves like the Dead Sea—lifeless and spiritually dead.

God wants to use you right where you are. Every day you probably come into contact with people who will never enter a church or talk with a pastor or open a Bible. You may be the bridge God uses to bring them to His Son, the Lord Jesus Christ. Anyone can be a servant, no matter how inadequate he or she may feel.

How can God's love flow through you in someone's life?

NOURISHED BY THE WORD

This Book of the Law shall not depart from your mouth, but you shall meditate in it day and night, that you may observe to do according to all that is written in it. For then you will make your way prosperous.

JOSHUA 1:8

Strengthening our spiritual roots begins with God's Word.

A wonderful friend of ours, Robert Morgan, wrote a little book about Bible memorization and stated, "Our minds are vaults especially designed to stockpile the seeds of God's Word." In his book, he tells the story of an eighty-nine-year-old woman in his church who said, "Oh, Pastor Morgan, I'm so glad you are having us memorize [Bible] verses. I've already gotten started on them. It's going to help me keep my mind fresh and young!"[1] It made me smile to realize that she would keep her mind fresh and young . . . she had not allowed it to get old. There is no better deposit to make in the human mind and heart than to fill them with the treasures found in the Word of God.

Are the truths of God nourishing your root system? We must never cease being filled with the abundant gifts from God that bring hope and satisfaction.

Which Bible verse will you memorize today?

_____

_____

WISDOM FOR GENERATIONS

*Let no one despise your youth, but be an example to the believers
in word, in conduct, in love, in spirit, in faith, in purity.*

1 TIMOTHY 4:12

The apostle Paul wrote these words as an aged man, counseling his spiritual son, Timothy, to grab hold of scriptural doctrines and teach them to the young *and old*. Here is a wonderful picture of God's truth impacting one generation to another. This is God's wisdom; this is His master plan.

My prayer is that you will sense God encouraging you to impact those around you, regardless of age. Look for the Lord's purpose in every face or voice you encounter daily, for the time He has given you is not without purpose. Prepare for each day by asking the Lord to open your eyes to what is going on around you. You may feel lonely, but perhaps the Lord will use your smile to draw someone else close to you. You may experience pain, but the Lord may use your resolve to strengthen another who doesn't have the will to go on. We can reject the opportunity to be used of God, or we can seize opportunities to impact others as a testimony to Him.

How does the Lord give you direction?

_____

_____

FAITH BEYOND UNDERSTANDING

*Nicodemus said to Him, "How can a man be born when he is old? Can
he enter a second time into his mother's womb and be born?"*
JOHN 3:4

Even though the new birth seems mysterious, that does not make it untrue.
Most people don't understand how electricity operates, but we know that
it lights our homes and runs our televisions and radios. Most do not understand
how the sheep grows wool, the cow grows hair, or the fowl grows feathers—but
we know they do. We don't have to fully understand, but we accept by faith the
fact that at the moment we repent of sin and turn by faith to Jesus Christ we
are born again.

It is the implantation or impartation of divine nature into the human soul
whereby we become the children of God. We receive the breath of God. Christ
through the Holy Spirit takes up residence in our hearts. We are attached to
God for eternity. That means that if you have been born again you will live
as long as God lives, because you are now sharing His very life. The long-lost
fellowship man had with God in the garden of Eden has been restored.

Are you born again?

_____

_____

A CHANGE OF DIRECTION

I will instruct you and teach you in the way you should go;
I will guide you with My eye.

PSALM 32:8

The word *conversion* means "to turn around," "to change one's mind," "to turn back," or "to return." In the realm of religion, it has been variously explained as "to repent," "to be regenerated," "to receive grace," "to experience religion," or "to gain assurance."

I remember one confirmed alcoholic who came to one of the opening meetings of a crusade and said to me, "Mr. Graham, I'm not sure there's a word of truth in what you're saying, but I'm going to give your Christ a trial, and if He works even a little bit the way you say He will, I'll come back and sign up for life!"

Weeks later he told me that he didn't quite understand it, but every time he started to take a drink it seemed as though something or someone stopped him. Christ had given him victory over his vicious habit. He returned to his family and is now living his life for Christ. In other words, he turned around; he changed his way of thinking—he had been converted!

What habit do you need a victory over today?

_____

_____

REPENTANCE AND FAITH

From that time Jesus began to preach and to say,
"Repent, for the kingdom of heaven is at hand."
MATTHEW 4:17

When you fall in love completely with Jesus Christ, you will not want to do the things He hates and abhors. You will automatically renounce all the sins of your life when you surrender by faith to Him. Therefore, repentance and faith go hand in hand. You cannot have genuine repentance without saving faith, and you cannot have saving faith without genuine repentance.

Repentance is a very unpopular word. But the first sermon Jesus ever preached was "Repent, for the kingdom of heaven is at hand" (Matthew 4:17). This was God speaking through His Son. Jesus had come with a heart filled with love and compassion, but He immediately called upon men to acknowledge their guilt and turn from their ungodliness. He said repentance must come before He could pour out His love, grace, and mercy upon men. Jesus refused to gloss over iniquity. He insisted upon self-judgment, upon a complete about-face. He insisted upon a new attitude before He would reveal the love of God. This does not limit the grace of God, but repentance makes way for the grace of God.

Have you fallen in love with Jesus?

_____

_____

A CHRISTIAN VIEW OF THOSE WHO SUFFER

I know that the LORD will maintain the cause of
the afflicted, and justice for the poor.
PSALM 140:12

A Christian will be concerned about suffering humanity around him. The poverty and suffering of thousands of people in your own neighborhood will become a concern to you. You will join with organizations and associations to help alleviate the suffering of humanity around you. Many people spend so much time in lofty enterprises that they make no contribution to suffering immediately at hand. Who is our neighbor? Whoever is closest to us. It could be a wife, a husband, a child, or those living next door. Our neighbor is that one closest to us—in our city or country, then the world.

The Bible says the common people heard Jesus gladly. Wherever He went, He healed the sick. He comforted the sorrowful; He gave practical encouragement. Years ago, an Anglican bishop told me that he could think of no social organization in England that did not have its roots in some evangelical awakening. The Christian will be interested and dedicated to causes that help those who suffer in our world.

Who is your neighbor?

_____

_____

EVIDENCE IN SCRIPTURE

*And now I stand and am judged for the hope of the
promise made by God to our fathers.*
ACTS 26:6

I f I did not believe that Christ overcame death on the cross and bodily rose
from the grave, I would have quit preaching that the resurrection empowers faith in Jesus Christ. I am absolutely convinced that Jesus is living at this
moment at the right hand of God the Father. I believe it by faith, and I believe
it by evidence found in the Scriptures.

Luke, a physician and disciple of Jesus, was one of the most brilliant men
of his day; he made this startling statement about the resurrection in the book
of Acts: "He . . . presented Himself alive after His suffering by many infallible
proofs, being seen by them during forty days" (1:3).

These "infallible proofs" have been debated for two thousand years. Many
people have come to know the truth while they tried to prove Jesus' resurrection a lie. Others ignore the facts recorded in the best-selling book of all
time, the Bible. The bloodstained cross is gruesome, but the empty cross is full
of hope.

Do you believe in Jesus by evidence or faith or both?

_____

_____

GROWING STRONG

His divine power has given to us all things that pertain to life and
godliness, through the knowledge of Him who called us.

2 PETER 1:3

How can we develop a faith strong enough to see us throughout our lives? The key is this: God wants us to be spiritually strong and has provided us with every resource we need. We need God's strength to face life's challenges—and He wants to give it to us.

Tragically, many Christians never discover this. They have committed their lives to Christ . . . they may be active in their churches . . . they pray and read their Bibles on occasion—but they remain spiritually immature and weak in the face of life's temptations and setbacks.

We may be old in years, but if our faith is immature, we will be fearful and unprepared. But it doesn't need to be this way. Just as a baby needs food and exercise in order to grow, so we need the spiritual food and exercise God has provided for us. Without them our faith is weak, but with them spiritual strength increases, and we are better prepared for whatever life has in store for us.

What are you doing now that will make you spiritually mature when you're older?

_____

_____

THE GIFT OF GOD'S WORD

"I am the LORD your God, . . .
Who leads you by the way you should go."
ISAIAH 48:17

How does the Bible help us develop spiritually? First, it points us to the truth—about God, about ourselves, about the world, and most of all about Jesus and His love for us. The Christian faith isn't just a matter of personal opinion or unfounded optimism. It is rooted in the unchanging truth of God, revealed to us in the pages of His written Word. The Bible is the constant rain that waters our root system of faith.

How can we be sure we make right decisions in life? By applying biblical principles. The world has its own values and goals, but they will never give us the lasting security and peace we seek.

Don't be intimidated by the Bible or think it is impossible to understand. Even if you read only a few verses a day, God can still use it to reshape your life. Take advantage of opportunities to learn the Bible from others—your pastor, respected teachers on Christian radio, and Christian books; but never let these things replace your personal reading of Scripture. It is a priceless gift to you.

How are you incorporating Bible reading into your daily life?

_____

_____

THE GIFT OF THE HOLY SPIRIT

The Spirit Himself bears witness with our spirit that we are children of God.

ROMANS 8:16

When we come to Jesus, God Himself comes to live within us. We may not feel any different; we may be unaware of His presence; we may even doubt if anything has really happened to us. But it has. God now lives within us! He does this through His Holy Spirit. Although we can't see Him, He is that part of God who is working and active in our world.

Why does the Holy Spirit come to live within us? One reason is to assure us of our salvation. He came to help us discover God's will—to illuminate our minds and make us yearn for God. He takes spiritual truth and makes it understandable to us. The Holy Spirit also encourages and strengthens us in times of trouble. And He has come to change us from within, to make us more like Christ.

Don't try to live the Christian life in your own strength. Instead, turn to God in submission and faith, and trust His Holy Spirit to help you.

How does the Holy Spirit strengthen you?

_____

_____

THE GIFT OF FELLOWSHIP

We took sweet counsel together, and walked unto the house of God in company.
PSALM 55:14 KJV

We are not meant to be isolated from and independent of each other, either as human beings or as Christians. We need other people in our lives, and they need us. This is especially true as we seek to grow in faith. The Bible says, "Let us not give up meeting together, as some are in the habit of doing, but let us encourage one another" (Hebrews 10:25). A solitary Christian is inevitably a weak Christian because he or she is failing to draw strength from what God is doing in the lives of fellow brothers and sisters in Christ.

If you aren't presently part of a church fellowship, ask God to guide you to a church where you can grow in your faith through biblical preaching and teaching and worship. The church is a storehouse of spiritual food. This is where our souls are fed, nourished, and developed into maturity. It is there we can "encourage one another and build each other up" (1 Thessalonians 5:11 NIV).

Who are the people who encourage you in your faith?

_____

_____

THEN AND NOW

"I am going away. . . . If you loved Me, you would rejoice because I said, 'I am going to the Father.'"

JOHN 14:28

This old house is empty now, with mostly only me, the trees are crowding up the hill as if for company."[2]

These words reflected my late wife's thoughts after all the children were gone, what is now called *empty-nest syndrome*. Ruth simply called it *then and now*. I watched how she transitioned to this stage of life with grace.

God designs transitions and provides the grace to embrace what follows. When Jesus prepared to leave His earthly dwelling, He told His beloved disciples where He was going. And He gave them work to do: "Feed My sheep" (John 21:17). How wonderful that the Lord did not leave the world void of His presence but sent His Holy Spirit to be our constant companion.

While I will never grow accustomed to life without Ruth, she would be the first to scold me if I didn't look for God's plan for the *here and now*. I also know that God will guide us into whatever He has for us if we are watching and waiting attentively.

How has God's grace helped you navigate a difficult transition?

WORK WELL

Whether you eat or drink, or whatever you do, do all to the glory of God.
1 CORINTHIANS 10:31

Work is a part of God's plan for our lives. Work is not something we do just to put food on the table; it is one of the major ways God has given us to bring glory to Him. In God's eyes work has dignity and importance, which means we should do our work with pride and diligence and integrity.

But our work was never meant to become the center of our lives. That place belongs only to God, and when we allow our work to dominate and control us, then it has become an idol to us. Someone who brags about working seventy hours a week probably thinks he is the master of his job—but in reality he has become its slave. In addition, because his life is so wrapped up in work, his sense of self-worth often comes to depend on his ability to work. Society only reinforces this view. But God says you are greater than your work, and your work is only a part of His plan for you.

Have you allowed work to become the center of your life?

_____

_____

RECOGNIZE HIS VOICE

"My sheep hear My voice, and I know them, and they follow Me."
JOHN 10:27

I have never heard the voice of the Lord audibly, but the Lord has spoken to me many times throughout my life. You might ask, "How can someone recognize His voice?" To recognize the voice of the Lord, we must belong to Him.

Ruth never had to identify herself when she called me on my many trips around the world. When I picked up the phone and heard her speak, I knew the voice of my wife. That was years before mobile phones and caller ID. I never had to ask my children to identify themselves by name when they phoned. We recognize the voices of those who are dear to us and those with whom we commune.

Likewise, if we are communicating with the Lord Jesus through prayer and meditating on His Word, our spirits will identify with His voice. The Lord would not expect us to hear His voice if He did not make it possible. "I will give them hearts that recognize me as the LORD" (Jeremiah 24:7 NLT); and "Obey My voice, and I will be your God" (Jeremiah 7:23).

How does obedience help you hear the Lord's voice more clearly?

_____

_____

FOUNTAIN OF LIFE

The fear of the LORD is a fountain of life.
PROVERBS 14:27

Juan Ponce de León, the Spanish explorer who traveled at one time with Christopher Columbus, went in search of a magic water source that people called the Fountain of Youth. Instead, he found Florida—what became America's retirement haven.

The world's idea of a fountain of youth is a mirage. Only the Bible provides an oasis for the soul. If the "fear of the LORD is a fountain of life," we must first understand what "fear of the LORD" means. It is contrary to being afraid of Him. This is a reminder to be in reverential awe of God, to love Him with our whole being and commit ourselves joyfully to Him in all things.

Jesus sums it all up in the closing book of the Bible: "I will give of the fountain of the water of life freely to him who thirsts" (Revelation 21:6–7).

The fountain of life is real, friends. We can draw strength from its resources and stand strong in our resolve to be overcomers, looking forward to the inheritance and being in the presence of the Savior of our souls.

Are you thirsty today for God's love?

_____

_____

RESTORING PEACE IN RELATIONSHIPS

If it is possible, as much as depends on you, live peaceably with all men.

ROMANS 12:18

How do we restore a legacy that has been marred by something that may have happened many years ago, but continues to haunt us because it was never resolved? Often these have to do with broken relationships that have never been healed. Perhaps this has been true in your own life. If so, face it honestly, and do whatever you can to change it. As we grow older and look back over our lives, how will we view these unresolved conflicts?

"My mother and I always had a difficult relationship," one woman wrote me, "and for the last ten years we didn't even speak. Now she's gone, and I'd give anything to have just one minute with her to tell her I'm sorry." Whether it's with parents, children, friends, or family, a broken relationship often brings regret—regret over what happened, regret over the years that have been lost, regret because the time for healing has passed. Don't live with regret. As far as it depends on you, restore peace in your relationships.

Is there someone you need to reconcile with?

OLD AND NEW

I write no new commandment to you, but an old commandment
which you have had from the beginning.
1 JOHN 2:7

While we all benefit in some ways from modern technology, I wonder what state our world would be in if we suddenly lost electrical power. Would the younger generations know how to grow crops, or drop anchor and wait for the catch? Would they know how to survive by the sweat of the brow? New is good. Old is necessary.

The Bible has a lot to say about the old and the new. In today's text John is reminding his readers that the proof of knowing God is following the commandments that He gave long ago, that He gave "from the beginning." The love of God is then perfected in the one who obeys (1 John 2:5). Anything "from the beginning" is old, including God's love, present before the beginning of time. When man did not fathom the inexpressible love of God the Creator, He sent love down to earth in the form of His Son, the Lord Jesus Christ. Our redemption is rooted in Jesus' sacrifice of Himself, keeping us firmly planted.

How does it affect your sense of peace knowing that the Lord is beyond time?

_____

_____

BLESSED ASSURANCE

*This is the testimony: that God has given us eternal life, and
this life is in His Son. He who has the Son has life; he who
does not have the Son of God does not have life.*

1 JOHN 5:11–12

Are you trusting Jesus alone for your salvation? If you aren't, or if you are unsure, I urge you to turn to Jesus Christ in repentance and faith today and by a simple prayer ask Him to come into your life as your Lord and Savior.

Don't let another day go by without Christ. Don't doubt God's promises about the certainty of Heaven, and don't doubt what Jesus Christ has already done to save you by His death and resurrection. When doubts assail you (and the devil will be sure they will), remember this: If you have put your faith and trust in Christ, you now belong to Him. You have been adopted into His family, and you are now His beloved son or daughter. Because of this, the Bible says, nothing "in all creation, will be able to separate us from the love of God that is in Christ Jesus our Lord" (Romans 8:39 NIV). You are now part of His family—forever!

What is one wonderful thing about being God's child?

_____

_____

LEADING THE WAY

In all things showing yourself to be a pattern of good works; in doctrine showing integrity, reverence, incorruptibility.
TITUS 2:7

A police officer pulled over a distinguished-looking woman, the story goes, and asked why she had exceeded the speed limit. The old gentleman sitting in the passenger seat laughed and said, "Well, young man, we were speeding to get to the place before we forget where we're going!" Getting where we are going is important. Equally important are those who are following us because they are on the same journey; they just don't realize it yet. Older generations may have a hard time keeping up with the younger, but let's remember that as long as we are still breathing, we are leading the way. Are we good examples?

While we have all made mistakes and would like to turn back the clock to correct some things, we know this is not possible. But the lessons we have learned from our failures and successes can help those following behind. The impact we can potentially have on them can mean the difference between leaving good memories or letting our lessons go to waste.

What failure have you experienced that you can share to help someone else?

_____

_____

REDISCOVER THE WORD

Jesus Christ is the same yesterday, today, and forever.

HEBREWS 13:8

I f you and the Bible have had a long absence from each other, it might be good for you to renew your acquaintance by reading again the gospel of John. While this is considered one of the most profound books in the Bible, it is also the clearest and most readily understood.

Next you might acquaint yourself with the Gospel as taught by Mark, Luke, and Matthew, noting how these men of widely different personalities and writing styles set forth the eternal story of redemption through Jesus. You will become aware of the powerful, universal truth that underlies all Gospel teaching.

When you have read each of the Gospels individually, start at the beginning of the New Testament and read straight through all the books in order. When you have done that, you will have developed such a taste for Bible reading, you will have found it such a fountain of inspiration, such a practical counselor and guide, such a treasure chest of sound advice, that you will make Bible reading a part of your daily life.

How has God met you as you have read your Bible recently?

_____

_____

ACCEPTING BY FAITH

Faith comes by hearing, and hearing by the word of God.
ROMANS 10:17

I have never been to the North Pole, and yet I believe there is a North Pole. How do I know? Because somebody told me. I read about it in a history book, I saw a map in a geography book, and I believe the authors. I accept it by faith.

So we must believe what God has to say about salvation.

Faith is not some peculiar, mysterious quality for which we must strive. Jesus said we must become as little children, and just as little children trust their parents, so we must trust God.

Suppose I were driving along the road at fifty miles an hour and I came to the crest of a hill. Would I immediately slam on my brakes, stop my car, get out, walk to the top of the hill, and look over to see if the road continues? No. I would trust the highway department and go on ahead even though I couldn't see the road ahead. I would accept it on faith. So it is with saving faith in Christ!

Do you fully trust the Lord?

_____

_____

FRESH START

"Unless one is born again, he cannot see the kingdom of God."
JOHN 3:3

If I could come and have a heart-to-heart chat with you in your living room, you perhaps would turn to me and confess, "I am confused. I have transgressed God's laws. I have lived contrary to His commandments. I thought I could get along without God's help. I have tried to make up my own rules and I've failed. The bitter lessons that I've learned have come through suffering and tragic experience. What wouldn't I give to be born again! What wouldn't I give to be able to go back and start all over—what a different road I'd travel if I could!"

If those words strike a familiar chord in your heart, I want to tell you some glorious news. Jesus said you can be born anew! You can have the fresh and better start for which you've prayed. You can lose your despised and sinful self and step forth a new person, a clean and peaceful being from whom sin has been washed away.

What is one of God's mercies that you are grateful for today?

_____

_____

ABIDING PEACE

Let the peace of God rule in your hearts, to which also
you were called in one body; and be thankful.
COLOSSIANS 3:15

Do you know the peace of God? Everyone who knows the Lord Jesus Christ can go through any problem, and face death, and still have the peace of God in his heart. When your spouse dies, your children get sick, or you lose your job, you can have a peace that you don't understand. You may have tears at a graveside, but you can have an abiding peace, a quietness.

A psychiatrist was quoted in the newspaper as saying that he could not improve upon the apostle Paul's prescription for human worry in Philippians 4:6–7. Be anxious for nothing. How many times do you and I fret and turn, looking for a little peace? God's peace can be in our hearts—right now.

Colossians 3:15 says, "Let the peace of God rule in your hearts." Some of you believe that you know Jesus Christ as your Savior, but you haven't really made Him your Lord. You're missing the peace of God in your struggles and turmoils and trials and pressures of life. Is the peace of God in your heart?

When in your life have you experienced God's peace?

_____

_____

The Privileges of Assurance

*If any of you lacks wisdom, let him ask of God, who gives to all
liberally and without reproach, and it will be given to him.*

James 1:5

There are certain special privileges that only the true Christian can enjoy. There is, for example, the privilege of having divine guidance. Also the Christian has a sense of true optimism, the assurance that everything will turn out well in the end.

The Christian also has a worldview. This worldview sets forth God's purpose and the end toward which all are proceeding. It assures us that in spite of every disaster, God is still on the throne and in command of everything. Satan himself is held back by God's power and given an opportunity to exercise his evil influence only as God sees fit and only as long as God sees fit to let him do it. The Scriptures teach us that God has a definite plan for each period of history, for every nation, and for every individual. The Scripture discloses God's plan for the return of Christ when His kingdom shall be established. Thus, for the Christian, life has a plan and an assurance that God will ultimately triumph over all unrighteousness.

Are you really living as though Jesus is in control of tomorrow?

CHRISTIAN HOPE

"Look, I am coming soon!"
REVELATION 22:12 NIV

Aside from the superiority of the Christian life over all other ways of living, we cannot overlook the advantage that the Christian will have for all eternity. Job said, "If a man die, shall he live again?" (Job 14:14 KJV). He answered his own question when he said, "For I know that my Redeemer liveth, and that he shall stand at the latter day upon the earth" (Job 19:25 KJV).

What a prospect! What a future! What a hope! What a life! I would not change places with the wealthiest and most influential person in the world. I would rather be a child of the King, a joint-heir with Christ, a member of the Royal Family of Heaven!

I know where I've come from, I know why I'm here, I know where I'm going—and I have peace in my heart. His peace floods my heart and overwhelms my soul!

In Christ we are relaxed and at peace in the midst of the confusions, bewilderments, and perplexities of this life. The storm rages, but our hearts are at rest. We have found peace—at last!

Do you feel anxiety or the peace of God?

_____

_____

THE WAY BACK TO GOD

"Assuredly, I say to you, unless you are converted and become as little children, you will by no means enter the kingdom of heaven."

MATTHEW 18:3

A man will not find God until he finds the way back to God.

The way back to God is not an intellectual way. It is not a moral way. You cannot think your way back to God because human thought-life will not coordinate with divine thought-life, for the carnal mind is at enmity with God. You cannot worship your way back to God because man is a spiritual rebel from God's presence. You cannot moralize your way back to God because character is flawed with sin.

The natural questions come to you—What shall I do? Where shall I start? Where do I begin? What is my road back to God? There is only one way back to God. It is significant that Jesus did not tell the little children to become as His disciples, but His disciples to become as little children. By childlike faith, everyone has a chance, from the feebleminded to intellectuals. Thus Jesus demanded a conversion. This is how to begin! This is where it starts! You must be converted and come to Him as a little child.

What is one way that your faith is like that of a little child?

_____

_____

WHAT IS FAITH?

For by grace you have been saved through faith, and
that not of yourselves; it is the gift of God.
EPHESIANS 2:8

The Bible declares that *faith* is absolutely essential. You ask, "Well, if faith is so important, what is faith? What do you mean by *faith*? What is a definition of faith? How can I know if I have proper faith? How much faith must I have?"

Wait just a minute—not so many questions at a time! I'll try to answer them as we go along.

Are we actually saved by faith? No, we're saved by grace *through faith*. Faith is simply the channel through which God's grace to us is received. It is the hand that reaches out and receives the gift of His love. In Hebrews 11:1, we read, "Now faith is the substance of things hoped for, the evidence of things not seen." Weymouth has translated it this way, which makes it easier to understand: "Now faith is a confident assurance of that for which we hope, a conviction of the reality of things which we do not see." *Faith* literally means "to give up, surrender, or commit." Faith is complete confidence.

Do you believe that God is who He says He is?

_____

_____

February

GROW YOUR KNOWLEDGE

The heart of the prudent acquires knowledge,
And the ear of the wise seeks knowledge.
PROVERBS 18:15

To have faith, you must have a *knowledge* of what God has said. Just to know that you are a sinner and that Christ died for you is enough knowledge. But on anything as important as this you should be as well informed as possible, and the only place to learn about salvation is in the Bible!

Many people say, "But I cannot understand much of the Bible, therefore I don't try to read it." That is not the wise attitude. There are many things in the Bible that I do not understand. My finite mind will never understand all about the infinite. I do not understand all about television, but I do not refuse to turn on my television set. I accept it by faith.

But God does not ask the impossible. He does not ask you to take a leap in the dark concerning conversion. Believing in Christ is based on the best evidence in the world, the Bible. Even though you do not understand it all, you can accept it at face value because God said it.

What have you learned in the Bible that you didn't understand at first?

_____

_____

INFLUENCING THE IMPRESSIONABLE

I am reminded of your sincere faith, which first lived in your grandmother . . .
and in your mother . . . and, I am persuaded, now lives in you also.

2 TIMOTHY 1:5 NIV

I am grateful that my children were influenced by their grandparents. They spent much time with my children and made a profound impact. When my father-in-law told stories of his time in China as a missionary doctor, and he got to the gory details, Ruth's mother would scold him. The children would laugh with delight, coaxing their grandfather to continue. They still talk about it today. They also refer often to the strength they still draw from their grandparents' wisdom. After all, it is part of their heritage, and they have passed it on to their children and grandchildren. This is a lasting legacy.

Society seems to lose more ground with each passing generation. An elderly couple admitted they had "no earthly idea" how to influence their teenage grandchildren—they simply could not relate to them. I believe that is, perhaps, the problem—we are looking for an *earthly* solution. We should, instead, try looking into God's Word. That's where we will find the answers.

How can you influence a younger person?

_____

_____

CHRISTIAN LIVING

"Just as you want men to do to you, you also do to them likewise."
LUKE 6:31

Whether we are playing a game, driving a car, or baking a cake, there are certain rules that must be followed for our safety as well as our success. Living by God's rules, what we call "Christian living," ensures personal growth.

The Bible teaches that the Christian life is one of constant growth. When you were born again, you were born into God's family. My wife, Ruth, and I have many grandchildren. And each of them is precious to us. Each is an accepted, treasured member of our family. And that's the way God feels about you.

It is God's purpose that you will grow into full stature and become mature in Christ. It would be against the law of God and nature if you were to remain a baby and become spiritually stunted. In 2 Peter 3:18, the Bible says that we are to grow. This implies steady development, constant enlargement, increasing wisdom.

As you continue into the new year, commit to growing spiritually. Devote yourself to becoming spiritually mature, and you will find this year one of your most rewarding yet.

How can you devote yourself to growing spiritually?

_____

_____

TIMELESS TRUTH

*All Scripture is given by inspiration of God, and is profitable for doctrine,
for reproof, for correction, for instruction in righteousness.*

2 TIMOTHY 3:16

In setting down their forthright messages, biblical scribes have never attempted to gloss over the realities of life. The sins of the great and small are freely admitted, the weaknesses of human nature are acknowledged, and life in biblical times is recorded as it was lived. The startling thing is that the lives and motivations of these people who lived so long ago have such a modern flavor! As we read, the pages seem like mirrors held up before our own minds and hearts, reflecting our own prides and prejudices, our own failures and humiliations, our own sins and sorrows.

Truth is timeless. Truth does not differ from one age to another, from one people to another, from one geographical location to another. Men's ideas may differ, men's customs may change, men's moral codes may vary, but the great all-prevailing Truth stands for time and eternity.

The Bible has a single, clear, bold message for every living being—the message of Christ and His offer of peace with God.

How does God's message of peace affect your life?

_____

_____

YOU AND THE BIBLE

The entrance of Your words gives light;
It gives understanding to the simple.
PSALM 119:130

I f you do not have a Bible in your home, go out and get one now—get the one that suits you best, get the size that is most comfortable for you to handle, that is most pleasant for you to read, and then settle down and find out for yourself why this one Book has endured.

A knowledge of the Bible is essential to a rich and meaningful life. The words of this Book have a way of filling in the missing pieces, of bridging the gaps, of turning the tarnished colors of our life to jewel-like brilliance. Learn to take your every problem to the Bible. Within its pages you will find the correct answer. Most of all, the Bible is a revelation of the nature of God.

A Christian once asked, "Do you know a book that you are willing to put under your head for a pillow when you are dying? Very well," he went on, "that is the Book you want to study when you are living. There is only one such Book in the world!"

How do you use your Bible?

_____

_____

WHERE IS PEACE?

When a man's ways please the LORD, He makes even
his enemies to be at peace with him.

PROVERBS 16:7

I know men who would write a check for a million dollars if they could find peace. Millions are searching for it. But, as we look around, we find that there is little personal, domestic, social, economic, or political peace anywhere. Why? Because we all have the seeds of destruction within us.

Peace can be experienced only when we have received divine pardon—when we have been reconciled to God and when we have harmony within, with our fellow man, and especially with God. Through the blood of the cross, Christ has made peace with God for us and is Himself our peace. If by faith we accept Him, we are justified by God and can realize the inner serenity that can come to man through no other means. When Christ enters our hearts, we are freed of that haunting sense of sin. Cleansed of all feeling of contamination and unfitness, we can lift up our heads secure in the knowledge that we can look with confidence into the face of our fellow men.

Have you ever searched for peace in the wrong place?

_____

_____

PEACE IN BODY

Beloved, I pray that you may prosper in all things and
be in health, just as your soul prospers.
3 JOHN V. 2

There are physical benefits that accrue from Christian living. Sin and the sense of inner unworthiness impair physical and mental well-being. The sense of guilt and sin that natural man carries within himself renders him unfit for the performance of his duties, renders him sick in both mind and body. It was no accident that Jesus combined healing with His preaching and teaching when He was on earth. There is a very real relationship between the life of the spirit and the health of the body and mind.

Peace with God and the peace of God in a man's heart and the joy of fellowship with Christ have in themselves a beneficial effect upon the body and mind and will lead to the development and preservation of physical and mental power. Thus, Christ promotes the best interest of the body and mind as well as of the spirit, in addition to inward peace, the development of spiritual life, the joy and fellowship with Christ, and the new strength that comes with being born again.

Do you feel the peace of well-being that only comes from the Lord?

_____

_____

WHO IS GOD?

Can you search out the deep things of God?

JOB 11:7

Who is God? What is He like? How can we be sure He exists? When did He begin? Can we know Him?

Everyone has asked these questions either aloud or to himself.

No less a wise man than Benjamin Franklin said, "I have lived a long time and the longer I live the more convincing proofs I see that God governs in the affairs of men."

We call upon God in our hours of greatest difficulty and trial. Some try to let the thought of Him fill every waking moment. Others say they don't believe in Him, that He doesn't exist. And still others say, "Explain Him to me and maybe I'll accept God."

For those who are wondering what God is like, it has been simply stated: God is like Jesus Christ. Just as Jesus came to make God visible to mankind and to become our Redeemer, even so, on His return to Heaven, He sent the Holy Spirit to indwell believers and enable them to live so as to make Christ visible to an unbelieving world.

What is your favorite characteristic of God?

_____

_____

41

WHAT IS GOD LIKE?

What may be known of God is manifest in them, for God has shown it to them.
ROMANS 1:19

What is God like?
Everyone should ask that question, and everyone should seek to know beyond a shadow of a doubt exactly who God is and what He is capable of accomplishing.

It is the absence of the knowledge of God and man's refusal to obey Him that lie at the root of every problem that besets us. It is man's confusion about God's plan that has the world in chaos. So let us learn all we can about Him.

God has revealed Himself in the book called the Bible. In it we have a revelation of God—and based on it our minds can be satisfied and our hearts filled. We can rest assured that we have the correct answer, that we are on our way to knowing and understanding the true nature of God.

If we read the Bible as carefully and as regularly as we read the daily news, we would be more familiar with God!

What has the Lord revealed to you about His nature through His Word?

_____

_____

JESUS SPEAKS PEACE

May the God of peace who brought up our Lord Jesus from the dead . . . make you complete in every good work to do His will.

HEBREWS 13:20–21

My colleagues George Beverly Shea and Cliff Barrows sang a song together that I always loved: "Jesus Speaks Peace to Me."[1] Study what the Bible says about the Source of peace; you will be blessed.

Jesus is the Author of peace. Jesus fills our hearts with peace. Jesus gives us peace in trouble. Jesus gives us the fruit of peace. Jesus Himself is our peace. Jesus speaks peace. Jesus will rule in peace. And Jesus, in peace, will crush Satan.

Jesus' peace is a certainty. The world, however, cannot offer peace. It fights for peace, negotiates for peace, and maneuvers for peace, but it has none to give. So it remains restless.

A quiet revolution is going on in the world today. It has no fanfare, no media coverage, and no propaganda, yet it is changing the course of lives. It is restoring purpose and meaning as people of all races and nationalities are finding peace with God.

How has the Lord's peace been restorative to you?

THE PEACE OF GOD

To be spiritually minded is life and peace.
ROMANS 8:6

E veryone who knows the Lord can go through any problem—and face death—and still have the peace of God in his heart, for He makes it possible.

A psychiatrist once said he could not improve upon the apostle Paul's prescription for human worry. Paul said, "Be anxious for nothing, but in everything by prayer and supplication, with thanksgiving, let your requests be made known to God; and the peace of God, which surpasses all understanding, will guard your hearts and minds through Christ Jesus" (Philippians 4:6–7). The peace of God can be in our hearts—right now (Colossians 3:15). There is no human philosophy that can achieve such changes or provide such strength.

Christ promotes our inward peace by developing our spirits. "Now may the God of peace Himself sanctify you completely; and may your whole spirit, soul, and body be preserved blameless" (1 Thessalonians 5:23).

What a life! I know where I've come from. I know why I'm here. I know where I am going. His peace floods my heart and overwhelms my soul, even in the midst of despair!

How has the Lord guarded your mind from things that steal your peace?

_____

_____

SAFE IN THE STORM

"Peace, be still!"
MARK 4:39

A colleague who traveled frequently throughout the Middle East was in a car with some missionaries driving through the Jordanian desert, along the King's Highway, when a sandstorm blew up. They were on a mountain pass with low visibility. Though an experienced traveler, my friend said his knuckles were white until one of the missionaries said, "Don't worry. I've been this way before." They pulled off in a safe place and enjoyed a peaceful visit until the storm passed. That's what peace with God is like.

Even the birds know peace: though the thunder and lightning rage, the little bird can sleep in the crevice of the rock, its head tucked serenely under its wing, sound asleep through the storm.

Jesus was asleep in a boat when a storm like that arose. The disciples were terrified and woke Him: "Lord, we will perish; save us!"

Jesus "said to the sea, 'Peace, be still!' And the wind ceased" (Mark 4:39).

In Christ, we can be at peace in the midst of the confusions, bewilderments, and perplexities of this life. The storm rages, but our hearts are at rest.

What safe place has the Lord provided you in the past?

_____

_____

FEEDING THE SOUL

Do you not know that you are the temple of God
and that the Spirit of God dwells in you?
1 CORINTHIANS 3:16

I n love, Paul corrected the Corinthian Christians with these words and instructed them that unless they were continually filled with the Holy Spirit, their service would not be empowered with strength from above. His words of discipline must have been difficult to hear, even though they were necessary. "Now no chastening seems to be joyful for the present, but painful; nevertheless, afterward it yields the peaceable fruit of righteousness" (Hebrews 12:11).

Just as we feed the physical body, we must also feed the soul. How do we do this? By an act of the will in obedience to the Spirit, allowing God to plant seeds of truth from His Word, which brings the power. We must acknowledge the presence of the Holy Spirit that indwells us, praying for God's Word to instruct us and asking Him to give us wisdom to obey Him. This empowers our faith. "The . . . righteous know what is acceptable" (Proverbs 10:32). This is how to increase the "fruits of . . . righteousness" (2 Corinthians 9:10).

How does the Lord correct you?

_____

_____

PEACE WITH GOD

We have peace with God through our Lord Jesus Christ.

ROMANS 5:1

L asting peace is foreign to human thinking. But where can we find it? We must first look within our darkened souls and get right with God.

The Bible says Jesus "came and preached peace to you who were afar off and to those who were near" (Ephesians 2:17).

Peace is possible, and there is a peace that you can have immediately—*peace with God* (Colossians 1:20). The greatest warfare going on in the world today is between man and God. It would be the greatest tragedy if I didn't tell you that unless you repent of your sins and receive Christ as your Savior, you are going to be lost—there will be no peace in Hell.

It's not just head belief; it's heart belief too. We must bring everything to the cross, where the Lord Jesus Christ died for our sins.

God made peace by the shedding of His blood. The war that exists between us and God can be over quickly, and the peace treaty will be signed in the blood of His Son, Jesus Christ.

Have you brought everything to the cross?

_____

_____

PEACE IN THE CROSS

And by Him to reconcile all things to Himself, by Him, whether things on earth or things in heaven, having made peace through the blood of His cross.
COLOSSIANS 1:20

The world will never know peace until it finds it in the cross of Jesus Christ. You will never know the peace with God, peace of conscience, peace of mind, and peace of soul until you stand at the foot of the cross and identify yourself with Christ by faith.

Accepting Christ's sacrifice changes men's standing before God. It is a change from guilt and condemnation to pardon and forgiveness. The forgiven sinner is not like the discharged prisoner who has served out his term and is discharged but with no further rights of citizenship. The repentant sinner, pardoned through the blood of Jesus Christ, regains his full citizenship. "Who shall lay any thing to the charge of God's elect? It is God that justifieth. Who is he that condemneth? It is Christ that died, yea rather, that is risen again, who is even at the right hand of God, who also maketh intercession for us" (Romans 8:33–34 KJV). Jesus has made peace with God possible through His intercession and sacrifice.

Have you thanked Jesus today?

_____

_____

THE LESSONS OF LOSS

The LORD is near to those who have a broken heart,
And saves such as have a contrite spirit.

PSALM 34:18

A teenage daughter of a friend of our ministry reflected on watching her grandfather die at home. She said with tears in her eyes, "I'll never forget the loving care Papa received from my grandmother. It taught me to care for the sick and dying. More than that, it taught me about living bravely in the midst of difficulties."

There is much the young can learn from those who have traveled the distance. Likewise, the elderly would be wise to consider the contribution the young make even to our own lives. They will see our mistakes, and they will see our triumphs. We will hopefully recognize their struggles and accomplishments and encourage them as they face the unknown future. The Bible says, "To everything there is a season, a time for every purpose . . . a time to gain, and a time to lose" (Ecclesiastes 3:1, 6). In times of loss there are lessons to be gained. Let's not miss the purposes of God even in times of sorrow and disappointment, for He is always with us on our journey.

What have you learned from someone in a different stage of life than yours?

_____

_____

GOD OF HOPE

May the God of hope fill you with all joy and peace in believing,
that you may abound in hope by the power of the Holy Spirit.
ROMANS 15:13

Our God is the God of hope. But what is hope?

Hope is the breath of nature that surrounds us every day.

Hope is seen in a sprig that shoots up from the crevasse of a sun-dried rock, proving the water of life within.

Hope is the first ray of sunshine that peeks above the horizon—without fail—every morning with blazing truth, telling us we can make it through.

Hope is dispatched when the moon rises in the dark night, foreshadowing that a new day will dawn.

Have you glimpsed the glow of hope? Strike a match and burn a candle. You will discover that the whisper of its flame brings life to a room, making the candle useful. Is your flame alive and making a difference in the world? You see, hope pierces the darkness.

Hope brings comfort to our aching souls. It perseveres, persuades, prevails. And it is God's gift to us.

How have you offered a glimpse of God's hope to another person?

END OF CONSTRUCTION

You formed my inward parts; . . .
The days fashioned for me.
PSALM 139:13, 16

Years ago my wife, Ruth was driving along a highway through a construction site. Carefully following the detours and mile-by-mile cautionary signs, she came to the last one that said, "End of Construction. Thank You for your patience." She arrived home, chuckling and telling the family about the posting. "When I die," she said, "I want that engraved on my stone." She was lighthearted but serious about her request. She even wrote it out so that we wouldn't forget. While we found the humor enlightening, we appreciated the truth she conveyed through those few words. Every human being is under construction from conception to death. Each life is made up of mistakes and learning, waiting and growing, practicing patience and being persistent. At the end of construction—death—we have completed the process.

Death says, "This is the finality of accomplishment." While we cannot add anything more to our experience, believers in Christ have the hope of hearing the Savior say, "Well done, good and faithful servant" (Matthew 25:21).

In what way are you a work in progress?

_____

_____

SHARE THE BURDEN

Bear one another's burdens, and so fulfill the law of Christ.
GALATIANS 6:2

I heard once about a pastor who always ended his sermons with these words: "Remember: everyone you are going to meet this week is carrying a heavy burden." Over the years I have found this to be true; I have never met a person who wasn't weighed down by some kind of problem or burden. But God wants to help carry everyone's burdens—one way He does that is by sending someone into the person's life who can share the burden.

Are there those in your church or neighborhood carrying a burden right now? Ask God to help you be a friend to them. Perhaps you can understand what they are going through, and you can help relieve the weight of their burden by your concern. Sometimes all they need is someone who will listen. Remember that God is "the Father of compassion and the God of all comfort, who comforts us in all our troubles, so that we can comfort those in any trouble with the comfort we ourselves have received from God" (2 Corinthians 1:3–4 NIV).

How can you help someone with a burden today?

_____

_____

DON'T LIVE WITHOUT HOPE

"For God so loved the world that he gave his one and only Son, that whoever believes in him shall not perish but have eternal life."

JOHN 3:16 NIV

"You are free to have your own opinion," a young man wrote me once, "but as far as I'm concerned once you are dead, that's it. Life after death is just a myth."

My reply came from the bottom of my heart. "Your letter deeply saddened me," I wrote, "because it means you are living without hope—hope for this life, and hope for the life to come. Have you honestly faced how empty and meaningless this will make your life?" I then urged him to turn to Jesus Christ and put his life into His hands, for He alone can give us hope for the future.

Is death really the end? No—absolutely not. The Bible tells us that although our bodies will die, our spirits will live on—either in Heaven or eternally separated from God in Hell. But God doesn't want anyone to perish. We were meant for Heaven, our final home. For those who belong to Him, Heaven is our destiny, and Heaven is our joyous hope.

Do you look to the future without fear?

WHAT IS HEAVEN LIKE?

Eye has not seen, nor ear heard, nor have entered into the heart of man the things which God has prepared for those who love Him.

1 CORINTHIANS 2:9

I don't believe I have ever known a person (or at least a Christian) who did not want to know what Heaven is like—including me! This is not mere curiosity, however, like wondering about someplace we have never visited. Instead, we know that Heaven is our final home—the place where we will be spending all eternity. Why wouldn't we want to know about it?

Admittedly the Bible doesn't answer all our questions about Heaven. One reason, I've realized, is that Heaven is so much greater than anything our limited minds can ever imagine. Even if God answered all our questions about Heaven, we wouldn't be able to understand them! Only in Heaven will we be able to grasp completely its endless glory and wonder and joy. Then, the Bible says, we "will share in the glory to be revealed" (1 Peter 5:1 NIV).

Even if the Bible doesn't tell us everything we want to know about Heaven, it does tell us everything we *need* to know. And everything it tells us about Heaven should make us want to go there!

What do you look forward to most in Heaven?

_____

_____

HEAVEN IS PERFECT

*He will wipe every tear from their eyes. There will be no more
death or mourning or crying or pain, for the old order of things
has passed away. . . . Nothing impure will ever enter it.*

REVELATION 21:4, 27 NIV

One of the Bible's greatest promises about Heaven is that it is glorious
and perfect. This shouldn't surprise us: since God is perfect, so, too, is
Heaven, His dwelling place. Why is this important? Because it reminds us that
in Heaven everything imperfect will be banished (1 Corinthians 13:10). Think of
all the sins and evils that afflict us now: disease, death, loneliness, fear, sorrow,
temptation, disappointment. But in Heaven all those will be banished! Every
evil and sin will be destroyed; every doubt and fear will be removed; every disappointment and heartache will be healed.

In Heaven we will be perfect—and someday so will all creation. Sin will no
longer have any power over anything—for sin and Satan will be bound forever,
and we will become like Christ.

What will it be like to become like Christ?

_____

_____

JESUS IS RETURNING

"Of that day and hour no one knows, not even the
angels of heaven, but My Father only."
MATTHEW 24:36

When will Christ appear again? Bible scholars don't always agree on the details, but one fact is clear: someday Christ will come again to defeat all the forces of sin and evil and establish His supreme authority over creation. Jesus Himself warned us against trying to set an exact timetable for His return (Mark 13:32). In God's time, this present world order will come to an end, and Christ will return to rule in power and glory and justice.

The fact of Christ's return should fill us with hope and joy and expectation. But it also should remind us of another truth: when Christ comes again, He will judge the world with perfect justice. On that day those who have rebelled against God and rejected His offer of salvation in Christ "will go away to eternal punishment, but the righteous to eternal life" (Matthew 25:46 NIV). These are sobering words, and if you have never turned from your sins and opened your heart and life to Jesus Christ, I pray you will do so now, before it is too late. Don't gamble with your eternal soul!

How does knowing Christ will come again make you more optimistic?

HEAVEN IS JOYOUS

You will show me the path of life; in Your presence is fullness of joy; at Your right hand are pleasures forevermore.

PSALM 16:11

Not only will Heaven be glorious and perfect, but it also will be joyous. Its glory, its perfection—these alone would be enough to bring us unimaginable joy. But Heaven will be joyous for other reasons also.

Heaven will be a place of joyous reunion with all those who have gone to Heaven before us. I am often asked if we will recognize each other in Heaven—and my answer is always a resounding yes! The Bible tells us that in Heaven we won't be isolated spirits, separated from each other and floating aimlessly around the clouds (as cartoons sometimes suggest). Instead, we will be united together: "We who are still alive and are left will be caught up *together with them* in the clouds to meet the Lord in the air. And so *we* will be with the Lord forever" (1 Thessalonians 4:17 NIV, emphasis added).

Perhaps, however, you don't look forward to meeting someone who has hurt you or someone you have hurt. Don't worry about this. In Heaven they will be perfect—and so will you!

Who do you want to meet again in Heaven?

_____

_____

HEAVEN RESOLVES ALL

For now we see only a reflection as in a mirror; then we shall see face to face.
1 CORINTHIANS 13:12 NIV

Life can be confusing, and every one of us has watched as a great evil seemed to be winning the day, asking God, "Why did You let this happen? It doesn't make any sense." But someday all our doubts and questions will be resolved, and we will understand. As part of this we will be able to look back over our lives and rejoice in God's goodness and grace to us.

In addition, Heaven will be joyous because all our burdens will be lifted—never to return. One of the Bible's most comforting pictures of Heaven is that it will be a place of rest: "Blessed are the dead who die in the Lord from now on. . . . They will rest from their labor" (Revelation 14:13 NIV).

The Bible tells us a final truth about Heaven's joy: our experience of Heaven will express itself in joyous worship. On this earth our worship is imperfect, incomplete, superficial. But in Heaven our worship will be glorious because we will see our Savior face-to-face.

Do you look forward to having perfect rest?

_____

_____

HEAVEN IS ACTIVE

The throne of God and of the Lamb shall be in [the city], and His servants shall serve Him.

REVELATION 22:3

To be honest, I'm not even sure I want to go to Heaven," someone e-mailed me once. "It sounds so boring, just sitting around on a cloud doing nothing." This is a misunderstanding of Heaven. In spite of the popular image, we won't be sitting on clouds and strumming harps. Instead, the Bible says we will be busy. God will have work for us to do! The difference is that in this life we get tired, but in Heaven we will have unlimited energy to serve Christ.

What will we do? The Bible doesn't say exactly; if it did, we probably wouldn't understand it anyway! It does, however, tell us that God will grant us the privilege of participating in Christ's rule: "And they will reign [with Him] for ever and ever" (Revelation 22:5 NIV). We definitely won't be bored in Heaven!

My Crusade song leader Cliff Barrows once joked that in Heaven I will be unemployed while he'll still have a job—they won't need evangelists, while the heavenly choirs will still need directors. But I'm not worried; God will find me something to do!

What work do you think the Lord has for you in Heaven?

Now Is the Time

"I am the way, the truth, and the life. No one comes to the Father except through Me."
JOHN 14:6

Do you know the way, the truth, and the life? No one ever grows too old to accept Christ's forgiveness and enter into His glorious presence. When we look back over our experiences along life's journey, we may have regrets about the choices we made, but remember, that was *then* . . . this is *now*. Some reading this may say, "But I rejected Christ my whole life. It's too late for me." I say to you, my friend, that was *then* . . . this is *now*. The Bible's promises were true then, they are true now, and they will be true forever. "Behold, *now* is the accepted time; behold, *now* is the day of salvation" (2 Corinthians 6:2 , emphasis added).

For those who have received the most precious gift of Christ's redeeming blood . . . you have reason to look forward to the glories of Heaven, for you will be perfected, you will be joyful, you will be active, and you can be certain that you are *nearing home*.

Do you believe in your heart that your past is behind you?

_____

_____

RUNNING TOWARD HOME

Teach us to number our days,
that we may gain a heart of wisdom.
PSALM 90:12

It doesn't seem so long ago that I was a young dreamer, filled with great expectation. Since there were few things in life that I loved more than base-ball, as a young man I dedicated myself to the sport. I often pictured myself hitting a big-league grand slam into the stadium seats and hearing the crowd roar as I ran the bases—*nearing home.*

I never would have guessed what lay in store. After giving my heart to the Lord Jesus Christ—repenting of my sin and putting my entire life into His hands—I laid down my dreams, along with my bat, and fully embraced God's plan by faith, trusting that He would lead me all the way. He did, He is, and He will.

As I look back, I see how God's hand guided me. I sense His Spirit with me today, and most comforting is the knowledge that He will not forsake me during this last stretch as I am nearing home in Heaven. If that doesn't give me a sense of hope and peace, nothing else will.

How have you felt the Lord's guidance from an early age?

_____

_____

PREPARING FOR HOME

"I go to prepare a place for you."
JOHN 14:2

Nothing thrills me more than seeing the Holy Spirit at work. The Word of God travels to the farthest corners of the earth, proclaiming the Good News of salvation. It still excites me just to think about the impact.

Jesus Christ did conquer death, and by His resurrection He was victorious. Before He left earth, He imparted to His followers the greatest of all strategies: go into the world and preach the Gospel. After listening to His words, they looked up to see their Savior nearing His heavenly home.

What home are you preparing for in your life? Some people spend their lives building ultimate dream homes so they can enjoy their twilight years. Some find themselves exchanging their bank accounts for residence within the gates of a retirement center or nursing home. But choosing your eternal home is the most important decision you will ever make. For the Christian, the last mile of the way is a testimony to God's faithfulness, for He has prepared a place for you.

Regardless of where you lay your head at night, I hope your thoughts are about your heavenly home.

Are you prepared to enter your heavenly home?

_____

_____

MARCH

CHARACTER AND FAITH

My little children, let us not love in word or in tongue, but in deed and in truth.
1 JOHN 3:18

My parents had a profound impact on me. My mother's kind and gentle character and concern for the spiritual welfare of others are reaping fruit still today. I recall also with deep gratitude my father's example of honesty, integrity, discipline, and hard work.

Over the years countless others have influenced me and changed me by the examples of their lives—although I am sure they were unaware of it. The same has probably been true of people in your life.

The greatest legacy you can pass on is the legacy of your character and your faith. If our character is bad, marked by lack of integrity or any other negative quality, this is how we will be remembered. But if our character and integrity have been shaped by Christ over the years, others can't help but see this and remember it.

Why is faith our greatest legacy? Because the memory of what we were like—not just our personalities but our character and our faith—has the potential to influence others for Christ. How do you want to be remembered?

What kind of legacy are you leaving?

_____

_____

PRAYING FOR FAMILY

*Now to Him who is able to do exceedingly abundantly above all that
we ask or think, according to the power that works in us . . .*

EPHESIANS 3:20

Over the years Ruth and I tried to follow several practices in our relationships with our family. One of them is to pray for them consistently.

How do you start? Don't pray only in general terms (the kind of prayer that
vaguely asks God to bless them). Make your prayers specific, and make them
daily. Pray not only that God will keep them safe but that He will guard them
from the temptations and evils that assail people today. Pray that God will give
them a desire to do what is right and avoid what is wrong, and to seek His will
for their lives. Pray about any decisions you know they will be making or difficulties you know they are facing. Let them know you are praying for them
because you love them and care deeply about what happens to them.

Remember, God knows their needs far better than you do, and He is able to
do what we cannot do. Commend your family into His hands, and trust in Him.

What are you praying for your loved ones?

_____

_____

FIXING BROKEN RELATIONSHIPS

Pursue peace with all people, and holiness, without which no one will see the Lord.

HEBREWS 12:14

Don't live with regret over a broken relationship that could have been healed—if you had only taken the first step. Why don't we do this? Often it is because of pride; we hate to admit we were wrong or at least that we had a part in causing the split. Sometimes it is because we are afraid of opening our lives to still more hurt. Whatever the reason, do not let it keep you from seeking to heal the conflicts of the past.

It is not always possible to mend a broken relationship, of course; some people simply refuse to be reconciled. Some people also refuse to accept responsibility for what they have done. If so, you probably can't solve their problems—but you can solve yours by reaching out and trying to be reconciled. Peace isn't possible in every case, but we are to make the effort.

Ask God to give you a forgiving spirit, not only reconciling you with others, but being an example of Christ's forgiveness and grace. It isn't easy, but it will be one of the most important things you ever do.

How can you be an instrument of reconciliation?

_____

_____

THE BLESSING OF FORGIVENESS

You meant evil against me; but God meant it for good, in order to
bring it about as it is this day, to save many people alive.

GENESIS 50:20

*F*orgiveness is one of the most beautiful words in the human vocabulary and is best illustrated by God's forgiveness of sin. When God's people practice forgiveness with their fellow man, sweetness replaces harshness. A marvelous example of this is revealed in the life of Joseph, when he forgave his brothers for selling him into slavery as a young man. Joseph assured his brothers that while they intended to do him evil, God meant it for good by using him to save many people during the famine that swept the land (Genesis 50:20). Because of Joseph's demonstration of forgiveness, he was greatly blessed by God in his old age. The Bible says, "Joseph saw Ephraim's children to the third generation. The children of Machir, the son of Manasseh, were also brought up on Joseph's knees" (Genesis 50:23). What a legacy!

If we cannot find it in our hearts to forgive, how can we know God's blessings? May we take advantage of every opportunity to forgive and see the blessings that come from the hand of God.

What difficult situation have you seen the Lord use for good?

_____

_____

BECOMING MORE LIKE HIM

Whom He foreknew, He also predestined to be conformed to the image
of His Son, that He might be the firstborn among many brethren.
ROMANS 8:29

What is God's plan for spiritual maturity? The Bible tells us that God's will is for us to become more and more like Jesus. He wants to change us from within, taking away everything that dishonors Him and replacing it with Christ's love and purity. This is spiritual maturity: to become more and more like Christ in our "love, joy, peace, patience, kindness, goodness, faithfulness, gentleness, self-control" (Galatians 5:22–23 ESV).

Will we ever reach this goal? No, not completely in this life—but someday we will enter God's presence forever, and then we will be totally free from sin's grip.

Does this mean it is hopeless to strive for spiritual maturity right now? No! God wants to begin changing us from within and making us more like Christ here on earth. In Heaven that process will be complete; sin's power over us will be destroyed, and we will inherit that heavenly home Christ has prepared for us.

Which fruit of the Spirit can you strive for today?

_____

_____

THIS PRESENT LIFE IS NOT THE END

[God] has given us new birth into a living hope through the resurrection of Jesus Christ from the dead, and into an inheritance that can never perish, spoil or fade—kept in heaven for you.

1 PETER 1:3–4 NIV

How do we know Heaven isn't just wishful thinking on our part? Each of us has an inner sense or feeling that death is not the end, because God "set eternity in the human heart" (Ecclesiastes 3:11 NIV).

Repeatedly Jesus told His disciples not only that Heaven exists but that someday they would go there. He declared, "I am the resurrection and the life. He who believes in me will live, even though he dies; and whoever lives and believes in me will never die" (John 11:25–26).

But can we know that there is life after death? The only way would be for someone to die—and then come back to life and tell us what lies beyond the grave. And that's exactly what happened when Jesus Christ rose again from the dead. More than that, however, Jesus' death and resurrection tell us that sin and death have been defeated forever. Heaven is God's promise to you and to all who put their faith and trust in Jesus Christ as their Lord and Savior.

How do you know you are going to Heaven?

_____

_____

HEAVEN IS GLORIOUS

It shone with the glory of God, and its brilliance was like that
of a very precious jewel, like a jasper, clear as crystal.

REVELATION 21:11 NIV

We sometimes speak of a beautiful sunset or a warm spring day as "glorious," but even earth's most awe-inspiring nature is but a shadow of the glory of Heaven. When the apostle John was given a glimpse of Heaven's grandeur, he barely could find words to describe it, comparing it to the most wondrous objects on earth—only far greater.

Why is Heaven glorious? It isn't simply because of its incredible beauty, overwhelming as that will be. Heaven is glorious for one supreme reason: Heaven is the dwelling place of God. "And I heard a loud voice from the throne saying, 'Now the dwelling of God is with men, and he will live with them. They will be his people, and God himself will be with them and be their God.' . . . They will see his face, and his name will be on their foreheads" (Revelation 21:3; 22:4). Think of it: if you know Jesus Christ, someday you will be safely in God's presence forever! I can barely imagine what that will be like—but it will be glorious beyond description.

What will you say to Jesus when you meet Him in Heaven?

_____

_____

OUR FINAL HOME

As long as we are at home in the body we are away from the Lord ... [but we] would prefer to be away from the body and at home with the Lord.

2 CORINTHIANS 5:6, 8 NIV

It has been a great privilege for me to be an evangelist; my greatest joy has come from seeing people all over the world respond to the life-changing message of Jesus Christ. But on a personal level it has had its downside because I was away from home so much, sometimes for months at a time. But no matter how short or long the trip was, when I landed in Charlotte or Asheville, I knew I was nearing home. Home was a place of rest and peace; it also was a place of love and joy and security.

In a far greater way, Heaven is our home—our final home—our ultimate place of complete peace and security and joy forever. Here our homes are imperfect, even at best; sadly, for many people home may be a place of conflict and unhappiness. But this isn't true of Heaven. When we belong to Christ, we know that when we die we finally will be at peace—for we will be home.

What does it feel like to long for home?

_____

_____

BLOOMING AT NIGHT

They shall still bear fruit in old age; they shall be fresh and flourishing.
PSALM 92:14

I n old age ... blossom at the end like a night-blooming cereus."[1] This statement was written by a missionary to India, the late Dr. E. Stanley Jones. He made a profound impact on all those around him because of his extraordinary faith and service to others. Later in life his work was acknowledged by Franklin D. Roosevelt and Mahatma Gandhi. In spite of a stroke at age eighty-seven that disabled him and impaired his speech, he addressed a world congress in Jerusalem from his wheelchair shortly before he died.

The night-blooming cereus (a family of flowering cacti) that he spoke of brings a beauty to the desert when it opens up at nightfall. Some say these plants produce fruit large enough for people to consume. Dr. Jones certainly knew something about blossoming and producing fruit.

Do we do the same? At every stage of life, are we producing fruit that replenishes others, or do we complain about our circumstances? No matter our age, we must not miss the chance to impact the younger generations by exemplifying reliance on Him and hope in His unchanging promises.

How can you be a blessing to other generations?

_____

_____

MATURE FRUIT

Be mature and complete, not lacking anything.
JAMES 1:4 NIV

We cannot pretend to be something we are not; a Christlike character cannot be faked. If Christ is not real to us or if we haven't learned to walk with Him and submit our lives to Him every day, then our spiritual impact will be far less than it might have been. People are very sensitive to hypocrisy; if they sense it in us, they will dismiss our pretenses and pay no attention to our advice. On the other hand, if they can sense our faith is sincere and our love is authentic, then they will respect us and take us seriously (even when they know we are not perfect).

This is why it is important to begin building our lives on the solid foundation of Jesus Christ now, instead of waiting until it is too late and the problems of old age overwhelm us. Every gardener knows that mature fruit does not appear overnight. It takes time to grow—and so does the fruit of the Spirit in our lives. Start tending your garden today, so you may be "mature and complete."

In what place in your life do you most need spiritual growth?

_____

_____

PAIN IS A TOOL

Let those who suffer according to the will of God commit their
souls to Him in doing good, as to a faithful Creator.
1 PETER 4:19

I had the great privilege to visit with Louis Zamperini, a World War II veteran who spent two and a half years as a POW in a Japanese prison camp.

When Louis was rescued in 1945 and was welcomed home as a war hero, he enjoyed short-lived celebrity, followed by hard times. He had reason to be bitter and cynical. His wife, though, persuaded him to attend our 1949 crusade in Los Angeles. When Louis returned the second night, he said that the Holy Spirit gripped his heart.

"Billy," he told me during our visit, "within a matter of moments my life was changed forever. Since that night I have never had another nightmare about my captivity. The Lord radically transformed me."

For the rest of his life, he served the Lord, investing the fruit of his experience in the lives of others. For anyone experiencing pain, think of Louis; find a way to use your situation to point others to Him. What a privilege we have to remind one another that we have the Lord Jesus to comfort us.

How can the Lord redeem your circumstances for your good?

_____

_____

WHEN CALLINGS CHANGE

"Which of you by worrying can add one cubit to his stature? . . .
But seek first the kingdom of God and His righteousness,
and all these things shall be added to you."
MATTHEW 6:27, 33

We never know what the future holds for us, but God does. This is why Jesus urged us not to be paralyzed by fear of the future but to trust our lives into God's hands.

I often think of my father-in-law, Dr. L. Nelson Bell. For twenty-five years he and his wife, Virginia, served the people of China as medical missionaries. One of my strongest memories of Dr. Bell was how he cared for his wife after she suffered a series of debilitating strokes. He gave up almost all his outside responsibilities, stating simply, "This is my calling now."

You may not be able to do everything you once did or everything you would like to do. Instead of feeling guilty or frustrated, however, thank God that you can still do some things—and make it your goal to do them faithfully and do them well. Commit yourself to Jesus Christ, and seek to do His will no matter what comes your way.

Do you submit to the Lord when your plans change?

Lasting Legacy

According to the grace of God which was given to me, as a wise master builder I have laid the foundation, and another builds on it.

1 Corinthians 3:10

I remember being moved when I read the last will and testament of the late J. P. Morgan. He is noted as perhaps the most influential banker in history. I have often wondered about the reaction of his children when they read their father's will after his death in 1913. I hope they sensed the power of his words and gained strength from them: "I commit my soul into the hands of my Saviour, in full confidence that having redeemed it and washed it in His most precious blood He will present it faultless before the throne of my heavenly Father; and I entreat my children to maintain and defend, at all hazard, and at any cost of personal sacrifice, the blessed doctrine of the complete atonement for sin through the blood of Jesus Christ, once offered, and through that alone."[2]

Having your house in order is one of the most important things parents can do for their children. More than anything else, let them know where you stand with the Lord Jesus Christ, for this will be your lasting legacy.

Is your house in order?

_____

_____

POWER WITHIN

To this end I also labor, striving according to His
working which works in me mightily.
COLOSSIANS 1:29

The headline of an article that appeared in 2010 on a Tokyo website stated, "A robot suit that gives super strength to the elderly." The caption stated that the heavy-duty suit weighs sixty-six pounds and will be originally priced at 1 million yen (approximately $12,000). I asked myself, "How many my age have the strength to carry around sixty-six pounds for an hour, much less all day?"

Apparently the secret was not in the suit but in the eight electric motors and sensors responding to commands through a voice-recognition system, enabling the body to lift and bend without strain to the muscles. While this futuristic invention may never be seen in our department stores, the brainstorming behind it reveals man's desire for strength and power beyond himself.

Paul reminded us in Colossians 1:29 that he depended on Christ's mighty power that works within, and we can claim this as well. Just as the sensors built into the power suit respond by voice recognition and infuse the suit with power, we are told to respond to God's voice, and He will be our strength.

What is one way you rely on the Lord's strength?

_____

_____

GOD'S MIGHTY VOICE

The voice of the LORD is powerful;
The voice of the LORD is full of majesty.
PSALM 29:4

D o we listen for God's voice in our everyday activity? Sometimes He speaks, but we don't hear. We can't blame it on the batteries going dead in our hearing aids. God speaks to the human heart. His voice is described as full of majesty (Psalm 29:4), a still, small voice (1 Kings 19:12), and a glorious voice (Isaiah 30:30).

We are to obey His voice (Deuteronomy 13:4) and hearken to the voice of His Word (Psalm 103:20 KJV).

Many people have told me that they believe God speaks through His Word, but they don't believe He actually hears their pleas. Scripture dispels this. For those who fear and honor the Lord, He hears the voice of weeping (Psalm 6:8).

If ever you feel lonely and weak, listen for God's words of comfort: "Hear my voice" (Isaiah 28:23), and "Lift up your voice with strength" (Isaiah 40:9). He hears the voice of your words (Deuteronomy 5:28 KJV) and attends to your voice in prayer (Psalm 66:19). I hope these reminders from Scripture boost your spirit.

Have you ever heard the Lord's voice?

_____

_____

INTERFERENCE

Then the LORD God called to Adam and said to him, "Where are you?"
GENESIS 3:9

Telecommunications have changed our world. Now there are few instances when anyone is disconnected. But sometimes phone reception is difficult. It is not unusual for a call to be dropped or interrupted because of interference. Often people nearly scream into the phone, "Can you hear me?" A reply comes back, "I can hear you. Can you hear me?" It's sometimes a comical exchange.

Sometimes the same happens when we try to communicate with God. It certainly happened to Eve. The first question God asked Eve was, "What is this you have done?" (Genesis 3:13). If Eve had had a mobile phone, she may have suggested there was interference on the line.

But there is nothing humorous about broken communication with the Lord. When it happens, I can assure you that we are the interference—not Him. Sometimes we don't want to hear what He has to say because we already know what the Word of God has told us. But we must not let anything keep us from communicating daily with God. Not only does He want to communicate *with* us, He also wants to hear *from* us.

Have you allowed interference to separate you from the Lord?

_____

_____

WHEN CHRIST IS THE FOCUS

*Neither death nor life, . . . nor any other created thing, shall be able to
separate us from the love of God which is in Christ Jesus our Lord.*
ROMANS 8:38–39

How do we overcome the perils that steal our zest for life? Let the promises of God's Word uphold you every day. Turn constantly to Him in prayer. Focus your thoughts on Christ, and maintain your connection with other believers who can encourage and help you. God's Word is true: nothing can separate us from Him.

In the weeks before her death, my wife, Ruth, repeated this scripture over and over to us. Ruth was always thinking of others. This was her secret for getting through so much of life with joy. She never focused on her problems; she turned her attention to Christ, and He always led her to someone who needed a word of encouragement or a listening ear.

The Lord blesses people who bless others, and He gives grace to those who focus on the things that please Him. But most of all, as we learn to trust every day into His hands, we grow closer to Christ. And that is life's greatest joy.

Have you shared the Lord's love today?

_____

_____

STIRRED UP

Be strong . . . for I am with you.
HAGGAI 2:4

Haggai was stirred up by the Lord to rebuild the temple in Jerusalem following the Babylonian captivity. In turn he stirred up God's people: "You expected much, but see, it turned out to be little. . . . Why? . . . Because of my house, which remains a ruin, while each of you is busy with your own house" (Haggai 1:9 NIV).

What stirs me about this is how Haggai mobilized God's people to take care of God's business and build up His house by giving them hope: "Be strong . . . for I am with you."

We may be successful in putting our personal affairs in place, but if we do it at the sacrifice of the more important—putting our spiritual affairs in order—we miss the joy and purpose of life.

Are you concerned only about taking care of business in this world? Or are you setting Christ at the center of your life? Ask the Lord to stir you up by considering all He has done for you, and depend on the strength of His Spirit to build a spiritual life.

What is one way you can draw on the Lord's strength?

_____

_____

OPPORTUNITIES ARE EVERYWHERE

We are ambassadors for Christ, as though God were pleading through us.
2 CORINTHIANS 5:20

During a visit to the Billy Graham Library, a woman relayed a story: "My sweet mother struggled with my belief that all people were born sinners, according to Scripture. I prayed for years that she would come to recognize her own sin and be saved. When my mother was on her deathbed, she took my hand and said, 'My dear, when I'm gone, take heart. The Lord has saved me.'

"'Mother, how did this come about?'

"'When I was committed to this bed of infirmity, I realized I had come to the end of myself. I felt lost in my own house. My home health care attendant would patiently read to me from the Bible: "Now set your heart and your soul to seek the LORD your God"' (1 Chronicles 22:19).

"'When I met the dear lady who had faithfully led my mother to the Lord, it gave me great comfort to know that God will use us to minister to others if we make ourselves available."

The living never run out of opportunity to witness; the question is, how will we take advantage of the opportunities that come to us?

Do you have opportunities to tell others about Jesus?

LIVING WITH GRIEF

To everything there is a season, a time for every purpose
under heaven: a time to be born, and a time to die

ECCLESIASTES 3:1–2

It has been years since my wife, Ruth, went home to be with the Lord. Not a day passes that I don't imagine her walking through my study door or us sitting together on our porch as we did so often, holding hands as the sun set over the mountaintops.

Grief is a reality; those who say we shouldn't grieve the loss of loved ones "because they're better off now" have never understood the enormous hole that is left in our hearts when loved ones die. A major part of our lives has been ripped from us, and just as it takes time to heal from a major surgery, so it takes time to heal from the loss of loved ones.

My experience may not be the same as yours, but grief comes eventually to us all. No matter what our present experience is, the Bible's words are true: "I do not want you to be ignorant, brethren, concerning those who have fallen asleep, lest you sorrow as others who have no hope" (1 Thessalonians 4:13). We will meet again.

Who do you grieve for?

THE CURE FOR PEER PRESSURE

We have heard with our ears, O God, our fathers have told us, the deeds You did in their days, in days of old.

PSALM 44:1

A reporter interviewing a 104-year-old woman asked, "What is the best thing about being 104?" She simply replied, "No peer pressure." This may bring a smile because there is so much truth in it. As the old grow older, we are more likely to forget what it was to be young and impressionable.

In my day boys felt the peer pressure to smoke. Later generations felt strong pressure to experiment with drugs and sex. Because the Word of God has been absent from our public school system for decades, and because families have virtually stopped attending church together, there are only shades of godly influence that instruct them to live moral lives and reverence God.

That is where we come in. What a privilege we have to prepare the way for those who are watching. To us, our experiences are old news. To the young, it is information they have never heard and considered.

The Bible instructs generations to pass on what has been learned. With whom can you share what you've learned along life's way?

What is one lesson you are grateful the Lord taught you in your youth?

_____

_____

HEAVEN IS CERTAIN

But if we walk in the light, as he is in the light, we have fellowship with one another, and the blood of Jesus, his Son, purifies us from all sin.

1 JOHN 1:7 NIV

Heaven is glorious, Heaven is perfect, Heaven is joyous, and Heaven is active; but can we know—really know—that it is also certain? Can we know *for certain* that we will go there when we die and that it will be our eternal home? The Bible says yes!

Only one thing will keep you out of Heaven, and that is your sin. God is absolutely pure and holy, and even one sin—just one—would be enough to banish you from His presence forever. But Jesus Christ came to take away your sins by His death on the cross and His resurrection from the dead. The Bible says, "The blood of Jesus, his Son, purifies us from all sin."

As long as you trust in yourself—your goodness, your religious deeds, your inner hopes—for your salvation, you will never have any lasting assurance of your salvation. Our salvation depends instead solely on Jesus Christ and what He has already done for us. Our faith and trust must be in Him, and not in ourselves.

Is your trust in God or yourself?

_____

_____

GRIEVING WITH GOD

Cast your burden on the LORD, and He shall sustain you;
He shall never permit the righteous to be moved.
PSALM 55:22

At some point in each life, grief comes to call. When it happens to you, take your burden to God.

How does God help us cope with grief? First, He assures us of His presence. We are never alone if we know Christ; He lives within us by His Spirit. Even when you don't feel His presence, it doesn't change the fact that He is with you every moment of the day (Isaiah 41:10).

He also assures us of His promises. Read them, learn them, memorize them, trust them, and let them grow and bear fruit in your soul.

Shortly after Ruth's death, I leafed through one of her old Bibles. She had underlined hundreds of verses, often adding a brief comment of her own in the margin. She especially had underlined passages in the Psalms that spoke of God's promise to be with us in times of hardship or sorrow or loneliness. In the midst of your grief, turn daily to God's Word, and let its promises encourage and sustain you.

Which promise of God sustains you the most in times of sadness?

_____

_____

LEAVING A LEGACY

A good person leaves an inheritance for their children's children.

PROVERBS 13:22 NIV

Children are not like computers; we can't program them so they will always do exactly what we want them to do or turn out exactly the way we wish they would. It is one of life's mysteries: two children can be brought up in the same way yet turn out to be exact opposites as they grow older. The best we can do is provide the right environment—love them and train them and pray for them and provide them the tools they will need to make wise decisions.

Even if we don't have grandchildren or if we are childless or single, we still have an important and unique legacy to pass on to the next generation—and beyond. They are observing us, and they will learn from our lives.

Think about it: How will they learn about the realities of life and how to cope with them? Or how about the importance of building their lives on a strong foundation of faith in Christ and His Word? The answer is obvious: they will learn these things by observing us and the legacy we leave.

If a young person was observing you today, what would he or she see?

_____

_____

ROOTS STRENGTHEN IN TIME

As you therefore have received Christ Jesus the Lord, so walk in
Him, rooted and built up in Him and established in the faith.
COLOSSIANS 2:6–7

A cable news network carried a press conference on the announcement of the new iPad. Before the presentation was finished, creators of the product told plans of its coming replacement. Keeping up with the latest and greatest is difficult, and it seems to take attention away from the past.

A popular technology accessory company posted on its website, "We are surrounded by so much technology that we begin to forget our roots."[3] It's true. People can become so encumbered with being "connected" to information that they "disconnect" from others. Technology can weaken relationships and push the reality of life out of the way—especially between older and younger generations.

I encourage you to never give up on seeking creative ways to engage with others in a meaningful way. Let's remember to teach them by example that roots are important. It is our responsibility to build them up: "Encourage one another and build one another up" (1 Thessalonians 5:11 ESV).

What connection do you need to strengthen today?

_____

_____

STANDING STRONG

The fruit of the righteous is a tree of life.

PROVERBS 11:30

My neighbor planted a young purple-leaf plum tree to shade her yard. But five years after planting it, the tree was stunted, sick, and battered by strong winds. No matter how she staked it, it would not stand tall. A friend examined it and noticed it was planted close to a downspout, so it never needed to stretch its roots to find water. It eventually would die.

Contrast this tree with the maple sapling planted on the edge of her property. A bare-root plant, the sapling was forced to reach up for sun and out for water. Five years later, it was tall and healthy. The Christian life should look like this. After our roots of faith are planted in the fertile ground of truth, we should grow strong as we understand God's Word, draw close to the Holy Spirit, talk to God daily in prayer, and fellowship with our brothers and sisters in Christ. As we drink from the springs of life, our roots will grow deeper when we are serving Christ. Only with a deep root system can we endure the storms of life.

Do you feel like the plum tree or the maple?

_____

_____

GROWTH THROUGH SERVING

Grow in the grace and knowledge of our Lord and Savior Jesus Christ.
2 PETER 3:18

Volunteer service has become very popular in recent decades. Some companies even require employees to give so many hours a year to a volunteer agency. Better than that is when people do it because they truly have a desire to help others, not just to fulfill a requirement.

Through my son Franklin's organization, Samaritan's Purse, I've heard touching stories about physicians who leave their lucrative practices to help a missionary doctor for a few weeks in developing countries. Multiple thousands every year volunteer to send out shoe box gifts for children through Operation Christmas Child. Opportunities abound.

I would encourage you to pray and ask the Lord to show you what you can do to share your time and talents with others. Get involved in your local church and other ministries that point people to Christ. This will stretch you and challenge you to grow deeper in your own faith. Take to heart what Peter wrote: "Grow in the grace and knowledge of our Lord and Savior Jesus Christ." In doing so, you help others do the same.

What volunteer activities would you like to do?

_____

_____

GAINING EXPERIENCE

Is not wisdom found among the aged? Does not long life bring understanding?

JOB 12:12 NIV

Our society is made up of obsessive contradictions: the young want to be rewarded with big jobs without obtaining experience, the middle-aged brag about working out at the gym but can't wait to retire in order to rest, and the old want to drink from the fountain of youth. The truth is that instant success robs young people of the journey; but it is along the journey that we obtain knowledge, collect memories, and have a sense of achievement that makes life a rewarding experience.

I am reminded of a young teenager who pulled up a chair beside his grandfather and said, "Poppy, the wrinkles on your face are starting to cover up the scar you are so proud of!" The wise grandfather smiled, patted the boy on the back, and said, "Son, scars, wrinkles, and rusty bones have lots of stories to tell." That afternoon the grandson learned about his heritage. A few years later, he enlisted in the United States military. When asked why, he replied, "I want to earn my scars and wrinkles like my grandfather did." Your journey in life is just as valuable as the destination.

What is the best lesson you have learned?

_____

_____

THE INDESTRUCTIBLE BOOK

"Heaven and earth shall pass away, but my words shall not pass away."
MATTHEW 24:35 KJV

The British and Foreign Bible Society was on Jerusalem Street, one of the main streets of Old Warsaw in World War II. When the Germans began bombing the city, the wife of the director went to the storeroom and carried some two thousand Bibles down to the basement. She was trapped by the bombing and later captured by the Germans and put in a prison camp. She managed to escape and after the war was over was able to get to those two thousand Bibles and distribute them to people in need. Warsaw was flattened, but on Jerusalem Street one wall of the old British and Foreign Bible Society remained standing. On it were these words, painted in large letters: "Heaven and earth shall pass away, but my words shall not pass away."

Now, as we approach what appears to be another decisive hour in world history, let us reexamine this indestructible Book of wisdom and prophecy. It has endured and been man's unfailing source of faith and spiritual strength, and it is available to you.

What did your first Bible look like?

_____

_____

THE GLORY OF THE SPIRIT

"God is Spirit, and those who worship Him must worship in spirit and truth."

JOHN 4:24

As human beings deprived of the unlimited vision that God originally intended His creatures to have, we cannot comprehend the glory and the magnitude of the Spirit that lies so far outside ourselves.

When we hear the word *spirit*, we immediately try to reduce it to our puny size, to make it fit within the scope of our small minds. It is like trying to explain the sweep and majesty and awe-inspiring grandeur of the ocean to a person who has never seen a body of water larger than a mud puddle! How can such a person envision the boundless sea? How could you make a person believe that such a wonder really exists?

How infinitely more difficult it is for us to grasp what Jesus meant when He said, "God is Spirit." Jesus knew! His mind was not limited as our minds are limited. His eyes were not focused on the mud puddle of life. He knew full well the borderless reaches of the Spirit, and He came to try to give us some understanding of its wonders, its comfort, and its peace.

Can you grasp the concept of the Holy Spirit?

_____

_____

LIMITLESS GOD

The sea is His, for He made it;
And His hands formed the dry land.
PSALM 95:5

Whenever we think we have a full grasp of God, we are like the person who makes his way to the ocean, scoops up a few drops, and holds them in his hands.

"Ah," he exclaims, "at last I have made the ocean mine! I hold the ocean in my hands." True, he does have a part of the ocean, but at the same moment the world's millions could reach out their hands to be filled with seawater. They could each take as much as they wanted, as much as they needed—and still the ocean would remain unchanged. Its mightiness and power would be the same.

So it is with God. He can be everywhere at once, heeding the prayers of all who call out in the name of Christ, performing the mighty miracles that keep the stars in their places and the fish swimming in the sea. There is no limit to God. There is no limit to His wisdom. There is no limit to His power. There is no limit to His love. There is no limit to His mercy.

Have you ever been awe-inspired?

_____

_____

APRIL

JESUS' DEFINITION OF REPENTANCE

"The son said to him, 'Father, I have sinned against heaven and in your sight, and am no longer worthy to be called your son.'"
LUKE 15:21

Jesus told the parable of the prodigal son to dramatize what He meant by the word *repent*. When the prodigal son repented, he didn't just sit still and feel sorry about all his sins. He wasn't passive. He didn't stay where he was, surrounded by the swine. He got up and left! He turned his feet in the other direction. He sought out his father and humbled himself before him, and then he was forgiven.

Too many modern Christians think that repentance is little more than shaking their heads over their sins and saying, "My, but I'm sorry I did that!" and then continuing to live just as they have lived before.

To be sorry is not enough in repentance. Even reformation is not enough. There is no torture that you can give your body, no trials you can set for your mind that will be pleasing to almighty God. Our sins were atoned for by Christ on the cross. There He suffered sin's penalty. No suffering that we can undergo will lead us to repentance; only He can.

When you sin, do you remember to ask Jesus for His forgiveness?

_____

_____

UNCHANGING SAVIOR

But You are the same, and Your years will have no end.
PSALM 102:27

Three facts constitute the true story of man: his past is filled with sin; his present is overflowing with sorrow; and the certainty of death faces him in the future.

The Bible says, "It is appointed unto men once to die" (Hebrews 9:27 KJV), and to the average person this seems a stark and hopeless situation.

But Christ came to give us the answers to the three enduring problems of sin, sorrow, and death. It is Jesus Christ, and He alone, who is also enduring and unchanging, "the same yesterday, today, and forever" (Hebrews 13:8). As the hymn writer Henry F. Lyte wrote: "Change and decay in all around I see; O Thou who changest not, abide with me."[1]

All other things may change, but Christ remains unchangeable. In the restless sea of human passions, Christ stands steadfast and calm, ready to welcome all who will turn to Him and accept the blessings of safety and peace. For we are living in an age of grace, in which God promises that whosoever will may come and receive His Son.

Is the Lord your unchanging Rock in the storm?

_____

_____

SURRENDER ALL

*"Whoever wants to be my disciple must deny themselves
and take up their cross and follow me."*
MATTHEW 16:24 NIV

There is not one verse of Scripture that indicates you can be a Christian and live any kind of a life you want to. When Christ enters the heart, He expects to be Lord and Master. He commands complete surrender—mind, body, talents, and abilities. He expects nothing less than that all your work will be performed in His name.

We have the warning of Christ that He will not receive us into His kingdom until we are ready to give up all, until we are ready to turn from all sin in our lives. Don't try to do it partway. Don't say, "I'll live part of my life for Jesus and part for my own desires." Jesus expects 100 percent surrender, and when that is accomplished He rewards a thousandfold. But don't expect Jesus to hand out any 50 percent awards for 50 percent surrenders! God doesn't work that way. When you have determined that you are renouncing sin, forsaking sin, and yielding all to Christ, you have taken another step toward peace with God.

Are you living partly for yourself and partly for Jesus?

_____

_____

No Turning Back

Moses was learned in all the wisdom of the Egyptians,
and was mighty in words and in deeds.
ACTS 7:22

M oses considered the claims and obligations of God carefully. At forty he fled, a murderer. At eighty he returned a leader. He realized that if he were to embrace God he would have to do it at the sacrifice of the things that men usually hold most dear. He made no hasty examination. He came to no half-considered conclusions under sudden impulse or emotional reaction. He knew how much was at stake, and he arrived at his decision with the full use of his well-trained and superior mental faculties.

He did not select faith as a tentative measure. He burned all the bridges and ships that might have made retreat possible from his new position. When Moses had his great crisis moment at the age of eighty, he committed himself totally and without reservation for all time and under all circumstances to God and His commands.

Victory doesn't come to the halfhearted. When you come to Christ, every bridge has to be burned behind you, with no thought of ever turning back.

What bridges and ships have you held in reserve?

_____

_____

DEALING WITH OUR GRIEF

The LORD is close to the brokenhearted and saves those who are crushed in spirit.
PSALM 34:18 NIV

How should we cope with grief? Let me mention a few steps that have helped me.

First, don't be surprised by your grief or deny it or feel guilty over it. Don't be surprised, either, if it creeps up on you at unexpected times. Grieving is a process, and it doesn't go away overnight—even when we know our loved ones' suffering has ended, and they are now safely in Heaven.

A second step is this: don't focus only on the past, but also turn your heart and mind to the future. We still have people who love us and need us, and we still have responsibilities. God is not finished with us; He still has a plan for the remainder of our lives.

A third step is this: in time, begin reaching out to others who need your help. Then God also helps us by assuring us of His goodness. Have a spirit of gratitude for the life of our loved one, gratitude for all he or she meant to us, and most of all gratitude that death ushers a saved soul into God's presence forever. A daily "attitude of gratitude" will do much to move us beyond our sorrow.

How can you nurture a grateful heart?

_____

_____

A FRIEND IN SUFFERING AND SORROW

Casting all your care upon Him, for He cares for you.

1 PETER 5:7

I received a letter from a radio listener who for five years had been crippled into a sitting position by arthritis. For five long, painful years she was unable to stretch out or to lie down, yet she wrote, "I have spent many a day alone, but never a lonely day." Why? It was Christ who made the difference. With Christ as your Savior and constant Companion, you, too, although alone, need never be lonely.

You today who are lying on a hospital bed enduring the loneliness of suffering can rest assured that Christ can give you His grace and strength. While you lie there, you can know something of the ministry of intercession, the greatest ministry on earth, as you pray for others.

Perhaps in suffering and sorrow, you want someone to come along with a strong hand to help wipe the tears away, put the smile back on your face, and give you joy. Jesus can do just that. God loves His children. If you are willing to trust Him and give yourself to Him, He can carry your sorrow.

Have you felt the Lord's peace when you're hurting?

JESUS, THE GREAT FORGIVER

*"But I say to you, love your enemies, bless those who curse you, do good
to those who hate you, and pray for those who spitefully use you and
persecute you, that you may be sons of your Father in heaven."*
MATTHEW 5:44–45

Crucifixion is an evil death. The position of the victim on the cross results
in asphyxia, prohibiting adequate exhalation and inhalation of air.
Breathing is laborious and speaking insufferable. Yet in the midst of this agony,
Jesus ministered to humanity's vilest and also to the brokenhearted. This is
why the cross is often seen as the symbol of Christianity.

As the guards divided His garments by casting lots, Jesus said, "Father,
forgive them, for they do not know what they do" (Luke 23:34). Even from the
cross, Jesus spoke to His heavenly Father on behalf of His enemies.

We don't want the searchlight of the cross examining our hearts, telling us
that we're guilty before God. The blood of Jesus convicts, but it also cleanses.
The blood of Jesus brings reproach, but it also brings redemption. The blood of
Jesus frustrates evil, but it also brings forgiveness to the sinner. The blood of
Jesus cancels God's judgment on the repentant heart.

Who do you need to forgive today?

_____

_____

HE WENT TO THE CROSS

"Greater love has no one than this, than to lay down one's life for his friends."
JOHN 15:13

Jesus willingly died on the cross to identify with all those searching for truth. Are you among them? Have you heard what Jesus has said to you from the cross? You were there. I was there. Oh, it's true that we hadn't been born yet, but our sins were present that day. It wasn't just the soldiers, thieves, religious leaders, and passersby who took part in the crucifixion of Jesus Christ. Our sins also nailed Him to the tree.

No one could have forced Jesus to the cross had He been unwilling to go. This is the crux of the cross—Jesus chose to go to Calvary. He willingly laid down His life for the sins of the world. When Jesus hung on the cross, a great unseen cosmic battle raged in the heavens. And in the end Christ triumphed over all the forces of evil and death and Hell, giving us the greatest of all hope— eternal forgiveness. The greatest vision of sin is at the cross, where we also see the greatest vision of love. Jesus hung from the cross with us in mind.

What is one way you can thank Jesus for choosing the cross?

_____

_____

THE PRICE OF VICTORY

[Jesus] became the author of eternal salvation
to all who obey Him, called by God.
HEBREWS 5:9–10

Who doesn't like being on a victory team? Victory is something we all want to experience. The late Paul "Bear" Bryant, award-winning coach at the University of Alabama, said, "The price of victory is high, but so are the rewards."[2] Another Paul, the great apostle, said, "I press toward the goal for the prize of the upward call of God in Christ Jesus" (Philippians 3:14).

What is the greatest and most costly battle ever to take place? Who was the victor, and what was the reward? The greatest battle ever fought was between good and evil. This great battle took place at Golgotha—also known as Mount Calvary—a rugged hill outside the walled city of Jerusalem. Jesus Christ was Victor, paying the cost with His blood. The reward was the salvation of human souls. No one who witnessed Jesus on the cross that Good Friday would ever have thought such chaos would result in resounding victory. But it did, and this is what we celebrate in the Easter season.

How does knowing the price Jesus paid affect your view of Easter?

_____

_____

WHAT CHRIST DID FOR US

*For the wages of sin is death, but the gift of God is
eternal life in Christ Jesus our Lord.*

ROMANS 6:23

Our greatest need is to be reconciled to God and become part of His family—but one insurmountable barrier stands in the way, and that is our sin. Sin separates us from God and brings us under His judgment, and no matter how hard we try, we cannot erase our sins by our own efforts. We are alienated from God and guilty in His holy eyes.

Only God can take away our sins; He made this possible by sending His only Son into the world to die for us. Because He was divine, Jesus Christ was without sin. But on the cross all our sins were placed on Him, and by His death He took upon Himself the judgment and Hell we deserve. He did for us what we could never do for ourselves, and now He freely offers us the gifts of forgiveness and eternal life if we will accept them. Think of it: God now offers you the free gift of salvation—free because Jesus Christ has already paid the price for it.

What a gift we have been given by the Savior. Will you trust Him today?

Have you ever tried to earn salvation?

_____

_____

JESUS, THE GREAT SAVIOR

Whoever calls on the name of the LORD shall be saved.
JOEL 2:32

J esus preached from the cross the way of salvation and assurance. As Jesus emptied out His life's blood, He heard the thieves on either side of Him debating what they had heard about the Christ. One rejected salvation with sarcasm. But the other received Him, and Jesus assured him that very day he would be with Him in paradise (Luke 23:39–43).

Jesus knew the hearts of these convicted criminals, but only one became convicted of his sin. The Bible says conviction leads to repentance. The thief, who no doubt also labored to speak, confessed his sins, admitting that his deeds deserved the punishment of death. He acknowledged that Jesus was innocent of all wrongdoing. And by asking to be received in Jesus' kingdom, he proclaimed that Jesus truly was the King. The thief displayed this remarkable faith. He was hanging near the cross of Christ, and the very Word—the Lord Jesus—was near him, receiving his repentant heart.

He chose the only path to salvation. Christ is the way, His Word is the truth, and His death and resurrection bring life.

Which thief do you think you're more like?

_____

_____

SINNER OR SUBSTITUTE

While we were still sinners, Christ died for us.

ROMANS 5:8

God demands death, either for the sinner or a substitute. Christ was the substitute! One look from His blessed face and legions of angels would have swept the angry, shouting multitudes into Hell. The spikes never held Him to the cross—it was the cords of love that bound tighter than any nails that men could mold.

For you! For me! He bore our sins in His body upon the tree. As someone has said:

Behold Him on the Cross, bending His sacred head, and gathering into His heart in the awful isolation of separation from God the issue of the sin of the world, and see how out of that acceptance of the issue of sin He creates that which He does not require for Himself that He may distribute to those whose place He has taken. Standing overwhelmed in the presence of this suffering, feeling our own inability to understand or explain, and with a great sense of might and majesty overwhelming us, we hear the next words that pass His lips, "It is finished."

How do Jesus' last words, "It is finished," give hope to us today?

_____

_____

WHERE IS JESUS?

Come and see the works of God;
He is awesome in His doing toward the sons of men.
PSALM 66:5

An entertainment network once carried a story on the Billy Graham Library. Kristy Villa, the show's cohost, toured "The Journey of Faith" and said with a sense of awe, "I see all the crosses, but where is Jesus?" My colleague smiled and said, "He's in Heaven, and He is also present in the lives of those who believe in Him and follow Him as their personal Lord and Savior." The journalist threw her hands around her face and exclaimed, "Oh, that's right! Some worship a crucifix, but Christians worship a risen Christ." After a moment Villa said, "I have been in church my whole life, but I have never heard the emphasis put on an empty cross."

She may not have realized it, but she had just proclaimed the heart of the Gospel. She told her viewers, "This destination is a place you must come and see!"[3] When I heard this marvelous report, it made my heart leap, and I thought about the words of the psalmist: "Come and see." Have you beheld the empty cross?

How does the empty cross mean victory?

_____

_____

RISEN REDEMPTION

"If I go and prepare a place for you, I will come back and take you to be with me that you also may be where I am."

JOHN 14:3 NIV

When Jesus walked among men, many believed He had come to save them, but they lost all hope when He was taken down from the cross and buried in a tomb. His followers were despondent that He had not saved them from their enemies. They considered all that He had claimed and saw only the blaze of defeat. How could their Rescuer save them if He couldn't save Himself?

But the Special Force that had come down had not yet completed His mission. His followers had forgotten what He had told them: "I will come back" (John 14:3). Redemption was fulfilled, as promised, on the third day when He rose from the grave. His resurrection conquered the enemy of death, and shortly afterward, Jesus appeared to His dejected followers who had lost faith. They looked at Jesus, the Man who had shed His blood to put to death the curse of sin. He had returned to them in all of His glory. He had won the victory over death and over sin that entangled humanity.

How do you think the disciples felt before Jesus' resurrection?

_____

_____

BE A GOOD CITIZEN

I urge, then, . . . that petitions, prayers, intercession and thanksgiving
be made for all people—for kings and all those in authority, that we
may live peaceful and quiet lives in all godliness and holiness.
1 TIMOTHY 2:1–2 NIV

The Bible teaches that the Christian should be law-abiding. The Bible also teaches loyalty to country. A loyalty to and love of country do not mean that we cannot criticize unjust laws. The government of God should be our model.

The Bible also teaches that we are to cooperate with the government. Jesus was asked, "Is it lawful to give tribute?" Then He set the example forever by paying taxes. It takes money to run a government and to maintain law and order. The tax dodger is a civic parasite and an actual thief. No true Christian will be a tax dodger. Jesus said, we are to "render to Caesar the things that are Caesar's" (Mark 12:17). We ought to be more than taxpayers. To be simply law-abiding is not enough. We ought to seek and work for the good of our country. Sometimes we may be called upon to die for it. We are to be conscientious in our work as good citizens.

What can you pray for the leaders of your country?

_____

_____

THE LIVING LORD

He is not here; for He is risen, as He said.
MATTHEW 28:6

What do Socrates, Bach, and Shakespeare have in common? They are remembered as bigger than life, but they are dead and in the grave and can do nothing for you. Walk into the great cathedrals whose spires pierce the sky, and you will see paintings and sculptures memorializing robust men who are still revered and kind women who reached down to the lowly in compassion. But they, too, lie silent in death; they can do nothing for you.

But where is Jesus? Sadly, artists too often have depicted Him as feeble, weak, and dead—still hanging on the cross. This is not the truth; for the One who is depicted hanging lifeless and broken on the cross is instead full of the breath of life, full of glory. He drank the cup of sin for all by emptying His life's blood so that He could fill us with the gift of eternal life by His resurrection.

Christianity is the faith of the empty tomb, a religion centered not on a dead leader but on the living Lord.

Do you celebrate the fact that you worship a living Lord?

_____

_____

JESUS, THE FINISHER OF OUR FAITH

When Jesus had received the sour wine, He said, "It is finished!" And bowing His head, He gave up His spirit.
JOHN 19:30

"It is finished" is a proclamation of salvation's completed plan. Never again will blood be shed for sin. Jesus Christ has paid the ransom. On His own accord, He quietly, reverently, and deliberately bowed His head, knowing He had finished the work His Father had given Him to do.

Had Jesus been rescued from the cross by His Father, the ransom for sin would have never been paid. For this profound reason, God had sent Jesus on a rescue mission to save the souls of mankind, and Jesus was obedient to the Father's calling. God the Father and God the Son are one, unified in bringing about the great gift of our salvation.

How mysteriously wonderful it is that Christ willingly took your place and mine. We now have the opportunity to finish with the hope and certainty of eternal life because of victory in the cross of Christ—"Looking unto Jesus, the author and finisher of our faith" (Hebrews 12:2). We, too, can now sound the victory cry: "It is finished!"

Do you have the hope of eternal life?

_____

_____

YOU WERE THERE

He forgave us all our sins, having canceled the charge of our legal indebtedness, which stood against us and condemned us; he has taken it away, nailing it to the cross.

COLOSSIANS 2:13–14

With whom do you identify at the cross of Jesus Christ? Are you just passing by, scoffing at what Christ has done for you, or are you thirsting for the life that Jesus longs to give you? Do you identify with the thief who rejected Christ as Lord or the thief who repented?

There are some who might identify with the religious rulers who believed they were holy and righteous, yet in vengeance they betrayed, mocked, and murdered the righteous One.

Perhaps you see yourself sitting with the soldiers, gambling for a little piece of Jesus; or standing with Mary and John, waiting to be comforted by Jesus. Will you go down in defeat as the executioners did, or will you say with the centurion, "Surely He was the Son of God!" (Matthew 27:54 NIV)?

Jesus looked down from the cross on our sin and loved us in spite of it. Will you look to Him and be saved (Isaiah 45:22)?

Who do you identify with most at the cross?

_____

_____

THE JOY OF THE RESURRECTION

For if we have been united together in the likeness of His death,
certainly we also shall be in the likeness of His resurrection.
ROMANS 6:5

The resurrection completes the work that Jesus came to do so that we can live a resurrected life now. Christ did not stay on the cross. He was raised from the dead; He is alive!

In his last year as chancellor of Germany, Konrad Adenauer invited me for a visit. It surprised me that he knew I existed. When we met, he looked at me with his blazing eyes and said, "Young man, I've invited you for one thing. I want to know, do you believe in the resurrection of Jesus Christ?"

I said, "I do, sir!"

He replied, "So do I!" Then he made a powerful declaration: "Life has no meaning whatsoever if Christ is still in the grave!"

The risen Savior has promised to give immortality to all who believe on His name. There is a light that shines brighter than the noonday sun, and Christ's resurrection is what gives us hope; this is the first stage of eternal life in Him. The first glorious step on the journey is choosing Christ.

Do you live as though Christ is resurrected?

_____

_____

DEATH IS DEFEATED

For I know that my Redeemer lives.
JOB 19:25

Here is an age-old question, found in the Old Testament book of Job: "If a man dies, shall he live again?" (14:14). We expect death, but we usually have a glimmer of hope that medical science will discover something that will keep us alive a little longer. Death carries with it a certain dread. We never know when the moment of death will come for us.

How do we know there is something more beyond death? Look into the garden tomb, outside of that great walled city. Jesus had been buried there, and a few women came that first Easter to anoint the Lord's body. They were startled to find the tomb empty. An angel sat on the stone that had been rolled away from the door of the tomb and said, "He is not here; for He is risen, as He said" (Matthew 28:5–6).

The greatest news that mortal ears have ever heard is that Jesus Christ has risen from the dead. Only in this truth can we comprehend that out of death comes life, out of emptiness comes eternity.

What must it have been like that day at the tomb?

_____

_____

BELIEF IS ESSENTIAL

*"Believe Me that I am in the Father and the Father in Me, or
else believe Me for the sake of the works themselves."*
JOHN 14:11

The Bible teaches that faith is the only approach to God. "For he that cometh to God must believe that he is, and that he is a rewarder of them that diligently seek him" (Hebrews 11:6 KJV). The Bible also teaches that faith pleases God more than anything else. "Without faith it is impossible to please him" (Hebrews 11:6 KJV).

People all over the world torture themselves, clothe themselves in strange garments, disfigure their bodies, deny themselves the necessities of life, spend much time in prayer and self-sacrifice in an effort to make themselves acceptable in God's sight. But the greatest thing we can do to please God is to believe and obey Him.

I might go to a friend and flatter him, but if after all my flowery phrases I were to tell him I did not believe him, every flattering thing I said would have been in vain. I would have built him up only to let him down.

The greatest way we can please God is to *believe* His Word.

Do you have to make yourself acceptable to the Lord?

_____

_____

OUR CODE BOOK

The grass withers, the flower fades,
But the word of our God stands forever.
ISAIAH 40:8

Have we just been placed here by some unknown creator or force without any clue as to where we came from, why we are here, where we are going, or which way shall we turn? Is there any authority left? Can we find a code book that will give us the key to our dilemmas? Is there any source of authority to which we can turn?

The answer to the first question is no. The answer to all the rest is yes. We do have a code book. We do have a key. We do have authoritative source material. It is found in the ancient and historic book we call the Bible. This book has come down to us through the ages. It has passed through so many hands, appeared in so many forms—and survived attacks of every kind. Neither barbaric vandalism nor civilized scholarship has touched it. Neither the burning of fire nor the laughter of skepticism has accomplished its annihilation. Through the many dark ages of man, its glorious promises have survived unchanged.

How can you take advantage of having the "code book"?

_____

_____

THREE ASPECTS OF FAITH

I made haste, and did not delay
To keep Your commandments.
PSALM 119:60

When Churchill gave his masterful speeches to the British people during the war, he appealed to intellect, but at the same time he made his audience "feel." I remember hearing him one time in Glasgow. He challenged my thinking, but he made me feel like standing up and shouting and waving a flag! When you fall in love with Jesus Christ, your emotions are bound to be stirred.

Intellect says that the Gospel is logical. Emotion puts pressure upon Will and says, "I feel love for Christ," or "I feel fear of judgment." And then the middleman, called Will, is the referee. He sits there with his hand on his chin, in deep thought, trying to make up his mind. It is actually the will that makes the final and lasting decision. Intellect and emotion alone can't result in faith: the will decides to believe.

Has your will made the final decision?

_____

_____

WHY BE BORN AGAIN?

The natural man does not receive the things of the
Spirit of God, . . . nor can he know them.

1 CORINTHIANS 2:14

The Bible teaches that our old nature is totally corrupt. From its head to its feet "there is no soundness in it" (Isaiah 1:6). Its heart is "deceitful above all things, and desperately wicked" (Jeremiah 17:9).

The Bible also teaches that our old nature is a self-nature. It is incapable of being renovated. The Bible teaches that when we are born again, we put off the old man—we do not patch him up. The old self is to be crucified, not cultivated. Jesus said the cleansing of the outside of the cup and the platter leaves the inside just as dirty as before.

In being born again, you can decide right now to wipe out your sinful past and make a new start, a fresh start, a right start. You can decide now to become the person that Jesus promised you could be.

Do you live like a new person?

_____

_____

YOU MUST BE BORN AGAIN!

"You must be born again."
JOHN 3:7

The Bible teaches that unless we have experienced the new birth, we cannot get into the kingdom of Heaven. Jesus made it even stronger by saying we *must* be born again. There is nothing indefinite, nothing optional about that. He who would enter the kingdom of God must be born again.

Salvation is not just repairing the original self. It is a new self created of God in righteousness and true holiness. Regeneration is not even a change of nature or a change of heart. Being born again is not a change—it is a regeneration, a new generation. It is a second birth.

The life that comes from the new birth cannot be obtained by natural development or self-effort. Man does not by nature have this holiness that God requires for Heaven. "That which is born of the flesh is flesh" (John 3:6). In the new birth alone is the beginning of such a life to be found. To live the life of God we must have the nature of God.

What does it mean to have the nature of God?

_____

_____

FAITH VERSUS FEELING

But these [the Bible] are written that you may believe that Jesus is the Christ, the Son of God, and that believing you may have life in His name.

JOHN 20:31

Many people say they have doubts and uncertainties concerning the Christian life. Some come from genuine Christians who seem to have none of the joy of Christian faith because they have confused faith with feeling.

Faith always implies an object—that is, when we believe, we must believe something. That something I call the *fact*. Let me give you, then, three words that must always be kept in the same order. They will point the way out of uncertainty to a confident Christian life. These three words are *fact*, *faith*, and *feeling*. The order is essential. If you confuse them, eliminate one, or add one, you will remain in confusion, but when you let them guide you, you can develop the joy and confidence of one who can say, "I know [Him in] whom I have believed" (2 Timothy 1:12).

Do you ever get *fact*, *faith*, and *feeling* out of order?

_____

_____

FACT

*I delivered to you first of all that which I also received: that Christ
died for our sins according to the Scriptures, and that He was buried,
and that He rose again the third day according to the Scriptures.*
1 CORINTHIANS 15:3–4

If you are saved from sin, you are saved through a personal faith in the Gospel of Christ as defined in the Scriptures. Though it may at first seem dogmatic and narrow to you, the fact remains that there is no other way. The Bible says that we are saved when our faith is in this objective fact. The work of Christ is a fact, His cross is a fact, His tomb is a fact, and His resurrection is a fact.

The Bible does not call upon you to believe something that is not credible, but to believe in the fact of history. The Bible calls upon you to believe that this work of Christ, done for sin and for sinners, is effective in all who will risk their souls with Him. Trusting in Him for your eternal salvation is trusting in a fact.

Do you live like you believe in the resurrection?

_____

_____

FAITH

Having been justified by faith, we have peace with
God through our Lord Jesus Christ.

ROMANS 5:1

F aith is rationally impossible where there is nothing to believe. Faith must have an object. The object of Christian faith is Christ. Faith means more than an intellectual assent to the claims of Christ. Faith involves the will. It is volitional. Faith demands action. If we actually believe, then we will live. "Faith without works is dead" (James 2:26). It means an acknowledgment of sin and a turning to Christ. We do not know Christ through the five physical senses, but we know Him through the sixth sense that God has given every man—which is the ability to believe.

Believing is an experience as real as any experience, yet many are looking for something more—some dramatic sensation that will bring a physical thrill, while others look for some spectacular manifestation. Many have been told to look for such sensations, but the Bible says that a man is "justified by faith" and not by feeling. Whatever feeling there may be is only the result of saving faith, but it in itself is not what does the saving!

What have you done that shows your faith in Christ?

_____

_____

FEELING

Praise the LORD!
Blessed is the man who fears the LORD,
Who delights greatly in His commandments.
PSALM 112:1

When I understand something of Christ's love for me as a sinner, I respond with a love for Christ—and love has feeling. But love for Christ is above human love, though there is a similarity. It is a love that frees us from self.

In marriage there is commitment. There is also feeling. But feelings come and go. Commitment stays. We who have committed ourselves to Christ have feelings that come and go—joy, love, gratitude, and so on. But the commitment remains unchanged.

It is not the feeling of boldness and confidence that saves us, but it is our faith in God that saves us through His forgiveness. Boldness and confidence result from our having trusted in Christ. From Genesis to Revelation we are told to fear the Lord. It is the fear of the Lord that puts all other fears in proper perspective.

Which of the three words—*fact, faith,* and *feeling*—do you rely on the most?

SOLID FOUNDATIONS

"Whoever hears these sayings of Mine, and does them, I will liken him to a wise man who built his house on the rock."

MATTHEW 7:24

I heard about a family who hired a contractor to build their dream house. But their dream soon turned into a nightmare. The first hint of trouble was a slight depression in the soil around the foundation; then as time went on, cracks began to appear in the walls. They called in a structural engineer, who discovered that part of the concrete for the foundation had been poured over a debris pit. As it decayed, the ground gave way, and the walls began to shift, making the whole house dangerously unstable.

Just as this house needed a solid foundation, so we need the same for our lives—an unchanging system of beliefs, goals, and moral values that will keep us stable and secure, even in the midst of life's storms. Nothing prepares us for the future like a solid moral and spiritual foundation based on God's will for our lives.

How is the Lord the foundation of your life?

_____

_____

MAY

GOD'S LAW IS CLEAR

Prophecy never came by the will of man, but holy men of
God spoke as they were moved by the Holy Spirit.
2 PETER 1:21

In the wonders of nature we see God's laws in operation. Who has not looked up at the stars on a cloudless night and marveled in silent awe at the glory of God's handiwork? Even our astronauts have lauded the Lord as Creator of the vastness of space. Who has not felt his heart lifted in the spring of the year as he sees all creation bursting with new life and vigor? In it we see the magnitude of God's power and the infinite detail of His planning, but nature tells us nothing of God's love or God's grace. We do not find the promise of our personal salvation in nature.

Conscience tells us in our innermost being of the presence of God and of the moral difference between good and evil, but this is a fragmentary message, in no way as distinct and comprehensive as the lessons of the Bible. It is only in its pages that we find the clear and unmistakable message upon which all true Christianity is based.

Do you feel close to God in nature?

_____

_____

GOD IS LOVE

God is love.
1 JOHN 4:8

We aren't always sure ourselves what we mean when we use the term *love*. That word has become one of the most widely misused words in our language. We say we "love" to travel; we "love" to eat chocolate cake; or we "love" our new car. Why, we even say we "love" our neighbors—but most of us don't do much more than just say it and let it go at that! No wonder we don't have a very clear idea of what the Bible means when it says, "God is love."

Don't make the mistake of thinking that because God is love everything is going to be sweet, beautiful, and happy and that no one will be punished for his sins. God's holiness demands that all sin be punished, but God's love provides the plan and way of redemption for sinful man. God's love provided the cross of Jesus, by which man can have forgiveness and cleansing. It was the love of God that sent Jesus Christ to the cross!

What is one way God shows His love to you?

_____

_____

THE BEGINNING OF THE PROBLEM

*"Away with you, Satan! For it is written, 'You shall worship
the LORD your God, and Him only you shall serve.'"*
MATTHEW 4:10

Freedom is meaningless if there is only one possible path to follow. Freedom implies the right to choose, to select, to determine one's individual course of action.

God granted Adam freedom of choice in the garden, and He gave him every opportunity to exercise it. Then, like the wise Parent that He is, God waited to see what choice this child of His would make.

Adam chose to disobey God by eating of the Tree of Knowledge, and sin entered the world. And so we are all sinners by inheritance.

Before we label God as unjust or unreasonable for permitting sin to envelop the world, let us look at the situation more carefully. God in His infinite compassion sent His Son to show us the way out of our difficulties. He sent His Son to experience the same temptations that were set before Adam. Jesus completely triumphed over the Tempter, Satan, to reveal to all peoples of all succeeding generations His sinless character. He is our victory!

Do you think of God as a wise parent?

_____

_____

THE ONLY REMEDY

"The Son of Man did not come to be served, but to serve,
and to give his life as a ransom for many."

MATTHEW 20:28

Charles Wesley wrote:

> And can it be that I should gain
> An interest in the Savior's blood?
> Died He for me, who caused His pain? . . .
> Amazing love! how can it be
> That Thou, my God, shouldst die for me?

Sin overreached itself on the cross. Man's injustice that crucified Christ became the means for man to become free. Sin's masterpiece of shame and hate became God's masterpiece of mercy and forgiveness. Through the death of Christ upon the cross, sin itself was crucified for those who believe in Him. He proved the truth of all God's promises to man, and if you will accept Christ by faith today, you, too, can be forgiven for your sins. You can stand secure in the knowledge that through the love of Christ your soul is saved from damnation.

What did you gain when Christ died on the cross?

_____

_____

JESUS' MIGHTY WORDS

No man ever spoke like this Man!
JOHN 7:46

Jesus taught with such authority that the people of His day marveled. There were no loopholes in the moral conceptions and statements of Jesus Christ. His ethical vision was wholly correct, correct in the age in which He lived, and correct in every age that has followed.

The words of this blessed Person were prophetically true. He prophesied many things that are even yet in the future. Lawyers tried to catch Him with test questions, but they could never confuse Him. His answers to His opponents were clear and clean-cut. There were no question marks about His statements, no deception in His meaning, no hesitancy in His words. He knew, and therefore spoke with quiet authority. He spoke with such simplicity that the common people heard Him gladly. Though His words were profound, they were plain. His words were weighty, yet they shone with a luster and simplicity of statement that staggered His enemies. He dealt with the great questions of the day in such a way that, from simple to sophisticated, man had no difficulty in understanding Him. And we can study His words today.

What is the difference between a person today speaking with authority and Jesus speaking with authority?

_____

_____

SUFFERING SAVIOR

[Jesus] said, "It is finished!" And bowing His head, He gave up His spirit.
JOHN 19:30

The physical suffering of Jesus Christ was not the real suffering. Many men had become martyrs. The awful suffering of Jesus Christ was His spiritual death. He reached the final issue of sin, fathomed the deepest sorrow, when He cried, "My God, why hast thou forsaken me?" (Matthew 27:46 KJV). This cry was proof that Christ, becoming sin for us, had died physically, and with it He lost all sense of the Father's presence at that moment in time. Alone in the supreme hour of mankind's history, Christ uttered these words! Light blazed forth to give us a glimpse of what He was enduring, but the light was so blinding, as G. Campbell Morgan says, "that no eye could bear to gaze that we men may know how much there is that may not be known."

I know only one thing—He bore my sins in His body upon the tree, and I am able to go to Heaven and merit that which is not my own, but is His by every right. His work was finished.

How do you think Jesus felt when He said, "Why hast thou forsaken me?"

_____

_____

EXAMINE YOUR FOUNDATIONS

The solid foundation of God stands, having this seal:
"The Lord knows those who are His."
2 TIMOTHY 2:19

Tragically, many people never stop to examine the foundations on which they are building their lives. They assume they are on the right road and their foundations will always be secure. For some the foundation may be self-indulgence or pleasure or entertainment. Others build upon financial success or social position. Still others think that if they can only find the right person . . . or discover the ideal place to live . . . or clinch the best-paying job . . . then they will always be happy and secure. But in moments of crisis, these dreams are shattered, leaving them disillusioned and wondering what went wrong.

Why is it that money, success, and pleasure don't provide a solid foundation? Because they ignore the soul. If we feed our bodies but starve our souls, we will find ourselves weak and unprepared for life's inevitable challenges.

God has a purpose for each of us, and He desires that we build upon Him, the very foundation He has put in place. When you examine your foundation, make sure it's in Him.

What false things have you relied on for security?

_____

_____

CONVERSION IS FOR EVERYONE

A highway shall be there, and a road, and it shall be called the Highway of Holiness. The unclean shall not pass over it, but it shall be for others.

ISAIAH 35:8

Conversion is so simple that the smallest child can be converted, but it is also so profound that theologians throughout history have pondered the depth of its meaning. God has made the way of salvation so plain that "the wayfaring men, though fools, shall not err therein" (Isaiah 35:8 KJV). No person will ever be barred from the kingdom of God because he did not have the capacity to understand. The rich and the poor, the sophisticated and the simple—all can be converted.

Conversion simply means "to change." In conversion as you stand at the foot of the cross, the Holy Spirit convicts of sin. He directs your faith to the Christ who died in your place. You must open your heart and let Him come in. At that precise moment the Holy Spirit performs the miracle of the new birth. You actually become a new moral creature. You become a partaker of God's own life. Jesus Christ, through the Spirit of God, takes up residence in your heart. This is available to everyone.

What would cause you to be barred from Heaven?

_____

_____

THE FEELING OF FAITH

The fear of the LORD is the beginning of knowledge.
PROVERBS 1:7

Desire, love, fear—all are emotions. Emotion cannot be cut out of life. No intelligent person would think of saying, "Let's do away with all emotion." To remove all personality from deep feeling is impossible. We cannot imagine life without the warm overtones of feeling. Suppose we had a family in which everyone acted only from a cold sense of duty. Suppose I asked my wife to marry me after I had explained to her first of all that I had no feelings for her at all.

As the great British Methodist preacher Dr. W. E. Sangster said, "Carry the same principle over into religion. Require that the Herald of God announce the offer of His King, freely to pardon and fully to bless, but firmly forbid that any transport of joy should accompany either the announcement of the news or its glad reception, and you ask the impossible."

There is going to be a tug at the heart. Emotion may vary in religious experience. Some people are stoic and others are demonstrative, but the feeling will be there. Ours is not a cold faith, but one that encompasses every part of us.

Do people see you as a joyful Christian?

_____

_____

THREE MANIFESTATIONS OF FAITH

Humble yourselves under the mighty hand of God,
that He may exalt you in due time.

1 PETER 5:6

The Bible teaches that faith will manifest itself in three ways. It will manifest itself in doctrine—in what you believe. It will manifest itself in worship—your communion with God and the fellowship of the church. It will manifest itself in morality—in the way you live and behave.

The Bible also teaches that faith does not end with trust in Christ for your salvation. Faith continues. Faith grows. It may be weak at first, but it will become stronger as you begin to read the Bible, pray, go to church, and experience God's faithfulness in your Christian life. After you have repented of sins and accepted Him by faith, then you must trust Him to keep you, strengthen you, enable you, sustain you. You will learn more and more how to rely on Christ for every need, in meeting every circumstance and every trial.

When you have saving faith in Jesus Christ, you have taken an additional step toward having peace with God.

What can you do when your faith is weak?

_____

_____

THE MEANING OF JUSTIFICATION

All things are of God, who has reconciled us to Himself through
Jesus Christ, and has given us the ministry of reconciliation.
2 CORINTHIANS 5:18

The moment you are born again, you are justified in the sight of God. By being justified is meant "just-as-if-I'd" never sinned. Justification is that act of God whereby He declares an ungodly man to be perfect. God places you before Him as though you had never committed a sin.

Your sins have been forgiven. God has buried them in the depths of the sea and placed them behind His back of forgetfulness. Every sin is completely wiped out. You stand before God as a debtor, and you have received your discharge; you have become reconciled to God.

But more than all of that, you have been adopted into the family of God. You are now a child of God. You are now a member of the royal family of Heaven. You have royal blood in your veins. You are a child of the King. Even your friends will begin to notice the change that has taken place in your life. You have now been born again.

Do you realize as a Christian that you have royal blood flowing through you?

_____

_____

A NEW POST

By this we know that we know Him, if we keep His commandments.
1 JOHN 2:3

In Texas they tell a story about a man who used to hitch his horse every morning in front of the saloon. One morning the saloonkeeper came out and found that the horse was hitched in front of the Methodist church. He saw the man walking down the street and called out, "Say, why is your horse hitched in front of the Methodist church this morning?"

The man turned around and said, "Well, last night I was converted in the revival meeting, and I've changed hitching posts."

That's what it means to be born again. That's what it means to be converted. That's what it means to be separated from the world. It means that you change hitching posts.

It means a change of habits, motivations, lifestyle, and everything in your life. Commitment to God will inevitably have a transforming effect. You will know that you have been born again because you will want to obey God in every way. Do your actions and choices reveal that you've hitched yourself to the Lord?

Have you tied yourself to God's hitching post?

_____

_____

THE PART GUILT PLAYS

And it shall be, when he is guilty in any of these matters,
that he shall confess that he has sinned in that thing.
LEVITICUS 5:5

I n an article that appeared in the *New York Times* (29 November 1983)
Dr. Helen Block Lewis, a psychoanalyst and psychologist at Yale University,
described guilt as a feeling that "helps people stay connected" to their fellow
human beings. "Guilt is one of the cements that binds us together and keeps us
human," she explained. "If it occurs to you that you've done something to injure
someone else, guilt compels you to do something to fix it, to repair the bond."

Samuel Rutherford said to "pray for a strong and lively sense of sin; the
greater the sense of sin, the less sin." A sense of sin and guilt not only tells you
when you are in trouble, but like the sense of pain, it can keep you out of it.
Without a sense of pain, one could put his hand on a hot stove and feel nothing.
The Bible teaches that Christ cleanses the conscience "to serve the living God"
(Hebrews 9:14).

Do you have a strong sense of sin that drives you to the Lord for help?

_____

_____

IN THE SPIRIT'S POWER

We do not wrestle against flesh and blood, but against principalities, against powers, against the rulers of the darkness.

EPHESIANS 6:12

I believe unselfconsciousness is characteristic of the fruit of the Holy Spirit. The person who says, "I am Spirit-filled" sets himself up for some pretty uncomfortable scrutiny. Did any apostle or disciple say of himself, "I am filled with the Holy Spirit"? But of many it was said, "They were filled with the Holy Spirit." The person who is self-consciously loving, self-consciously joyful, self-consciously peaceful has about him the odor of self.

It is only the consecrated, Spirit-filled Christian who can have victory over the world, the flesh, and the devil. It is the Holy Spirit who will do the fighting for you. This is a spiritual warfare. You cannot fight against these three enemies all by yourself, in your own self-power and self-consciousness. Only as we become channels and let the Holy Spirit do the fighting through us are we going to get complete victory. Don't hold back anything from Christ. Let Him be completely the Lord and Master of your life.

How can you be unselfconscious about your faith?

_____

_____

141

SYSTEMATIC PRAYER

Be joyful in hope, patient in affliction, faithful in prayer.
ROMANS 12:12 NIV

Try to have a systematic method of prayer. Prayer combined with Bible study makes for a healthy Christian life. The Bible says, "Pray without ceasing" (1 Thessalonians 5:17). If you have special prayer periods that you set aside during the day, your unconscious life will be saturated with prayer between the prayer periods. It is not enough for you to get out of bed in the morning and just bow your knee and repeat a few sentences. There should be stated periods in which you slip apart with God. For the overworked mother or one living under extremely busy circumstances, this may be impossible. But here is where "prayer without ceasing" comes in. We pray as we work. As we have said, we pray everywhere, anytime.

There will be many interruptions, but keep at it! Don't be discouraged. Soon you will find that these periods of prayer are the greatest delight of your life. Without constant, daily, systematic prayer, your life will seem barren, discouraging, and fruitless. Without constant prayer, you never can know the inner peace that God wants to give you.

What times of day can you commit to prayer?

_____

_____

RELY ON THE HOLY SPIRIT

If the Spirit of Him who raised Jesus from the dead dwells in you, He who raised Christ from the dead will also give life to your mortal bodies through His Spirit who dwells in you.

ROMANS 8:11

To grow spiritually you must rely constantly on the Holy Spirit. Remember that Christ dwells in you through the Holy Spirit. Your body is now the dwelling place of the Third Person of the Trinity. Do not ask Him to help you as you would a servant. Ask Him to come in and do it all.

It is impossible for you to hold out in your Christian life—but He can hold you. Just relax and rest in the Lord. Do not fret about important decisions—let Him make them for you. Do not worry about tomorrow—He is the God of tomorrow. Do not worry about the necessities of life—He is there to provide. A victorious Christian is one who, in spite of worries, is confident that God is in control. In reliance on the Holy Spirit, you will find that many of your troubles will disappear.

What struggles should you release to the Holy Spirit?

_____

_____

ATTEND CHURCH REGULARLY

"Where two or three are gathered together in My
name, I am there in the midst of them."
MATTHEW 18:20

Christianity is a religion of fellowship. Following Christ means love, righteousness, service; and these can only be achieved and expressed through social relations. These social relationships are to be found in the church.

There is a visible church, and there is an invisible church. The invisible church is made up of true believers down through the centuries and the world over. We are told in the Scriptures "not [to forsake] the assembling of ourselves together" (Hebrews 10:25). Christians need fellowship—the fellowship of fellow believers.

If you are a true follower of Christ, you will not let inconvenient circumstances stop you from going to church. There are many people who say they can stay at home on Sunday morning and worship God in their own minds. But this is not enough; the mind and the body should participate in rendering to God a complete act of worship.

What part of gathering together for worship do you enjoy the most?

_____

_____

GRACE IN ACTION

For judgment is without mercy to one who has shown
no mercy. Mercy triumphs over judgment.
JAMES 2:13

C hristians ought to be gracious, and this is one of the most important of Christian virtues. The very power of our conviction sometimes inclines us toward feeling that we are right and that other people are wrong, based on our own ideas rather than Scripture. The many different and frequently warring factions within the church emphasize the terrible human tendency to gather into select groups, built upon convictions on trivial matters, each insisting that they and they alone have the right answer. As the late Dr. Harry Ironside once said, "Beware lest we mistake our prejudices for our convictions."

To be sure we must deplore wickedness, evil, and wrongdoing, but our commendable intolerance of sin too often develops into a deplorable intolerance of sinners. Jesus hates sin but loves the sinner.

The teachings of Jesus deal frequently with our attitudes toward our fellow men. Study them and live by them. Only then can you demonstrate to a confused world the transforming power of the indwelling Christ.

Are you considered gracious?

_____

_____

QUESTIONS ABOUT HEAVEN

"In that day you will ask Me nothing."
JOHN 16:23

You may ask, "Will we know each other in Heaven?" The Bible indicates in a number of places that it will be a time of grand reunion with those who have gone on before.

Others say, "Do you believe that children will be saved?" Yes. The Bible indicates that God does not hold a child accountable for his or her sins until he reaches the age of accountability. There seems to be plenty of indication that the atonement covers their sin until they reach an age at which they are responsible for their own right and wrong actions.

The Bible also indicates that Heaven will be a place of great understanding and knowledge of things that we never learned down here.

Many of the mysteries of God—the heartaches, trials, disappointments, tragedies, and the silence of God in the midst of suffering—will be revealed there. Elie Wiesel said that eternity is "the place where questions and answers become one." And in John 16:23 Jesus says, "And in that day ye shall ask me nothing" (KJV). All our questions will be answered!

Does it bring joy to know all your questions will be answered someday?

_____

_____

THREE THINGS IN THE CROSS

*"I am the way, the truth, and the life. No one comes
to the Father except through Me."*

JOHN 14:6

In the cross of Christ I see three things: First, a description of the depth of *man's sin*. Do not blame the people of that day for hanging Christ on the cross. You and I are just as guilty. It was not the people or the Roman soldiers who put Him to the cross—it was your sins and my sins that made it necessary for Him to volunteer this death.

Second, in the cross I see the overwhelming *love of God*. If ever you should doubt the love of God, take a long, deep look at the cross, for in the cross you find the expression of God's love.

Third, in the cross is the *only way of salvation*. If there had been any other way to save you, He would have found it. If reformation or living a good moral and ethical life would have saved you, Jesus never would have died. A substitute had to take your place.

Remember these three things, and you'll begin to understand the power of the cross.

Do you daily thank Jesus for His sacrifice?

_____

_____

FORGIVEN DEBTS

Having canceled the charge of our legal indebtedness, which stood against
us and condemned us; he has taken it away, nailing it to the cross.
COLOSSIANS 2:14 NIV

Years ago King Charles V was loaned a large sum of money by a merchant in Antwerp. The note came due, but the king was bankrupt and unable to pay. The merchant gave a great banquet for the king. When all the guests were seated, the merchant had a large platter placed on the table before him and a fire lighted on it. Then, taking the note out of his pocket, he held it in the flames until it was burned to ashes.

Just so, we have all been mortgaged to God. The debt was due, but we were unable to pay. Two thousand years ago God invited a morally corrupt world to the foot of the cross. There God held your sins and mine to the flames until every last vestige of our guilt was consumed.

Many people have wondered, "I cannot understand why Christ had to die for me." At the cross, your debt was burned to ashes. This sacrifice is the very heart of Christianity.

What comes to mind knowing your debt has been paid?

_____

_____

SAME PROBLEMS, SAME SOLUTION

"These things I have spoken to you, that in Me you may have peace. In the world you will have tribulation; but be of good cheer, I have overcome the world."

JOHN 16:33

Not so long ago many of man's physical diseases were termed incurable. Today, we have drugs so effective that many age-old diseases are disappearing. But with all this progress, man has not solved the basic problem of the human race. We still can't govern ourselves or live together in equality and peace!

We may create great new schools of art and music, we may discover newer and better vitamins, but there is nothing new about our troubles. They are the same old ones that man has always had, only they seem magnified and more abundant. They may seem to give sharper pain and deeper anguish; but fundamentally we are facing the same temptations, the same trials, the same testings that have always confronted mankind.

Since that tragic moment in the garden of Eden, when man gave up God's will for his own will, man has been plagued by the same problems. And the Gospel of Jesus Christ gives us their remedy.

Which of your troubles has always been around?

_____

_____

GOD IS A PERSON

As a father has compassion on his children,
so the LORD has compassion on those who fear him.
PSALM 103:13 NIV

The Bible reveals God as a *Person*. All through the Bible it says, "God loves," "God says," "God does." A person is one who feels, thinks, wishes, desires, and has all the expressions of personality.

Here on earth we confine personality to the body. Our finite minds cannot envision personality that is not manifested through flesh and bones. We know that our own personalities will not always be clothed in the bodies they now inhabit. We know that at the moment of death, our personalities will leave our bodies and go on to the destinations that await them. We know all this—yet it is difficult for us to accept it.

What a revelation if we could all realize that personality does not have to be identified with a physical being. God is not bound by a body, yet He is a Person. He feels, He thinks, He loves, He forgives, He sympathizes with the problems and sorrows that we face. How blessed we are that we can know God personally.

Do you think of the Lord as a person or a spirit or both?

_____

_____

AN EXAMPLE OF FAITH

*"He who finds his life will lose it, and he who
loses his life for My sake will find it."*
MATTHEW 10:39

I heard about a man some years ago who was rolling a wheelbarrow back and forth across Niagara River on a tightrope. Thousands of people were shouting him on. He put a two-hundred-pound sack of dirt in the wheelbarrow and rolled it over, and then he rolled it back. Then he turned to the crowd and said, "How many of you believe that I can roll a man across?"

Everybody shouted! One man in the front row was very excited in his professed belief. The tightrope walker pointed to this excited man and said, "You're next!" You couldn't see that man for dust! He actually didn't believe it. He said he believed it, he thought he believed it—but he was not willing to get in the wheelbarrow.

Just so with Christ. There are many people who say they believe on Him, who say they will follow Him. But they never have gotten into the wheelbarrow. We must make sure we have committed and surrendered ourselves wholly, 100 percent to Christ—the object of our faith.

Is there anything holding you back from complete faith in the Lord?

_____

_____

Witness by the Word

"So shall My word be that goes forth from My mouth;
It shall not return to Me void,
But it shall accomplish what I please,
And it shall prosper in the thing for which I sent it."
Isaiah 55:11

Some time ago I came across this question: Which is more important, to witness by one's life or to witness by the Word? And my answer was, "Which is more important, the left or right wing of an airplane?" Thinking this very clever, I repeated it one day in a car as I was driving some missionaries out to lunch. One of them spoke up and said, "That's very clever. But it's just not true." Surprised, I asked what she meant.

"All the way through the Scriptures," she replied, "God has promised to bless His Word, not our lives.... We are responsible to God for the way in which we live, but it is His Word that He has promised to bless, and this explains why a musician in a communist country can pick up a page torn from the Bible and be converted." Of course, witness with your life, but know that the real power is in God's Word.

Does the Lord bless His Word or our lives?

_____

_____

A CHURCH FOR EVERYONE

Behold, how good and how pleasant it is
For brethren to dwell together in unity!
PSALM 133:1

Some people find it easier to draw closer to God in magnificent buildings and with some form of ritual. Others find they can seek God only in stark simplicity. Some people find themselves more comfortable with formality; others feel more at home with informality. The important thing is not how we do it, but the sincerity and depth of purpose with which we do it, and we should each find and join the church in which as individuals we can best accomplish this.

Do not make the mistake of attaching yourself to a particular minister rather than to the body of the church itself. The ministry may change—it is healthy and stimulating that it should—but the tenets of the church remain the same, and it is to Christ that you owe allegiance. A stable church is built up when the members of the congregation recognize that it is their mutual love of Jesus Christ and the sincere desire to follow in His steps that hold them together.

What type of gathering helps you draw close to the Lord?

_____

_____

THE AFFAIRS OF THIS LIFE

"For what profit is it to a man if he gains the whole world, and loses his own soul? Or what will a man give in exchange for his soul?"
MATTHEW 16:26

The fact that we have daily fellowship with Christ should enable us to live realistically. Christ's way of life does not require that a man renounce legitimate interests or ambitions. Though the Scriptures may teach that Christ may return at any time, the Scriptures also exhort us to carry on business as usual until He comes.

For example, there was nothing wrong about the eating, drinking, marrying, and giving in marriage in Noah's day except that the people had become totally preoccupied with these activities to the neglect of the spiritual dimension of life (Luke 17:27). Nor was there anything wrong about the buying, selling, planning, and building in Lot's day except that they were carried on by sinful methods (Luke 17:28).

As someone has said, "The Bible was not written to encourage people to take an interest in the affairs of this life.... [But it] aims to encourage man to see his worldly affairs in the light of the greater importance ... of spiritual things."

How can you live wisely?

_____

_____

A NEW HOME

For this world is not our permanent home; we are
looking forward to a home yet to come.

HEBREWS 13:14 NLT

As the Bible pronounces Hell for the sinner, it also promises Heaven for the saint. A saint has been described as a sinner who has been forgiven. If that is you, a new home awaits you.

If you are moving to a new home, you want to know all about the community to which you are going. If you are transferring to another city, you want to know all about the city—its industries, parks, lakes, schools, and so on. Since we are going to spend eternity someplace, we ought to know something about it. The information concerning Heaven is found in the Bible. It is right that we should think about it and talk about it. In talking about Heaven, earth grows shabby by comparison. Our sorrows and problems here seem so much less when we have keen anticipation of the future. In a certain sense, the Christian has Heaven here on earth. He has peace of soul, peace of conscience, and peace with God. In the midst of troubles and difficulties, he has an inner peace and joy not dependent on circumstances.

Are you anticipating your heavenly home?

THERE IS A HEAVEN

*We are confident, yes, well pleased rather to be absent
from the body and to be present with the Lord.*
2 CORINTHIANS 5:8

Someone asked John Quincy Adams at the age of ninety-four how he felt one morning. He said, "Quite well. Quite well. But the house I live in is not so good." Even if the house we live in may be sick and weak, we can actually feel strong and confident if we are Christians. Jesus taught there is a Heaven.

The apostle Paul said time after time, "We know," "We are confident," "We are always confident." The Bible says that Abraham "looked for a city which hath foundations, whose builder and maker is God" (Hebrews 11:10 KJV).

Many people say, "Do you believe that Heaven is a literal place?" Yes! Jesus said, "I go to prepare a place for you" (John 14:2). The Bible teaches that Enoch and Elijah ascended in a literal body to a literal place that is just as real as Hawaii, Switzerland, or the Virgin Islands, or more so!

Many people have asked, "Where is Heaven?" We are not told in the Scriptures where Heaven is. Nor does it matter, because wherever it is, Christ will be there to welcome us home.

Does thinking about Heaven give you peace?

_____

_____

WHAT IS THE LAW?

Therefore no one will be declared righteous in God's sight by the works of the law; rather, through the law we become conscious of our sin.

ROMANS 3:20 NIV

I t is impossible to be converted by the keeping of the law. The Bible says, "By the law is the knowledge of sin" (Romans 3:20). The law is a moral mirror, the gauge by which man can see how far he has fallen. It condemns but does not convert. It challenges but does not change. It points the finger but does not offer mercy. There is no life in the law. There is only death, for the pronouncement of the law was, "Thou shalt die." It is the "straight stick" beside which the crookedness of human nature is obvious.

There are many people who say that their religion is the Sermon on the Mount, but the man or woman is yet to be born who has ever lived up to the Sermon on the Mount.

Examine your own motives before you decide that you are above reproach. Look into your own heart fearlessly and honestly. Let the law reveal you to yourself, and run straight to Christ. In Him salvation is found.

Are you relieved we don't live under the law?

_____

_____

THE UNIVERSAL QUESTION

Jesus answered, "Very truly I tell you, no one can enter the
kingdom of God unless they are born of water and the Spirit."
JOHN 3:5 NIV

When I was preaching in Hollywood, a group of people from the movie industry asked me to talk to them. After my address we had a discussion period, and the very first question asked was, "What is conversion?"

In almost every university and college group where I have led discussions, this same question is invariably asked: "What do you mean by 'born again'?" In my book *How to Be Born Again* (Word, 1976), I described the process this way:

This new birth happens in all kinds of ways. It may seem to happen over a period of time or in a moment. That encounter with Christ is the beginning of a whole new path in life under His control. Lives can be remarkably changed, marriages excitingly improved, societies influenced for good—all by the simple, sweeping surge of individuals knowing what it is to be born again.

How has your life been changed by being born again?

_____

_____

JUNE

THE NATURE OF CONVERSION

From the rising of the sun to the place where it sets,
the name of the LORD is to be praised.
PSALM 113:3 NIV

Conversion can take many different forms. The way it is accomplished depends largely upon the individual—his temperament, his emotional balance, his environment, and his way of life. Conversion may follow a great crisis in a person's life; or it could come after all former values have been swept away, when great disappointment has been experienced, when one has lost one's sense of power through material possessions or lost the object of one's affections.

Or again, conversion may take place at the very height of personal power or prosperity—when all things are going well, and the bountiful mercies of God have been bestowed generously upon you. Conversion can be an instantaneous event, or it can be a gradual unfolding. Many young people who have grown up in Christian homes and had the benefit of Christian training are unaware of the time when they committed their lives to Christ. Someone has said we may not know the exact moment when the sun rises—but we most certainly know once it has risen. What is your conversion story?

Is your conversion story a gift to share?

_____

_____

CONVERTED IN THOUGHT AND DEED

Faith by itself, if it does not have works, is dead.

JAMES 2:17

There is a vast difference between intellectual belief and the total conversion that saves the soul. To be sure, there must be a change in our thinking and intellectual acceptance of Christ.

But beyond intellectual and emotional experience, Christ demands a change in the way you live. Certainly there will be a change in the elements that make up emotion when you come to Christ—hate and love will be involved, because you will begin to hate sin and love righteousness. Your affections will undergo a revolutionary change. Your devotion to Him will know no bounds. Your love for Him cannot be described.

Even if you have an intellectual acceptance of Christ and an emotional experience, that still is not enough. There must be the conversion of the will! There must be that determination to obey and follow Christ. Our main desire must be to please Him. It is a total commitment to Jesus Christ, who takes up residence in your heart through His Holy Spirit.

Is your faith expressed through your will?

_____

_____

JOYFUL RESURRECTION

*"I am the resurrection and the life. He who believes
in Me, though he may die, he shall live."*
JOHN 11:25

When we stand at the graveside of a loved one, we sorrow. But those united with Christ in death are also united with Him in the joy of resurrection. There was no joy at the tomb of Lazarus. It was a somber and woeful time—until Jesus arrived! Mary and Martha had wept for their loss, and Jesus had delayed His appearance for the purpose of demonstrating His power over death and sorrow. He said to His disciples, "Our friend Lazarus sleeps, but I go that I may wake him up" (John 11:11).

Then the Lord cried out, "Lazarus, come forth!" (v. 43).

Words cannot describe the shock of seeing a dead man alive again—and the joy of knowing that we, too, shall one day hear the Lord Jesus call our names. Contemplate it for a moment and imagine hearing His voice speak your name. If that does not cause joy to bubble inside of you, it is doubtful anything else will.

The Lord Jesus welcomes His children into His kingdom. That is joy—eternal joy!

Do you joyfully anticipate the moment Jesus will call your name?

_____

_____

CONVERSION CHANGES EVERYTHING

Therefore, since we are receiving a kingdom which cannot be shaken, let us have grace, by which we may serve God acceptably with reverence and godly fear.

HEBREWS 12:28

When a person is converted, he may continue to love objects he loved before, but there will be a change of reasons for loving them. The converted person will love the good he once hated and hate the sin he once loved. There will even be a change of heart about God. Where he once may have been careless about God, he now finds himself in a state of complete reverence, confidence, obedience, and devotion. There will be a reverential fear of God, a constant gratitude to God, a dependence upon God, and a new loyalty to Him. Before conversion there may have been gratification of the flesh. Cultural and intellectual pursuits or the making of money may have been of supreme importance. Now righteousness, holiness, and living the Christian life will be placed above all other concerns, for pleasing Christ will be the only goal of real importance. In other words, conversion means a complete change in the life of an individual.

What sin did you once love but now hate?

_____

_____

WHAT IS REPENTANCE?

"I say to you that likewise there will be more joy in heaven over one sinner who repents than over ninety-nine just persons who need no repentance."
LUKE 15:7

If repentance could be described in two words, I would use the words *turn around*. Turn around from what? The answer can be given in one word: *sin*. The Bible teaches that sin is a transgression of the law. Sin is the rejection of all authority and the denial of all obligation to God. Sin is that evil principle that came into the garden of Eden when Adam and Eve were tempted and fell. Ever since the disaster in Eden, this evil poison has affected all men so that "all have sinned," and "there is none righteous, no, not one" (Romans 3:23, 10). Sin has destroyed our relationship with God, and as a consequence it has disturbed our relationships with each other, and even with ourselves.

We cannot possibly have peace with God or peace with each other in the world or even peace within ourselves until something is done about sin. We must renounce or turn our backs on sin and turn toward God, who gives peace through salvation to the repentant.

Is there some sin you are holding on to that you have not yet surrendered to the Lord?

_____

_____

LIFE'S GREATEST DECISION

"In an acceptable time I have heard you,
And in the day of salvation I have helped you."

2 CORINTHIANS 6:2

We all want a happy and secure life; we all want a solid and lasting foundation beneath us. But wishful thinking is not enough! We need to make a decision—a personal commitment to Jesus Christ and His will for our lives.

Have you committed your life to Jesus Christ? No matter how young or old you are, are you seeking to build your life on Him? The most important decision you will ever make is to give your life to Christ and become His follower. Don't wait until life's storms begin to batter you; then it may be too late. Open your heart and life to Him now.

If you have never invited Jesus Christ to come into your life, or if you are unsure of your salvation, I invite you to pause right now and ask Him to come into your life, to forgive you, and to save you—and He will.

Do you truly believe that you are forgiven?

_____

_____

THE RESULTS OF THE NEW BIRTH

It is the God who commanded light to shine out of darkness,
who has shone in our hearts to give the light of the knowledge
of the glory of God in the face of Jesus Christ.

2 CORINTHIANS 4:6

When you are born again, several results follow: First, it will increase your vision and *understanding*. The Bible says, "The eyes of your understanding being enlightened" (Ephesians 1:18). Things that you used to laugh at as foolishness you now accept by faith. Your whole mental process is changed. God becomes the hub of your intellectual thinking.

Second, your *heart* undergoes a revolution (Ezekiel 36:26). Your affections have undergone a radical change. Your new nature loves God and the things pertaining to God.

Third, your *will* undergoes a tremendous change. Your motives are changed (Hebrews 13:20–21). You will want to do only His will. There is a new self-determination, inclination, disposition, new choices. You seek to glorify God. You may stumble, but immediately you will be sorry, confess your sins, and ask forgiveness, because you have been born again. Your very nature has changed.

How can you tell your nature is changing a little each day?

_____

_____

THE MIRACULOUS BOOK

Search from the book of the LORD, and read: not one of these
shall fail; not one shall lack her mate. For My mouth has
commanded it, and His Spirit has gathered them.

ISAIAH 34:16

Sixteen hundred years were needed to complete the writing of the Bible. It is the work of more than thirty authors, each of whom acted as a scribe of God. They did not set down merely what they thought or hoped. They acted as channels for God's revelation; under His divine inspiration they were able to see the great and enduring truths and to record them so that others might see and know them too.

During these sixteen hundred years, the sixty-six books of the Bible were written by men in different languages—living in different times—and in different countries, but the message they wrote was one. When the great scholars gathered together the ancient manuscripts and translated them into a single modern tongue, they found that God's promises remained unchanged. Even today, these words are as fresh and meaningful to this generation as they were in Jesus' time.

Do you believe that God's promises never change?

_____

_____

A WAY OF ESCAPE

God is faithful, who will not allow you to be tempted beyond
what you are able, but with the temptation will also make
the way of escape, that you may be able to bear it.

1 CORINTHIANS 10:13

The moment you made your decision for Christ, Satan suffered a tremendous defeat. He is angry now. From now on he is going to tempt you and try to lead you into sin. He'll try to discourage you; to divert you; to dilute your testimony; to destroy your relationship to Christ and your influence upon others.

You ask, "How can I overcome him? What can I do?"

Don't be alarmed. God has made a way of escape. Remember this: Temptation by the devil is not a sign that your life is not right with God. It is actually a sign that you are right with God. Temptation is not sin. Also remember that God never tempts His own children. All doubts and temptations come from the devil. Satan can only tempt. He can never compel you to yield to the temptation. Remember also that Satan has already been conquered by Christ. His power is made inoperative in the life of a fully trusting and yielded Christian who is completely dependent upon God.

How are you protected from the lures of Satan?

_____

_____

THE WORLD'S BESTSELLER!

The law of the LORD is perfect, converting the soul;
The testimony of the LORD is sure, making wise the simple.

PSALM 19:7

I t is small wonder that the Bible has always been the world's bestseller! No other book can touch its profound wisdom, its poetic beauty, or the accuracy of its history and prophecy. Its critics, who claimed it to be filled with forgery, fiction, and unfulfilled promises, are finding that the difficulties lie with themselves and not the Bible. Greater and more careful scholarship has shown that apparent contradictions were caused by incorrect translations rather than divine inconsistencies. It was man and not the Bible who needed correcting. Someone has said, "The Bible does not have to be rewritten, but reread."

As we cast our eyes around for something that is real and true and enduring, we are turning once more to this ancient Book that has given consolation, comfort, and salvation to millions in the centuries past. The Bible embodies all the knowledge man needs to fill the longing of his soul and solve all his problems. It is the blueprint of the Master Architect, and only by following its directions can we build the life we are seeking.

How can reading God's Word help you?

_____

_____

RESIST AND PRAY

Resist him, steadfast in the faith, knowing that the same sufferings are experienced by your brotherhood in the world.

1 PETER 5:9

A poet once said, "The devil trembles when he sees the weakest saint upon his knees."

We can depend upon the blood of Christ when we are under attack. There are times when we simply must hide behind the person of Christ and ask Him to handle our problems. Jude says, "Yet Michael the archangel, when contending with the devil he disputed about the body of Moses, durst not bring against him a railing accusation, but said, The Lord rebuke thee" (v. 9 KJV). That's what we need to do—call upon God.

Now, the Bible says that we are to "resist the devil, and he will flee" from us (James 4:7 KJV). But before that, God says, "Submit yourselves . . . to God." If you have fully submitted, 100 percent yielded and surrendered yourself to Christ, then you can "resist the devil," and the Bible promises he will flee from you. The devil will tremble when you pray. He will be defeated when you quote or read a passage of Scripture to him and will leave you when you resist him.

Does the devil flee from you when you pray in Jesus' name?

_____

_____

THE WORLD

Do not love the world or the things in the world.
1 JOHN 2:15

Worldliness has been vastly misunderstood on the part of thousands of Christians. It needs a little clarification.

Suppose someone should offer me a hamburger after I had eaten a T-bone steak. I would say, "No, thank you, I am already satisfied." Christian, that is the secret. You are so filled with the things of Christ, so enamored of the things of God, that you do not have time or taste for sinful pleasures of this world. The Bible says, "The full soul loatheth an honeycomb; but to the hungry soul every bitter thing is sweet" (Proverbs 27:7 KJV).

You will find in your born-again experience that your pleasures have been lifted into an entirely new and glorious realm. Many non-Christians have accused the Christian life as being a set of rules, taboos, vetoes, and prohibitions. This is another lie of the devil. It is not a series of "don'ts" but a series of "dos." You become so busy in the work of Christ and so completely satisfied with the things of Christ that you do not have time for the things of the world.

Do you see the Christian life as a series of "don'ts" or of "dos"?

_____

_____

MAKING GOOD CHOICES

He who does the will of God abides forever.
1 JOHN 2:17

Many people ask, "Is this wrong?" or "Is that wrong?" "Is this sinful?" or "Is that sinful?" One simple question, earnestly and prayerfully asked, will clear this up. Just ask this question: "What would Christ have me to do?" Another question you can ask is, "Can I ask His blessing upon this?" or "Could I ask Christ to go along with me to this event?" Being omnipresent, He'll be there anyway. The point is, should you?

It does not mean that in society we are snobs or have a superiority complex, lest we be in danger of spiritual pride—which would be far worse than any worldliness. But you should always be able to tell the difference between the Christian and the unbeliever.

Christians should stand out like sparkling diamonds against a rough background. They should be poised, wholesome, cultured, courteous, gracious, but firm in the things that they do and do not do. They should laugh and be radiant, refusing to allow the world to pull them down to its level.

When have you declined to go somewhere because it wasn't Christ-honoring?

_____

_____

THE FLESH

Reckon yourselves to be dead indeed to sin.

ROMANS 6:11

The Bible teaches "the flesh lusteth against the Spirit, and the Spirit against the flesh" (Galatians 5:17 KJV). But what does this mean? The flesh is that evil tendency of your inward self. Even after you are converted, sometimes your old, sinful cravings will return. You become startled and wonder where they come from. The Bible teaches that the old nature, with all its corruption, is still there and that these evil temptations come from nowhere else. In other words, "a traitor is living within." "That wretched bent toward sin is ever present to drag you down." War has been declared! You now have two natures in conflict, and each one is striving for dominance.

It is the battle of the self-life and the Christ-life. This old nature cannot please God. It cannot be converted, or even patched up. Thank God, when Jesus died He took you with Him, and the old nature can be made inoperative. This is done by faith.

We are to re-yield and re-surrender ourselves to God that we can, by faith, reckon the old nature dead indeed unto sin.

Has your old self ever tried to make a resurgence?

_____

_____

FIGHTING OUR FOES

Be filled with the Spirit.
EPHESIANS 5:18

Abiding in Christ, as taught in John 15, is the only possible course for the Christian who has to be "in" the world but does not want to be "of" it. In relation to the devil, we resist him only as we submit ourselves to God. In relation to the world, the Bible says, "This is the victory that overcometh the world, even our faith" (1 John 5:4 KJV). In relation to the flesh, the Bible says, "Walk in the Spirit, and ye shall not fulfill the lust of the flesh" (Galatians 5:16 KJV).

Here is glorious news to you who have already been fighting these battles and temptations: You are not asked to fight the battle alone. Jesus left us with a Helper—the Holy Spirit—who comes alongside and walks with us.

Just as Christ came to make God visible and redeem mankind, so the Holy Spirit came to make Christ visible in the life of the believer and enable the individual Christian to offer Christ's redemption to a lost and dying world.

Are you battling temptations alone, or do you rely on the Holy Spirit?

_____

_____

FAITH IS A FACT

Do you not know that your body is the temple of the Holy
Spirit who is in you, whom you have from God?
1 CORINTHIANS 6:19

The Bible says that the moment you accepted Christ as Savior, the Holy Spirit took up residence in your heart. You say, "But I don't feel the Spirit of God in me."

You may or may not feel the Spirit. Accept Him by faith as a fact. He lives within you right now to help you live the Christian life. He is living in you in order to magnify, glorify, and exalt Christ in you so that you can live a happy, victorious, radiant, Christ-honoring life.

The Bible commands, "Be filled with the Spirit" (Ephesians 5:18). If you are filled with the Spirit, then you are going to produce the fruit of the Spirit, which is "love, joy, peace, longsuffering, gentleness, goodness, faith, meekness, temperance" (Galatians 5:22–23 KJV).

How do you know that you are filled? When you give all you know of yourself to all that you know of Him, then you can accept by faith that you are filled with the Spirit of God.

What kind of life can you live when you are filled with the Spirit?

_____

_____

RELEASE YOUR GRIP

"The one who comes to Me I will by no means cast out."
JOHN 6:37

A little child playing one day with a very valuable vase put his hand into it and could not withdraw it. His father, too, tried his best, but all in vain. They were thinking of breaking the vase when the father said, "Now, my son, make one more try. Open your hand and hold your fingers out straight as you see me doing, and then pull."

To the father's astonishment the little fellow said, "Oh, no, Father. I couldn't put my fingers out like that because if I did, I would drop my penny."

Smile, if you will—but thousands of us are like that little boy, so busy holding on to the world's worthless penny that we cannot accept liberation. I beg you to drop that trifle in your heart. Surrender! Let go, and let God have His way in your life.

Now, after you have given yourself completely to Christ in consecration, remember that God has accepted what you have presented. You have come to Him; now He has received you. And He will in no way cast you out!

What are you holding on to as the little boy held on to that penny?

_____

_____

THE FRUIT OF THE SPIRIT: LOVE AND JOY

The fruit of the Spirit is love, joy, peace, longsuffering, kindness,
goodness, faithfulness, gentleness, self-control.

GALATIANS 5:22–23

When you are filled with the Spirit, you will produce the fruit of the Spirit. Keep in mind that these fruits are of the Spirit. One does not produce them himself. They are supernatural in origin. The first is, according to Galatians 5, love, and from this root will grow all the others. We must differentiate between the gifts and the fruit of the Spirit. Gifts are given—fruits are grown. To grow something there must be a close, personal relationship between the vine and the branch. A person must be rooted and grounded in Christ.

Another fruit of the Spirit is joy. One of the characteristics of the Christian is an inward joy that does not depend upon circumstances. S. D. Gordon, the well-known devotional writer of a past generation, said: "Joy has its springs deep down inside. And that spring never runs dry, no matter what happens. Only Jesus gives that joy. He had joy, singing its music within, even under the shadow of the cross. It is an unknown word and thing except as He has sway within."

How can you root yourself in Christ so firmly that you produce fruits?

_____

_____

SCRIPTURE IS POWERFUL

For the word of God is living and powerful . . . and is a
discerner of the thoughts and intents of the heart.
HEBREWS 4:12

Suppose an archaeologist discovered the original diary of Genghis Khan or Alexander the Great, or the love letters of Cleopatra? Imagine the stampede into the bookstores across America to get copies of such books. Yet we have here a book that God Himself has written for mankind—how much more should we desire to know what it says?

Some parts of our world do not enjoy the freedom we have to read the Bible and study it together with fellow Christians. In most of the world, in fact, there's a veritable famine for the Word of God! I recall the story of a Chinese musician in the People's Republic of China. He was converted and strengthened spiritually through the reading of individual pages of the Scripture torn from a Bible and slipped to him by a friend. There are other stories of prisoners who survived years of labor and torture, and came out totally lacking in bitterness toward their captors because of God's Word. What a privilege to have access to this Book every day!

What kind of power do the Lord's words have in your life?

_____

_____

READ THE BIBLE DAILY

Desire the pure milk of the word, that you may grow thereby.

1 PETER 2:2

For one to grow properly, certain rules must be observed for good spiritual health. First, *read your Bible daily*. It is one of your greatest privileges. Your spiritual life needs food. What kind of food? Spiritual food. Where do you find this spiritual food? In the Bible, the Word of God. The Bible reveals Christ, who is the Bread of Life for your hungry soul and the Water of Life for your thirsty heart. Don't starve yourself. Read it, study it, meditate on it, and memorize it. Ninety-five percent of the difficulties you will experience as a Christian can be traced to a lack of Bible study and reading.

Hide the Word of God in your heart. A little portion well digested is of greater spiritual value to your soul than a lengthy portion scanned hurriedly. Even if you cannot remember all you have read or understand it all, go on reading. The very practice in itself will have a purifying effect upon your mind and heart. Let nothing take the place of this daily exercise.

What verse of Scripture can you memorize today?

_____

_____

LEARN TO PRAY

Delight yourself also in the LORD,
And He shall give you the desires of your heart.
PSALM 37:4

To grow, you must learn the secret of prayer. Your prayers may falter at first. But the Holy Spirit who lives within you will help you and teach you. Every prayer will be answered. Sometimes the answer may be "Yes" and sometimes "No," and sometimes it is "Wait," but nevertheless it will be answered.

Prayer is communicating. A baby's first response is to his parents. He isn't asking for anything. He is simply smiling back when his parents smile, cooing when they talk to him. What a thrill his first response brings to the entire family! In the same way, can you imagine the joy our first response to Him brings to God?

Your petitions should always be conditioned by "Thy will be done." Delighting ourselves in Him will direct our desires, so God can answer our petitions. Remember that you can pray anytime, anywhere. Washing dishes, digging ditches, working in the office, in the shop, on the athletic field, even in prison—you can pray and know God hears!

What is the most unusual place you have prayed?

_____

_____

A PLACE OF GROWTH AND SERVICE

Serve the LORD with gladness;
Come before His presence with singing.
PSALM 100:2

In certain countries today, church gatherings are not encouraged. For years people have been forced to meet privately in homes, perhaps just a single family or perhaps a few Christian friends gathering together. Christians need one another; we need to gather together to worship God, and nothing can take the place of church attendance.

There are many invalids, prisoners, and so on who are blessed to watch a church service via television or the internet, but others who stay home without excuse miss the fellowship of worshiping the Lord collectively. We do not go to church to hear a sermon. We go to church to worship God and to serve Him in the fellowship of other Christians. We cannot be a successful and happy Christian without being faithful in church. In the church we find our place of service. We are saved to serve. The happy Christian is the serving Christian.

Where do you think you'd like to serve in your church?

_____

_____

BE A WITNESSING CHRISTIAN

Always be ready to give a defense to everyone who
asks you a reason for the hope that is in you.
1 PETER 3:15

To grow in faith, be a witnessing Christian. If a cup is being filled continually, it is bound to overflow. God's purpose for you and me after we have been converted is that we be witnesses to His saving grace and power. We are to be commandos for Christ. We are to be minutemen for Him.

In the days of Western Union telegram services, a messenger's sole obligation was to carry the message to the person to whom it was addressed. He may not like to carry that message. It may contain bad news or distressing news. The messenger was not permitted to stop on the way, open the envelope, and change the wording. His duty was to take the message.

This is the same for God's messengers. We are holding a light. We are to let it shine! Though it may seem but a twinkling candle in a world of blackness, it is our business to deliver God's message according to His Word.

Is it hard or easy for you to share the light of Christ with others?

_____

_____

CHRIST'S AMBASSADOR

Those who are wise shall shine like the brightness of the firmament, and those who turn many to righteousness like the stars forever and ever.

DANIEL 12:3

We Christians are duly appointed and commissioned ambassadors of the King of kings. We are to let our flag fly high over our embassy. Suppose our ambassador to Russia should order the American flag pulled down because it is not popular in Russia—we would soon call him home! He would not deserve to represent the United States.

If we are not willing to let our flags fly in the home, in the office, in the shop, on the campus—then we are not worthy to be ambassadors for Christ! We are to take our stand and let all those around us know that we are Christians. We are to bear witness for Christ.

It has been my privilege to win others to a saving knowledge of Christ. I never cease to thrill at hearing of one who has listened, accepted Christ, and been transformed by His grace. Hearing this is worth more than all the money in the world.

Are you an ambassador for Christ?

_____

_____

SHARING THE WORD

Everyone who thirsts,
Come to the waters.
ISAIAH 55:1

When we share Christ's Gospel, we are blowing a trumpet. In the din and noise of battle, the sound of our little trumpet may seem to be lost, but we must keep sounding the alarm to those who are in danger.

We are kindling a fire. In this cold world full of hatred and selfishness, our little blaze may seem to be unavailing, but we must keep our fire burning.

We are striking with a hammer. The blows may seem only to jar our hands as we strike, but we are to keep on hammering. Amy Carmichael of India once asked a stone-cutter which blow broke the stone. "The first one and the last," he replied, "and every one in between."

We have bread for a hungry world and water for those who thirst. The people may seem to be so busy feeding on other things that they will not accept the Bread of Life, but we must keep on giving it, offering it to the souls of men.

We must persevere. We must never give up. Keep proclaiming the Word!

What can you do to keep your fire burning?

_____

_____

LET US LOVE

"By this all will know that you are My disciples, if you have love for one another."
JOHN 13:35

If you want to grow spiritually, let love be the ruling principle of your life. Be ruled by love.

Love does not necessarily imply approval of the one loved. If God had waited until He could approve of us before He sent His Son to redeem us, where would we be?

Of all the gifts God offers His children, love is the greatest. Of all the fruits of the Holy Spirit, love is the first.

The Bible declares that we who follow Christ should love one another as God loved us when He sent His Son to die on the cross. The Bible says that the moment we come to Christ, He gives us supernatural love and that His love is shed abroad in our hearts by the Holy Spirit. The greatest demonstration of the fact that we are Christians is that we love one another. If we learn this secret of God early in our Christian experience, we will have gone a long way toward a mature, happy Christian life.

Are you waiting to approve of someone before you love them fully?

_____

_____

LEARN HOW TO MEET TEMPTATION

Submit to God. Resist the devil and he will flee from you.
JAMES 4:7

Temptation is not sin. It is yielding to it that is sin. God never brings temptation to us. He allows it to test us. It is the work of the devil. Recognize it as such. One way to meet temptation is to quote a verse of Scripture. That puts Satan on the run, for he cannot stand the Word of God.

When Jesus was tempted in the wilderness, His response was the Word of God. He said three times, "It is written."

Speak God's Word and Satan will flee. Let Christ through the Holy Spirit do the fighting for you. Be like the little girl who said, "Every time I hear the devil knock, I send Jesus to the door."

Everyone has temptations, but some folks entertain them. They seem to enjoy being tempted. Get your eyes off the temptation and onto Christ!

Have you ever called on Christ to send the devil packing?

_____

_____

LIVE ABOVE YOUR CIRCUMSTANCES

I know how to be abased, and I know how to abound.
Everywhere and in all things I have learned both to be full
and to be hungry, both to abound and to suffer need.

PHILIPPIANS 4:12

Learn to live above your circumstances. God made you as you are! He placed you where you are! So you can best serve and glorify Him just as you are, where you are. Some people are always looking on the other side of the fence because they think the grass is greener. They overlook all the advantages and opportunities open to them right where they are.

Paul said he had learned how to abound and how to be abased. He had learned to be every inch a Christian even in prison. Don't let your circumstances get you down. Learn to live graciously within them, realizing the Lord Himself is with you.

These principles and suggestions may seem simple, but they work. I have seen them tested in the lives of thousands. I have tested them in my own life. They will give you peace of soul, happiness, peace of mind, and pleasure, and you will have learned the secret of living life with satisfaction.

Why do you think God placed you where you are?

_____

_____

THE CHRISTIAN AND THE CHURCH

In whom you also are being built together for a
dwelling place of God in the Spirit.
EPHESIANS 2:22

M an finds his greatest sense of security and satisfaction in the company of
others who share his interests and attitudes. Of all the many groups into
which humans have collected themselves throughout history, none has been so
powerful, so far-reaching, or more universal as the church.

Clubs, college fraternities, lodges, literary societies, political parties, military organizations—all of these, from private clubs to the high school "gang,"
represent man's need to find comfort and reassurance in the company of others
who approve of his way of life because their own way of life is similar.

Nowhere, however, has man found this comfort, this reassurance, this
peace to the extent that he has found it in the church, for all other groups are
obviously man-inspired. They draw artificial boundaries and set up only the
illusion of protection, while the church—the body of Christ on earth—is a living,
vibrant organism that draws its power from God Himself instead of relying
upon outside sources to give it meaning and vitality.

How is your church different from other groups you are in?

_____

_____

ORIGIN OF THE CHURCH

No other foundation can anyone lay than that which is laid, which is Jesus Christ.

1 CORINTHIANS 3:11

The word *church* is an English translation of the Greek word *ecclesia*, which means "the called-out ones," or an assembly of people. The word as applied to the Christian society was first used by Jesus Himself when He told Peter, "Upon this rock I will build my church; and the gates of hell shall not prevail against it" (Matthew 16:18 KJV).

Thus Jesus Christ Himself founded the church. He is the great cornerstone upon which the church is built. He is the foundation of all Christian experience, and the church is founded upon Him. Jesus proclaimed Himself to be the founder of the church and the builder of the church. The church belongs to Him and to Him alone. He has promised to live with, and in, all those who are members of His church. Here is not only an organization but an organism that is completely unlike anything else that the world has ever known: God Himself living with, and in, ordinary men and women who are members of His church.

How can you build your life on Jesus Christ?

_____

_____

July

THE "SOCIAL GOSPEL"

"Just as you want men to do to you, you also do to them likewise."
LUKE 6:31

Many people have criticized the "social gospel," but Jesus taught that we are to take the Gospel to the world. In fact, "social gospel" is a misnomer. There is only one gospel.

My son Franklin who heads up a Christian relief agency, said, "Proclaiming the Gospel must always have priority."

Christians, above all others, should be concerned with social problems and social injustices because of the Gospel. Down through the centuries the church has contributed more than any other single agency in lifting social standards to new heights. Child labor has been outlawed. Slavery has been abolished in Britain, the USA, and some other parts of the world. The status of women has been lifted to heights unparalleled in history, and many other reforms have taken place primarily as a result of the influence of the teachings of Jesus Christ. Christians are to take their place in society with moral courage to stand up for that which is right, just, and honorable.

What injustices concern you?

_____

_____

BEFORE DIFFICULT DAYS

Remember now your Creator in the days of your youth,
Before the difficult days come, . . .
Remember your Creator before the silver cord is loosed.

ECCLESIASTES 12:1, 6

When I was interviewed by *Newsweek* in 2006 and asked to give a statement about death, I commented that I had been taught all of my life how to die, but no one had ever taught me how to grow old. That statement triggered a lot of interest. I am certainly no expert on the subject of growing old, but now that I am gaining some experience, I have to admit that not all things get better with age. I have a newfound appreciation for Ecclesiastes 12.

As a young preacher, I did not relate to it as I do now. What impresses me is that Solomon, the wisest king ever to rule Israel, intended for the young to read it "in the days of . . . youth, *before* the difficult days come" (emphasis added).

Whether you are young, old, or somewhere in between, now is the time to recommit to following God's law daily, and "remember your Creator." You will need it later—that much is sure.

Is there a particular passage from the Bible you want to be sure to remember as you mature?

_____

_____

THE SERMON ON THE MOUNT

Seeing the multitudes, He went up on a mountain, and when He was seated His disciples came to Him. Then He opened His mouth and taught them.
MATTHEW 5:1–2

One day upon a mountain near Capernaum, Jesus sat with His disciples. He may have looked quietly and tenderly at each of these devoted disciples, as a parent looks at his children—loving each child separately, loving each one for a special reason, loving them in such a way that each child feels singled out and individually embraced. That is how Jesus must have loved His disciples.

There, on the mountain, Jesus preached the greatest sermon that human ears have ever heard. He explained the essence of Christian living. When He was through and a holy hush had settled on His wide-eyed listeners, they "were astonished at his doctrine: for he taught them as one having authority, and not as the scribes" (Matthew 7:28–29 KJV).

Indeed He did teach with authority, the authority of God Himself; and the rules He set forth were God's own rules, the ones that all Christians with the hope of salvation in their hearts must follow.

What must it have been like that day on the mountain when Jesus preached?

_____

_____

THE SUPREME CONSTITUTION

The law was given through Moses, but grace and truth came through Jesus Christ.

JOHN 1:17

America has a great document that is valued and respected. It was written more than two hundred years ago by a number of men who labored long and debated even longer over its many provisions. The framers of the Constitution knew they were writing the basic document granting its citizens freedom. It described their rights, their privileges, and their limitations.

Just as America has grown and prospered within the framework of our Constitution, so Christianity has flourished and spread according to the laws set forth in Scripture.

As the Constitution is the highest law of the land, so the Bible is the highest law of God, in which He makes His enduring promises and reveals His plan of redemption for the human race.

Have you adopted the Bible as your Constitution for life?

_____

_____

THE TRUE KING

The people refused to obey the voice of Samuel; and they said, "No, but we will have a king over us, that we also may be like all the nations."
1 SAMUEL 8:19–20

We may look with a suspicious eye at ancient Israel, but we are no different; many of us live under a three-ruler kingdom: me, myself, and I.

Just as America has grown and prospered within the framework of its Constitution, so Christianity has flourished from the principles set forth in the Bible. The secret strength of a godly nation is found in the faith that abides in the hearts and homes of its citizens. Will we humble ourselves and admit we have strayed too far from God?

We don't know the future for America, but we do know the future for the people of God. In Israel's case, God will do what He said He would do: protect the remnant of Israel and restore the throne of David.

We know that the Lord is going to restore the throne and that Jesus Christ will be enthroned and crowned King forever in His kingdom. So let us remain true and faithful believers, holding fast to the principles of our King, instead of one made in our image.

Who is the ruler of your kingdom, you or the Lord?

_____

_____

A CHRISTIAN VIEW OF MATERIALISM

For the love of money is a root of all kinds of evil, for which
some have strayed from the faith in their greediness, and
pierced themselves through with many sorrows.

1 TIMOTHY 6:10

The Christian attitude should prevail in the matter of economics. Jesus said a man's life does not consist in the abundance of the things he possesses. Money is a good slave but a bad master. Property is to be used, enjoyed, shared, given, but not hoarded. Paul said that the love of money was the "root of all . . . evil" (1 Timothy 6:10). Covetousness shackles its devotee and makes him its victim. It hardens the heart and deadens the noble impulses and destroys the vital qualities of life.

Beware of covetousness in every phase and form! All of us should keep ourselves from it through vigilance, prayer, self-control, and discipline. Life is not a matter of dollars and cents, houses and lands, earning capacity and financial achievement. Greed must not be allowed to make man the slave of wealth.

The Christian, above all others, should realize that we come into life with empty hands—and it is with empty hands that we leave it.

Do you feel money is more your servant or your boss?

_____

_____

GOD OWNS IT ALL

The earth is the LORD's, and all its fullness,
The world and those who dwell therein.
PSALM 24:1

Consider for a moment your possessions. Actually, we can possess nothing—no property and no person—along the way. It is God who owns everything, and we are but stewards of His property during the brief time we are on earth. Everything that we see about us that we count as our possessions only comprises a loan from God, and it is when we lose sight of this all-pervading truth that we become greedy and covetous.

When we clutch an object or a person and say, "This thing is mine," we are forgetting that we can't take it with us. This does not mean earthly riches are a sin—the Bible does not say that. The Bible makes it clear that God expects us to do the best we can with the talents, the abilities, the situations with which life endows us. But there is a right way and a wrong way to acquire money and a right way and a wrong way to achieve power. Choose God's way, and hold possessions lightly.

How can you think about possessions so that you hold them lightly?

_____

_____

SPIRITUAL AND MATERIAL VALUE

Honor the LORD with your possessions,
And with the firstfruits of all your increase.

PROVERBS 3:9

How do we make godly priorities when it comes to finances? Earn your money, as much as you can, according to God's laws, and use it as God leads. Give one-tenth of it to the Lord, the firstfruits (Proverbs 3:9), tithe faithfully, for the Bible says that this is right and just. Whenever you have any doubts about material values, get out your Bible and read what Jesus taught about money; read what He had to say about the earning of money and the use and distribution of wealth. Just ask yourself, "What would Jesus have done in this situation?" and be guided by that and that alone.

It was my privilege at one time to have among my close friends an extremely wealthy industrialist. One day he calmly told me that the day before he made thirteen million dollars on a deal. "But let me tell you what I discovered in the Scriptures this morning!" he exclaimed, changing the subject abruptly to his deepest interests. This man had his priorities in order.

How should you reprioritize your life to obediently give a tithe to the Lord?

_____

_____

DEEP ROOTS

"He who endures to the end shall be saved."
MATTHEW 24:13

A friend of mine makes beautiful bowls and candlesticks from old wood. "What is your favorite wood to work with?" I asked him one day.

"I suppose it would be from the trees that grow along the ridgetops of the Appalachian Mountains," he answered. "Because of the harsh climate, those trees grow very slowly. It's tough and hard to carve; but anything made from it will be durable and very beautiful."

Those trees have been stunted and twisted into grotesque shapes by the fierce, cold winds. But when I saw his work, I understood that what was once ugly and battered could be made into something exquisite by a masterful hand.

Like those trees along our windswept mountain ridges, we often find ourselves buffeted by storms—the storms of life. Like those trees, we need deep roots that will supply us with the spiritual nutrients needed to grow strong in our faith and to keep us anchored when we are tossed about by life's trials. And over time, we will become beautiful—and durable—under His hand.

What storms of life has your faith brought you through?

_____

_____

I'm a Christian Because . . .

He who has the Son has life.
1 John 5:12

M any think that going to church makes them a Christian. Others say that they are Christians because they believe in Jesus Christ. Some say they are Christians because they pray and read the Bible. Multitudes believe that going to confession makes them a Christian, while others believe they are Christians because they were born into a Christian home.

Do you fit into one or more of these categories? Do you really understand what it means to belong to Jesus? How many know beyond a shadow of doubt that they are a Christian and truly follow Him?

You see, the issue is not "What does becoming a Christian mean to you?" but "What did Jesus say about becoming one of His followers?"

The Bible teaches that belief in Him changes the person. "If anyone loves the world," the Bible says, "the love of the Father is not in him. For all that is in the world—the lust of the flesh, the lust of the eyes, and the pride of life—is not of the Father but is of the world" (1 John 2:15–16). Living the Christian life means trusting God every moment, and He will give us the faith to follow Him.

What makes you a Christian?

_____

_____

THE WAY OF THE CROSS

"Now my soul is troubled, and what shall I say? 'Father, save me from this hour'?
No, it was for this very reason I came to this hour. Father, glorify your name!"
JOHN 12:27–28 NIV

Jesus could have called legions of angels to His side on the cross. But He chose to die in order to spare us eternal death. He chose to suffer to grant us comfort. He chose to give up His earthly life that we might have everlasting life. This is my hope. Is it yours?

Jesus suffered the persecution of His own people. He suffered desertion by His own disciples. But worse than all that, He suffered abandonment from His Father in Heaven for the glory of God (Mark 15:34).

On the cross Jesus was severely afflicted with the sins of the world, but it was also on the cross that He completed the greatest of all of His works. The cross is where sin met the Savior. The cross is where the sinner finds salvation. The cross is where wretched souls can find victory in Jesus.

This is the bloodstained picture of sin that separates men and women from fellowship with God. We must crucify—put to death—our ways and go the way of the cross. When we do that, we participate in His great work of reconciliation.

What did Jesus sacrifice for you?

_____

_____

DOWN THROUGH THE CENTURIES

[Jesus] asked His disciples . . . "Who do men say that I am?" . . .
Peter answered and said to Him, "You are the Christ."
MARK 8:27, 29

S keptics claim that the Scriptures are not believable, yet testimonies about Jesus' life and resurrection come from historians, philosophers, scientists, churchmen, and, yes, even atheists.

As early as the first century, a Jewish historian named Flavius Josephus confirmed the impact Jesus Christ made in the hearts of His followers:

> About this time there lived Jesus, a wise man. . . . He won over many Jews and many of the Greeks. He was the Messiah. When Pilate . . . had condemned him to be crucified, those who had in the first place come to love him did not give up their affection for him. On the third day he appeared to them restored to life. . . . And the tribe of the Christians, so called after him, has still to this day not disappeared.[1]

Jesus is the Word of God in flesh. He was resurrected to fulfill that living Word, and He lives today.

Who do you say Jesus is?

_____

_____

SUPREME CREATOR

In the beginning God created the heavens and the earth.
GENESIS 1:1

We are daily faced with the miracle of life and the mystery of death, of the glory of flowering trees, the magnificence of the star-filled sky, the magnitude of mountains and of sea. Who made all this? Who conceived the law of gravity by which everything is held in its proper place? Who ordered the day and the night and the regular procession of the seasons? What about the infinity of the universe? Can we honestly believe (as someone has written), "This is all there is or was or ever will be"?

The only possible answer is that all these things and many more are the work of a Supreme Creator. As a watch must have a designer, so our precise universe has a Great Designer. We call Him God. His is a name with whom the whole human race is familiar. From earliest childhood we have breathed His name. The Bible declares that the God we talk about, the God we sing about, the God "from whom all blessings flow!" is the God who created this world and placed us in it.

How do you find inspiration from nature?

_____

_____

GOD IS SPIRIT

"A spirit does not have flesh and bones as you see I have."
LUKE 24:39

What do you think of when you hear the word *spirit*? What mental image does it bring to your mind? Do you think of a wisp of vapor drifting across the sky? Does *spirit* mean the sort of thing that frightens children on Halloween? Is *spirit* just a formless nothingness to you? Do you think that was what Jesus meant when He said, "God is Spirit" (John 4:24)?

Spirit is *without* body (Luke 24:39). It is the *opposite* of body. Yet it has being and power. This is difficult for us to understand because we are trying to understand it with our limited, finite minds.

The Bible declares that God is a Spirit—that He is not limited to body; He is not limited to shape; He is not limited to boundaries or bonds; He is absolutely immeasurable and undiscernible by eyes that can see only physical things. The Bible tells us that because He has no such limitations, He can be everywhere at once—that He can hear all, see all, and know all. There are no limits to God.

Is the Holy Spirit a person or a spirit or both?

_____

_____

INFINITE SPIRIT

Who has directed the Spirit of the LORD,
Or as His counselor has taught Him?
ISAIAH 40:13

I am eternally grateful to my mother for many things, but one of the most enduring blessings she brought into my life was to teach me in the catechism, at the age of ten, that "God is a Spirit, infinite, eternal, and unchangeable in His being, wisdom, power, holiness, justice, goodness, and truth." That definition of God has been with me all my life, and when a man knows in his heart that God is an infinite, eternal, and unchangeable Spirit, it helps to overcome the temptation to limit Him. It helps to overcome all doubt about His ability to accomplish things that we can't do ourselves!

Perhaps you are only now catching your first glimpse of God's unlimited power. Perhaps you are only now beginning to understand Him for what He actually is. For if God is the Spirit that Jesus declares Him to be, there is no problem of providence; there is no problem of His sovereignty in the affairs of men; there is no problem of His inspiration of the men who wrote the Bible. Everything fits into place once you understand who and what God really is.

Do you limit God?

_____

_____

GOD IS HOLY AND RIGHTEOUS

God is light and in Him is no darkness at all.

1 JOHN 1:5

From Genesis to Revelation, God reveals Himself as a holy God. He is utterly perfect and absolute in every detail. He is too holy to tolerate sinful man, too holy to endure sinful living.

If we could envision the true picture of His righteousness, what a difference it would make in the way we live as individuals and as nations! If we could but realize the tremendous gulf that separates unrighteous man from God's perfect righteousness! The Scriptures declare Him to be the Light in whom there is no darkness at all—the one Supreme Being without flaw or blemish.

Here again is a difficult concept for imperfect man to understand. We can scarcely imagine the overwhelming holiness of God—but we must recognize it if we are to understand and benefit from the Bible.

Man is a sinner, powerless to change his position, unless he cries out for mercy sincerely. But because the God we worship is a pure God, a holy God, a just and righteous God, He sent us His only begotten Son to make it possible for us to have access to Him.

How thankful are you to have direct access to God?

_____

_____

UNFATHOMABLE LOVE

God demonstrates His own love toward us, in that
while we were still sinners, Christ died for us.
ROMANS 5:8

Never question God's great love, for it is as unchangeable a part of God as is His holiness. No matter how terrible your sins, God loves you. Were it not for the love of God, none of us would ever have a chance in the future life. But God is love! And His love for us is everlasting!

The promises of God's love and forgiveness are as real. But, like describing the ocean, its total beauty cannot be understood until it is actually seen. It is the same with God's love. Until you actually accept it, until you actually experience it, until you actually possess true peace with God, no one can describe its wonders to you.

Your finite mind is not capable of dealing with anything as great as the love of God. It might have difficulty understanding how a black cow can eat green grass and give white milk—but you drink the milk and are nourished by it. How much more you can be nourished by God's love.

What is one example of how the Lord loves you?

_____

_____

A TUG ON THE HEART

Those who are led by the Spirit of God are the children of God.
ROMANS 8:14 NIV

Whenever anyone asks me how I can be so certain about who and what God really is, I am reminded of the story of the little boy who was out flying a kite. The kite went up and up until it was entirely hidden by the clouds.

"What are you doing?" a man asked the little boy.

"I'm flying a kite," he replied.

"Flying a kite, are you?" the man said. "How can you be sure? You can't see your kite."

"No," said the boy, "I can't see it, but every little while I feel a tug, so I know for sure that it's there!"

Don't take anyone else's word for God. Find Him for yourself, and then you, too, will know by the wonderful, warm tug on your heartstrings that He is there for sure.

You have to receive God by faith in Jesus Christ. When that happens, there isn't any room for doubt. You don't have to question whether or not God is in your heart; you can know it.

Do you know the Lord in your heart as well as in your mind?

_____

_____

FREEDOM OF CHOICE

All have sinned and fall short of the glory of God.
ROMANS 3:23

The great preacher Dr. M. L. Scott, tells about a friend of his whose son had gone away to university for study. When he returned home for a visit, filled with his newly acquired knowledge, he said, "Dad, now that I've been to university, I'm no longer sure I can go along with your simple, childlike faith in the Bible."

The father sat there studying his son with unblinking eyes and said, "Son, that is your freedom—your terrible freedom." That is what God gave to Adam—his freedom to choose. His terrible freedom.

In the garden, Adam had total freedom—freedom to choose or to reject, freedom to obey God's commands or to go contrary to them, freedom to make himself happy or miserable. It is not the mere possession of freedom that makes life satisfying—it is what we choose to do with our freedom that determines whether or not we shall find peace with God and with ourselves.

Have you used your freedom well?

_____

_____

Choose the Right Path

"Blessed are those who hear the word of God and keep it!"
LUKE 11:28

There is not a single day that we do not face the same test that was set before Adam. There is not a day that we do not have a chance to choose between the path of the devil's clever promises and God's sure Word.

From the beginning of time until the present moment, man's ungodly quest for power, his determination to use his gift of free choice for his own selfish ends, has brought him to the brink of doom.

God, meanwhile, in His infinite understanding and mercy, has looked on, waiting with a patience and compassion that passes all understanding. He waits to offer individual salvation and peace to the ones who will come to His mercy. The same two paths that God set before Adam still lie before us. We are still free to choose. We are living in a period of grace while God withholds the eternal punishment we so justly deserve.

In your daily choices, are you choosing Him continually in obedience to His Word? As you stand at the crossroads today, choose obedience, and He will give you peace.

How have you chosen the right path of obedience to God?

_____

_____

DON'T DOUBT THE DEVIL

The God of peace will crush Satan under your feet shortly.
ROMANS 16:20

Who is responsible for the infamy, terror, and agony that we see all around us? How can we account for the sufferings that we all experience if evil is not a potent force? Education has, in truth, impeded our minds. Because of allegedly scientific findings, some have lost their belief in the supernatural powers of Satan, while others worship him.

George Galloway summed up this dubious contribution of current education when he said, "The theory that there is in the universe a power or principle, personal or otherwise, in eternal opposition to God is generally discarded by the modern mind."

The modern mind may discard it, but that doesn't cause the evil principle itself to disappear! Once asked how he overcame the devil, Martin Luther replied, "Well, when he comes knocking upon the door of my heart and asks, 'Who lives here?' the dear Lord Jesus goes to the door and says, 'Martin Luther used to live here but he has moved out. Now I live here.' The Devil, seeing the nail-prints in His hands, and the pierced side, takes flight immediately."

What can you do when you are confronted with evil?

_____

_____

THE END OF LONELINESS

There is a friend who sticks closer than a brother.

PROVERBS 18:24

Have you ever felt the loneliness of being friendless? You can have a friend who sticks closer than a brother. Jesus Christ can make life joyful, satisfying, and glorious to you. All over the world are millions of men and women who love and serve Jesus Christ. The moment you accept Him, you are closer to them than you are to your own blood relatives.

There is not a city in the United States that does not have a warm church to which you could go and meet the most wonderful people. There is a giant network of true Christians in every community of America. The moment you clasp their hands, you know that you have friends.

But first, you must repent, surrender, and commit your heart and life to Christ. Let Him forgive your past sins, and He will take you into His family; He will bring you to the hearth, and you will feel the warmth of the fire. If you are lonely today, I beg you, come to Christ and know the fellowship that He brings.

If you do not have Christian friends, how can you find them?

_____

_____

HE BRINGS YOU BACK IN

"What man of you, having a hundred sheep, if he loses one
of them, does not leave the ninety-nine in the wilderness,
and go after the one which is lost until he finds it?"
LUKE 15:4

Perhaps you at one time knew the joy and peace of being born into God's family. You tasted the complete happiness and satisfaction of Christ's presence with you, but you sinned. You went out from the presence of Christ, and you have found that it is night. Perhaps there is no loneliness quite so bitter as the loneliness of unrepentant sin.

There are thousands of lonely people who carry heavy burdens of grief, anxiety, pain, and disappointment; but the loneliest soul of all is the man whose life is steeped in sin.

I beg you, come to the foot of the cross and confess that you are a sinner; forsake your sins. Christ can give you power to overcome every sin and habit in your life. He can break the ropes, fetters, and chains of sin; but you must repent, confess, commit, and surrender yourself to Him first. Right now it can be settled, and you can know the peace, joy, and fellowship of Christ.

How can the Lord help heal your loneliness?

_____

_____

HOPEFUL LAST WORDS

God will wipe away every tear from their eyes; there
shall be no more death, nor sorrow, nor crying.

REVELATION 21:4

Last statements of the dying provide an excellent study for those who are looking for realism in the face of death.

Matthew Henry—"Sin is bitter. I bless God I have inward supports."

Martin Luther—"Our God is the God from whom cometh salvation: God is the Lord by whom we escape death."

John Knox—"Live in Christ, live in Christ, and the flesh need not fear death."

John Wesley—"The best of all is, God is with us. Farewell! Farewell!"

Richard Baxter—"I have pain; but I have peace. I have peace."

Adoniram Judson—"I am not tired of my work, neither am I tired of the world; yet when Christ calls me home, I shall go with the gladness of a boy bounding away from school."

How different are stories of Christians who confess sin and by faith receive Jesus Christ as their personal Savior!

What message would you like to leave behind when you are gone?

_____

_____

CORONATION DAY

When the Chief Shepherd appears, you will receive
the crown of glory that does not fade away.
1 PETER 5:4

P eople from all walks of life look forward to Heaven: a ninety-four-year-old saint, eager to be with her Lord; a woman on death row who had become a Christian and can now look beyond her approaching execution to the glory that lies ahead; and two women whose husbands had just died after many years of marriage (one just short of their forty-ninth wedding anniversary). Each is looking beyond death to the glory that lies ahead.

The great Dwight L. Moody on his deathbed said, "This is my triumph; this is my coronation day! It is glorious!"

The Bible teaches that you are an immortal soul. In other words, the real you—the part of you that thinks, feels, dreams, aspires; the ego, the personality—will never die. The Bible teaches that your soul will live forever in one of two places—Heaven or Hell. Christians can have confidence that they will spend eternity with God and not fear eternity without Him. God promises eternal glory to those who follow Him.

What do you hope your last words will be?

_____

_____

THE IDEA OF REDEMPTION

How much more shall the blood of Christ . . . cleanse your
conscience from dead works to serve the living God?

HEBREWS 9:14

As a teenager, I was invited to hear a traveling preacher. The advertisements called him a "fighting preacher." I liked a good scrap, so I went. Halfway through his message that night, he pointed in my direction and shouted, "Young man, you are a sinner!"

There were other guys around me, but I was convinced he had singled me out, so I ducked. But then the idea that someone would call me a sinner stirred up my fighting spirit. I told myself, "I live a good, moral life. I even belong to a church." Yet I found myself in great conflict and could not resolve my own guilt over wanting to experience happiness in my own way. I knew I was living beneath God's standard. In God's eyes I was no different from anyone else. I wasn't a murderer. I wasn't a thief. But I was a sinner.

God puts within each soul a longing to know Him. But sin is a barrier that keeps us from Him. We are bound *by* it unless we are freed *from* it. That's what Jesus' redemption does for us.

What barrier can keep you from God?

_____

_____

Accept Redemption

Thus says the LORD, who created you, . . . "Fear not, for I have redeemed you; I have called you by your name; you are Mine."
ISAIAH 43: 1

God's gift of redemption says, "I will buy you back with My blood because I love you. I will free you from the chains of sin. I will settle the conflict within and give peace to your soul. But you must come to Me with a repentant heart. You must be willing to be redeemed. You must exchange your sin-blackened heart for a new heart that is cleansed by My blood."

Redemption is the Bible's great theme.

God's redemption plan is what turned a sordid story into a great story. His rescue mission was executed through His Son, the Lord Jesus Christ. He completed His mission more than two thousand years ago, when He hung on the cross and shed His blood in ransom for the souls of mankind. He died for your sin and my sin. When He conquered death and was raised from the grave that could not hold Him in bondage, He reached out His nail-scarred hands and said, "I've come to free you from your bondage and give you new life."

How are you freed from sin?

_____

_____

REDEMPTION: THE GREAT STORY

After you heard the word of truth, . . . having believed, you were
sealed with the Holy Spirit of promise, who is the guarantee of our
inheritance until the redemption of the purchased possession.

EPHESIANS 1:13–14

God's redemption story is great because God gives each of us the choice to accept His forgiveness and live with Him eternally. The Bible says that "God is not the God of the dead, but of the living" (Matthew 22:32). God is alive and well and wants no less for those He loves.

From the cross Jesus offered each soul a gift that will last eternally—with no expiration date. His precious blood was applied to your sin. He has covered your sin with His blood, which takes the sting of sin away.

Will you receive Christ? Have you read His redemption plan? It's written in blood with you in mind. Have you reached out to accept it? You cannot buy it with money; it has already been purchased for you. But you must surrender all you are hanging on to for something far better—the redemption of your soul. Once you accept salvation, you will walk in a peace that comes only from God.

What is sin covered with?

_____

_____

POISONOUS PRANK

Would not God search this out? For He knows the secrets of the heart.
PSALM 44:21

Many years ago a distinguished Methodist minister was preaching on sin. Some deacons approached him afterward and said, "We don't want you to talk so plainly about sin; if you do, our people will more easily become sinners. Call their sins mistakes if you will, but do not call their mistakes sin."

The minister picked up a small bottle and showed it to the group of deacons. The bottle was clearly marked Poison.

"Would you like me to change the label?" the minister asked. "I can mark that this strychnine is the essence of peppermint to make you feel better, but if you take it you will still die. Don't you see that the milder you make the label, the more dangerous you make the poison?"

The truth is that every last one of us is born in sin, and while some may not think of themselves as sinners, God does. But He loves sinners more than we love sin. And that is why He sacrificed His only Son to pay the penalty for mankind's sin.

No love is greater than that.

What is one sin that our culture often calls good?

_____

_____

WHO CARES ABOUT THE LAW ANYWAY?

The wickedness of man was great in the earth, . . .
And the LORD was . . . grieved in His heart.

GENESIS 6:5–6

Would you enjoy sports without rules or boundaries? What would be the point? When a player on the field or court goes out of bounds, he has committed a transgression, and there is a penalty for that transgression. This is common sports language. We accept the rules; in fact, we love them. If we are rooting for our team, and the other team commits a transgression, we cheer.

Do you begin to see what is in our hearts? Do you think the Lord cheers when we go out of bounds? No, His heart is grieved. God's desire is for man to be victorious over sin.

God's commands are designed to show us His goodness and His desire for us to live a better way than what we would choose for ourselves.

Scripture says, "The law is holy, and the commandment holy and just and good" (Romans 7:12). God wants us to stay within the boundaries He set so that we can have victory over sin.

Why? Once again, because God loves sinners.

Is it easy or hard to play by God's rules?

_____

_____

LIVING HISTORY

He is not here, but is risen!
LUKE 24:6

Why is it that the biographies of so many others are believed when they were written long after their deaths?

Alexander the Great's biography, for instance, was written four hundred years after he died, so its author obviously never knew him. But Alexander's legacy lives on while people doubt the life of Christ as documented by the gospel writers who walked with Jesus.[2]

Many people down through the centuries never had a record of their own births. Yet the existence of Jesus is revealed in an intricate genealogy, recorded in the Bible, that has stood the test of time.

You will never meet Alexander the Great in this life because he is dead. But you can meet Jesus Christ in this life because He lives! The marks of His sacrifice on the cross are found in human hearts. Most gravestones bear the words: "Here lie the remains of . . ." But from Christ's tomb came the living words of an angel, declaring: "He is not here, but is risen!" Jesus' tomb is history's only empty grave.

Why do you think it's so hard for some people to believe in the resurrection?

_____

_____

AUGUST

EVIDENCE OF THE RESURRECTION

He rose again the third day according to the Scriptures.
1 CORINTHIANS 15:4

There is more evidence that Jesus rose from the dead than there is that Julius Caesar ever lived. It is strange that historians will accept thousands of facts for which they can produce only shreds of evidence. But in the face of the overwhelming evidence of the resurrection of Jesus Christ, they cast a skeptical eye. The Smithsonian Institution states:

> The Bible, in particular the historical books of the old testament, are as accurate historical documents as any that we have from antiquity and are in fact more accurate than many of the Egyptian, Mesopotamian, or Greek histories.
>
> These Biblical records can be and are used . . . in archeological work. For the most part, historical events described took place and the peoples cited really existed.[1]

The world of science cannot unequivocally deny the Bible, and neither can history, based on the evidence. The Lord's Word is dependable: Jesus is risen!

What goes through your mind when scientists and historians find proof of biblical events?

_____

_____

THE JESUS EFFECT

And there are also many other things that Jesus did.
JOHN 21:25

We have access to libraries of information that will keep generations busy, confirming the overwhelming evidence found in the Bible. Kenneth Scott Latourette, former president of the American Historical Society, stated:

Even if we did not have the four . . . Gospels we could gain a fairly adequate impression of [Jesus] and of the salient points of his life, teachings, death, and resurrection from . . . letters of his followers written within a generation of his death. . . .

It is evidence of his importance, of the effect that [Jesus] has had upon history and, presumably, of the baffling mystery of his being that no other life . . . has evoked so huge a volume of literature. . . . Some characteristics stand out so distinctly in the accounts . . . that they are a guarantee of authenticity, so obviously are they from life and not invented or even seriously distorted.[2]

Search the evidence for yourself, and be convinced.

Does it thrill you to realize how much has been written about Jesus?

_____

_____

THE LEAP OF FAITH TO ETERNAL LIFE

Faith is the substance of things hoped for, the evidence of things not seen.
HEBREWS 11:1

A lbert Einstein said this near the end of his life:

> There comes a point where the mind takes a leap . . . and comes out upon a higher plane of knowledge, but can never prove how it got there. All great discoveries have involved such a leap.[3]

This, my friend, may be the point in time for your higher plane—relying on more than others' testimonies and completely on faith in God alone because of what He says about Himself. "Most assuredly, I say to you, before Abraham was, I AM" (John 8:58). This leap of faith is given when you speak the name of Jesus in sincere truth, realizing that you are Hellbound without His forgiving grace and mercy. Ask Him to look into your barren heart and your hungry soul and fill it with the faith to believe that He will change you. No matter how much knowledge you gather, you will never know the Lord Jesus Christ without taking the certain leap of faith that salvation comes only from Him.

Have you asked the Lord to bolster your confidence to take a leap of faith?

_____

_____

SEARCHING SOULS

"My thoughts are not your thoughts,
Nor are your ways My ways."

ISAIAH 55:8

P op culture is searching for truth. But truth has become to many *whatever* they want it to be, bound up in lies from Satan that cause them to look in futility to others and, sometimes, to themselves.

God longs to fill our minds with His truth and heal our sick hearts. God's heart's desire is to love us and change us.

I was moved when I heard the story that at age sixteen the singer Jewel was traveling through Mexico and observed that everyone seemed to be looking "for someone to save them."[4] Her evaluation was true. She later wrote lyrics to what would become a major hit, "Who Will Save Your Soul?" in which she reveals people's worry about who will save their souls.[5]

I wish I could tell this talented young entertainer who is searching for God that humanity is not God and never will be. And aren't we glad? No one cares for us as God does, and no one but God loves us with an everlasting love.

What would you say to a person looking for someone to save his or her soul?

No Religion Can Save

Put on the new man who is renewed in knowledge according to the image of Him who created him.
COLOSSIANS 3:10

No religion will save your soul because religion did not die to redeem your soul. Only the Man Jesus Christ, the Son of God, died in order that your soul might live. And those whose souls bear the conviction of sin, guilt, and shame and who confess their need to holy God will receive the gift of salvation through redemption in Jesus Christ.

True Christianity is not religion. It is faith in Christ alone.

He is not something you *add* to your life. Becoming a Christian means that Jesus Christ comes into your life and takes over. It is a totally new outlook that is not satisfied with anything less than penetration into the furthest corners of the soul.

Nor is following Jesus a spectator sport—buying a ticket and sitting on the sidelines. Becoming a Christian means no longer living for yourself but for God in obedience to Him. You must leave the old life behind and step into a new way of living, where Christ makes possible what you think impossible.

Are you satisfied with life on the sidelines?

_____

_____

CONNECTED TO THE VINE

"I am the vine, you are the branches."
JOHN 15:5

Jesus often used nature to illustrate His truth, and one of His most powerful illustrations involved a vine and its branches.

The analogy is clear. Christians draw holy strength from the vine that makes holy living possible. You may say that it seems a little egotistical to claim to be holy. But read carefully what the Bible says: "As obedient children, do not conform to the evil desires you had when you lived in ignorance. But just as he who called you is holy, so be holy in all you do; for it is written: 'Be holy, because I am holy'" (1 Peter 1:14–16 NIV).

When Christ transforms us into new creations, we have new positions in Him, and He helps us to reflect the holiness of His character. Living a holy life means that you give yourself wholly to Christ. That doesn't mean you will be perfect, but your desire will be to live according to the ways of God. If you're living wholly unto Christ, you look different, talk differently, and act differently to the world, for you are bearing His fruit.

Does your life reflect God's presence in your life?

_____

_____

CLOTHED IN SALVATION

You were enriched in everything by Him in all utterance and all knowledge.
1 CORINTHIANS 1:5

We can have faith in Jesus Christ because He sacrificed everything—His life's blood. He is worthy of all our surrender of self to the Savior. We give it all up . . . and in return we get all of Him. This is what the Bible means to be "clothed with salvation" (2 Chronicles 6:41). What richness there is in Him.

That's not to say we should expect Jesus to make us rich . . . or beautiful . . . or give us whatever our hearts desire. Becoming a Christian means God will provide for our needs according to His standard, which is higher than ours. We exchange our wills for His will.

He changes our countenance to reflect His heart, which is righteous. He begins a work in us that will transform our selfish desires into what He desires so that we glorify Him. He replaces what is most important to us with Himself, and He becomes the most important thing in our lives. Why? Because He is going to guide our every step.

What godly desires has the Lord placed in your heart?

_____

_____

TWO ROADS

"Narrow is the gate and difficult is the way which
leads to life, and there are few who find it."

MATTHEW 7:14

I magine a very wide road filled with people, all walking in the same direction. In the center of that road is a narrow path that goes in the opposite direction. It can be a lonely road—but it's the right road. Jesus plainly pointed out these two roads. One is broad, lacking in faith, convictions, and morals. It is the easy, popular, careless way. It is heavily traveled, but it leads to destruction. The other road is narrow and unpopular.

People who follow the broad path are shallow. The path they choose is riddled with compromise. Standing for Christ means that you will walk the narrow way and stand for righteousness, goodness, morality, and justice.

Perhaps you are at a crossroads. You find yourself gazing into the faces of those living for popularity and self-pleasure. That road leads to Hell. You are right to look at the narrow path and consider the journey. It can bring persecution because of faith in Christ, but He will walk with you because this is the road that leads to Heaven.

How difficult is it to stay on the narrow path?

_____

_____

No Such Thing as a Little Sin

Whoever has been born of God does not sin, for His seed remains in him; and he cannot sin, because he has been born of God.

1 John 3:9

Two teenage siblings asked their father for money to go see a movie with their friends. Knowing the content of the movie was inappropriate, the father told them they couldn't go. The teens debated their position: there were only a few curse words and one minor immoral scene, but the rest of the movie was wonderful. The father still refused.

Sulking, they retreated to their rooms until they were called for supper. When it came time for dessert, their mother set a pan of freshly baked brownies on the table. The father cut large squares for his children and said, "Your mother has made your favorite dessert, but there is one thing you should know before you eat it. I had her mix in some manure."

"How could you?" they moaned.

"Oh, it's just a little bit," the father answered. "Enjoy!"

Needless to say, the entire pan of brownies was thrown out.

Even a little sin is enough to corrupt. So don't mix it in.

How can you have the strength to choose holiness over sin?

_____

_____

CHIEF OF SINNERS

Christ Jesus came into the world to save sinners, of whom I am chief.

1 TIMOTHY 1:15

When men and women believe they are good and powerful enough to control their own destinies, they prove what the Bible says about "having a form of godliness but denying its power" (2 Timothy 3:5). Notice what one man wrote after he came out of darkness into the light: "For we ourselves were also once foolish, disobedient, deceived, serving various lusts and pleasures. . . . But when the kindness and the love of God our Savior toward man appeared . . . He saved us . . . to the hope of eternal life" (Titus 3:3–7).

This murderer, named Saul, sought and persecuted those who were following Jesus. Then he heard God's plea to come to Him (Acts 9), was reformed from sinner to saint, and was transformed to Paul the apostle.

Don't think you're hopeless. Don't hide behind scoffing, mocking, false humility, and laughter that the world applauds. Behind the world's curtain is Satan, pushing people into his vile and wicked world. Flee the lures of Satan and come into the care of Christ's everlasting forgiveness, abundant grace, and merciful love.

Is it humbling to know Paul called himself the chief sinner?

COUNT THE COST

*"Which of you, intending to build a tower, does not sit down first
and count the cost, whether he has enough to finish it?"*
LUKE 14:28

Standing strong for Christ often means being subject to abuse and ridicule. This is a cost we must be willing to pay. I visited with a successful business-man who lost his job because he refused to cover for top executives who were padding their expense accounts. He was distraught, but he knew covering for dishonesty would tarnish his testimony for the Lord. He put his confidence in the Lord instead of the power of others and eventually led one of the perpetra-tors to Christ. He counted the cost and had the joy of winning a soul to Christ.

It won't be easy, but if you let others see Christ in you, He will strengthen you and give you a boldness you have never known. He doesn't ask us to live the Christian life alone. *I* cannot live the Christian life alone. But Christ can live it through me if I will let Him, and He will do the same for you. The reward of His shed blood was the saving of lost souls.

Who said that becoming a Christian was easy? It certainly was not Jesus—it cost Him His life's blood. We must count the cost as well.

What is our reward for choosing to follow Jesus?

_____

_____

THE LOVING WARNING FROM GOD

Thus says the LORD, "Behold, I am fashioning a disaster and devising a plan against you. Return now every one from his evil way."
JEREMIAH 18:11

God's warnings are always fortified with hope. Aren't you thankful when the fire alarm sounds, giving the opportunity to douse the flames or escape? Aren't you relieved to hear a siren when you're in trouble and know that help is on its way? If your ship begins to sink, will you refuse to board the lifeboat? The Bible has given us fair warning and shown us the way of escape. Will you heed it?

Jeremiah, known as the "doomsday prophet," was sounding the alarm. He warned the people that judgment would come if they didn't repent. But the people ignored him. They scoffed at the holy Word of God: "We will walk according to our own plans, and we will every one obey the dictates of his evil heart" (Jeremiah 18:12). Doesn't this sound familiar today?

Though God spoke often about the day of doom, His compassionate warnings provide a way of escape, a way to salvation. Are you heeding the warning or grasping for another way? My friend, God's way is the only way.

How can you be sure you are listening to God's fair warnings?

ESCAPING FLOODS AND FIRE

"There will be great tribulation. . . . Therefore you also be ready,
for the Son of Man is coming at an hour you do not expect."
MATTHEW 24:21, 44

Jesus was predicting that a dark night was coming and equated this warning with the one God gave to the people of Noah's day—destruction is coming once again to earth. The earth was destroyed by water before Christ's first coming; and it will be destroyed again by fire at Christ's second coming—but it will also be cleansed. Fire can destroy, but fire also purifies.

What miner who discovers gold does not put it through the refiner's fire to uncover its worth? God is the Master Miner and Refiner. The earth belongs to Him, but human sin has polluted it. He is coming back to reclaim what is rightfully His and has invited those whose sin has been cleansed to reign with Him.

He will restore humanity and its dwelling to the pristine condition that was in the beginning. For those who believe in Him, there is no reason to fear the end because the end is the new beginning. This is very good news; it is God's message of great hope to the world.

Do you feel a sense of peace or fear when you consider the destruction to come?

_____

_____

THE HUNDRED-YEAR WARNING

By faith Noah, being divinely warned of things not yet seen, moved with godly fear, prepared an ark.

HEBREWS 11:7

Can you imagine what the people thought when Noah began chopping down trees and building an enormous ark on dry land, far from any ocean? Noah knew nothing about sailing the high seas, and he certainly was at a loss as to how to build a boat, even with God's detailed instructions. But he believed God when He said it would rain and the land would flood, in spite of the fact that it had never rained upon the earth. Still, over a hundred-year period, Noah faithfully carried out God's command. Noah's faith defied all human rationale. Through his obedience, he exhibited faith in God and was called righteous.

Noah believed God by faith in "the evidence of things not seen" (Hebrews 11:1). That is authentic faith. He so revered God that he prepared the ark "for the saving of his household, by which he condemned the world and became heir of the righteousness which is according to faith" (v. 7). Would you commit yourself to an ark of salvation while it sits on dry land? Christ is the ark of salvation.

How can you develop the faith and obedience of Noah?

_____

_____

HE'S COMING BACK

Looking for the blessed hope and glorious appearing of our great God and Savior Jesus Christ, who gave Himself for us, that He might redeem us.
TITUS 2:13–14

There is coming a day of greater conflict than the world has ever known. Where do you stand on the battlefield of good versus evil? Is your name written in the Book of Life? Do you long to hear God call you by name? Are you ready for the dark night to end? Are you ready for a new day, a new world, a new way of life? Are you ready for God's provision of true hope and real change?

Friend, I can tell you that if you belong to the King of Heaven, you will be victorious when the end of time comes. I have read the last page of the Bible. If you know Him, everything's going to turn out all right. Jesus, the changeless One whose promises never change (Malachi 3:6), will break through the dark night and rise as the conquering Champion and reigning King of glory.

Do you think He is coming back? I don't think it; I *know* He's coming back—and soon. This is my hope.

> List two things that come to mind when you think of Jesus coming back.
>
> _____
>
> _____

HOW TO FIND CHRIST

Whoever calls on the name of the LORD shall be saved.

ROMANS 10:13

I can recall being approached by a student who said, "Mr. Graham, we hear a lot about what Christ has done for us, the value of religion, and what personal salvation is. But nobody tells us how to find Christ." This lament became a challenge to me to explain simply and plainly how to find Christ.

First, you must be convinced that you need Him.

Second, you must understand the message of the cross. It is only when we understand that Christ died in the place of sinners, for sin, that we find the elements of satisfaction.

Third, you must count the cost.

Fourth, you must confess Jesus Christ as Lord of your life.

Fifth, you must be willing for God to change your life.

Sixth, when you are saved, you must desire nourishment from God's Word, from prayer, and from fellowship with other believers.

As you persist, you'll find yourself growing. Christ will work in you and through you.

Have you called on the name of the Lord?

_____

_____

CHRIST DIED FOR YOU

I have been crucified with Christ; it is no longer I who live, but Christ lives in me.
GALATIANS 2:20

I remember a young reporter in Glasgow who attended our meetings as part of his assignment. He heard the Gospel night after night, but it seemed to make no impact upon him.

One day, however, a colleague asked him, "What are they preaching down there?" He tried to explain the Gospel he had heard, and in so doing, he found himself saying, "You see, it's this way. Christ died for me. . . . Christ died for my sins." And when he said that, he suddenly realized the words were true! The full meaning of the message burst in miraculously upon him, and then and there he received salvation by acknowledging his sin, receiving Christ's work on the cross for the forgiveness of his sin, and committing himself wholly to Jesus Christ.

When you see Him high and lifted up—the Son of God smitten, marred, bruised, and dying for you—and understand that He loved you and gave Himself for you, you will have taken a step toward the Christian's assurance of salvation.

Do you believe Christ died for you?

_____

_____

WHAT IS THE SOUL?

The LORD God formed man of the dust of the ground, and breathed into his nostrils the breath of life; and man became a living being.

GENESIS 2:7

M an was created with both body and brain, but he was not a living creature until God breathed into him the breath of life, making him a living soul.

You may ask, "Just what is the soul?" The soul is the real you, the real me—the very breath of life that comes from God.

The body is the house, the soul is the tenant, and every soul is precious to God. Jesus said that one soul is worth more than the whole world (Matthew 16:26).

God is the soul's Creator, and He holds in His hand "the breath of all mankind" (Job 12:10). Jesus is the soul's Savior: "But God will redeem my soul from the power of the grave" (Psalm 49:15). And the Spirit of God is the soul's guiding light: "The Spirit of truth . . . will guide you" (John 16:13).

Medical science has probed the organs and tissues of the human body after death, but it cannot probe the soul, for it is unseen and lives eternally. The soul—the spirit of man—never dies.

How would you describe the soul?

_____

_____

INEVITABLE CONSEQUENCES

For the wages of sin is death, but the gift of God is eternal life in Christ Jesus.
ROMANS 6:23

A young couple took their children to a park one day to play, but they learned there was poison ivy in some nearby bushes. They warned their children to stay away from the area. Where do you think the children ran when their parents were not looking? Right into the ivy.

The father ran and caught the youngest one before she could touch it. To the father's surprise, the child jerked away from his grip. She embraced the leaves, looked up into her father's sad face, and said, "Look, Daddy, pretty red flowers."

In spite of our children's disobedience, we do everything we can to alleviate the pain and discomfort that comes from consequences. But we cannot take away the results of disobedience. If this father could have taken the festering rash from his child, he would have, but it was not possible. Instead, he soothes her skin with medicine that will bring healing, hoping she will learn that disobedience drags behind it severe consequences.

This is the picture we see of God's loving response toward humanity's defiance.

Do you ever feel like a child running into poison ivy?

_____

_____

THE BEGINNING OF REDEMPTION

*The LORD God sent him out of the garden of Eden to
till the ground from which he was taken.*

GENESIS 3:23

Death was not part of God's plan for Adam and Eve. He did not intend for them to be imprisoned by sin. He gave them life. He gave them freedom in Paradise. God allowed them to walk with Him in the garden. He created them for His own pleasure. Instead, the man and the woman surrendered to Satan's enticement. They chose to step out of God's will and God's perfect garden and into self-will—Satan's paralyzing grip.

Adam and Eve paid a price for their disobedience. They were driven out of the Paradise of God, His very presence, into the world they had chosen.

But that is not the whole story. Genesis portrays not only the beginning of the human race but the start of God's redemptive work in history. The salvation of the human race was put in place at the very beginning. Because God so loved His creation, He initiated a way to make amends for man's sin. This is the greatest search-and-rescue mission ever carried out—redemption of those made in God's image.

What is God's redemption plan for mankind?

_____

_____

A STORY OF REDEMPTION

In Him we have redemption through His blood, the forgiveness
of sins, according to the riches of His grace.
EPHESIANS 1:7

God's message is for people of every generation. As a young man, my head resisted what my soul longed for—peace from an inner conflict. I fell miserably short of God's standard of goodness. I wanted to make my own decisions, never considering that some of my choices altered the happiness I desired.

God was not going to force His way on me. I could receive Him and live according to His high standard, or I could reject Him and live in a lowly state with Satan snapping at my heels. How could I resolve this bitterness of soul? The answer came when I considered the Bible's great redemption story. I came to the place of repentance for my sin against God, believing in what He had done for me. In order to know the peace that comes *from* God, I had to confess my sin and come *to* God.

On the night of November 1, 1934, I exchanged my will for God's way. I traded my calloused heart for a cleansed soul. I had been redeemed and knew firsthand the promise of the Bible: in His presence is fullness of joy.

At what point did you ask the Lord to save you?

_____

_____

WHAT IS A SINNER TO DO?

"I will pardon all their iniquities."

JEREMIAH 33:8

The Bible declares, "All unrighteousness is sin" (1 John 5:17). *All* is an important word. It encompasses not only *all* people but *all* actions, words, unspoken thoughts, and attitudes. Even when directed at others, these things are just as harmful to us. Anger toward others never relieves our hearts. Jealousy causes some to outwardly rage while others seethe inwardly. Gossip poisons our tongues and preys on our minds. Sin violates the very love of God and breaks the law of God set forth to protect us from these hateful and harmful dispositions. The Bible says, "For all have sinned and fall short of the glory of God" (Romans 3:23). We can pretend that we are not unrighteous, but in our hearts we know we are.

Humanity's chief trouble is sin. God's chief truth is the wonderful gift of His salvation. And Jesus Christ is the only remedy for sin. "If we confess our sins, He is faithful and just to forgive us our sins and to cleanse us from all unrighteousness" (1 John 1:9). Sin's masterpiece of hopelessness is overshadowed by God's masterpiece of forgiveness and mercy.

Have you confessed your sins?

_____

_____

CAN YOU BE REMADE?

*If anyone is in Christ, he is a new creation; old things have
passed away; behold, all things have become new.*
2 CORINTHIANS 5:17

A sculpture artist was chipping away at a chunk of stone.
A man asked him, "What are you doing?"

The artist replied, "I am sculpting an elephant."

The man asked, "How do you know what to chip away?"

The sculptor smiled and said, "I chip away anything that doesn't look like
an elephant."

This is what God wants to do with our lives. We were made in His image, but
sin distorted everything about us—our bodies, our hearts, and our minds. Sin is
not to be regarded merely as a human weakness. God calls sin an abomination.
When we submit to Him and place our lives in His care, He will chip away at
whatever keeps us apart from Him so that we can wholly be part of Him.

You see, God doesn't just rescue us from the bondage of sin. He doesn't just
redeem us. When He saves us, the Holy Spirit begins a transformation in us. He
forgives the curse of sin against us and remakes us to live for Him.

What is the Lord trying to reveal as He chips away at you?

_____

_____

HOW DO I REDEEM MYSELF?

"[I have] come to seek and to save that which was lost."
LUKE 19:10

A troubled young girl asked a question to anyone who would listen: "How can I redeem myself for what I've done? I'm not religious, and I've done a lot of bad things that I can't apologize for."

Someone answered back, "You should do good things in your life, help other people when you can, and you'll set things right for yourself."

Another person said, "Seek forgiveness of those you hurt and forgive yourself."

These things will never win eternal life in Heaven with Jesus Christ. Only He can forgive and set us free. Good deeds will not bring comfort to the soul because the bad and hurtful things we do to others are ultimately done against the One who created our souls.

Your soul belongs to God. He is the only One who can redeem your soul.

God made your soul. The Lord Jesus died to redeem your soul. And the Holy Spirit can fill your soul with God's love and guide you through life.

This is the way to have victory over sin.

Who brings peace to your soul?

_____

_____

WHO CAN SET US FREE?

Flee also youthful lusts; but pursue righteousness, faith, love,
peace with those who call on the Lord out of a pure heart.
2 TIMOTHY 2:22

Few people have ever met the ruler of a kingdom or a head of state. But the power of those leaders is real and affects all who live under their governance. Jesus Christ governs with love that demands obedience. His great love calls us to the foot of His cross so that we may receive His pardon for our transgressions. The Bible says, "Let the peace of God rule in your hearts" (Colossians 3:15).

Repentance is more than just being sorry for our sin; it is a complete turning away from our total depravity. When we do that, Jesus Christ frees us from the consequences of sin, which is guilt and ultimate eternal separation from His presence. Only then are we delivered from the clutches of Satan.

Perhaps you are saying, "Billy, this is archaic, hard to believe. You're asking me to believe that Someone I've never seen can forgive me of what I've done out in the open or even in private?" Jesus said, "Blessed are those who have not seen and yet have believed" (John 20:29).

How is Jesus different from a head of state?

_____

_____

GOD VERSUS YOU

He has delivered us from the power of darkness and conveyed
us into the kingdom of the Son of His love, in whom we have
redemption through His blood, the forgiveness of sins.
COLOSSIANS 1:13–14

Jesus stands ready to pardon your offense against Him and receive you into His care. So in the case of *God v. You*, do you make the plea for Jesus Christ to save you? He will if you admit your guilt and accept His pardon, then live for Him now and with Him in eternity. Or will you reject the pardon? Will you try to convince yourself and others of your innocence?

Satan is the one who has convinced you that you are blameless, and you go on dying each day in your guilt and despair, without hope. God desires to give you eternal life, free from the guilt of sin, but Satan desires your very soul to be forever lost with him.

You can be freed from Satan's stronghold. You don't have to spend the rest of your life on earth and through eternity imprisoned by your guilt. You can be pardoned. And when the King pardons, your name appears in the Book of Life. This is an eternal exchange: sin and death for hope and eternal life.

Do you accept the Lord's pardon?

_____

_____

ALL CAN BE SAVED

The grace of God that brings salvation has appeared to all men . . .
denying ungodliness . . . looking for the blessed hope.
TITUS 2:11–13

Faith is the key that unlocks the truth of God's bountiful grace. The world is blinded to the fact that God's redemption of humanity through His Son is limited. It is only as we accept Christ as our personal Savior by faith that we are born again—given new life in Christ—and are thus brought into the family of God. Scripture teaches that "all are justified freely by his grace through the redemption that came by Christ Jesus. God presented Christ as a sacrifice of atonement, through the shedding of his blood—to be received by faith" (Romans 3:24–25 NIV).

All is a wonderful truth—don't miss it. The Bible's message is inclusive—for *all*. God's message is also exclusive—only those who call upon His name can be saved. But God's Word makes it clear that He desires that *all* be saved.

Sin has crippled human nature, but God has provided the cure. There is no sin that the blood of Jesus Christ cannot cleanse. And that's good news indeed.

Are you still feeling guilt over past sins?

_____

_____

FROM SEEDLING TO TREE

He shall be like a tree
Planted by the rivers of water,
That brings forth its fruit in its season.

PSALM 1:3

I t is no accident that the Bible compares us to trees, urging us to grow spiritual roots that are deep and strong. But a tree wasn't always a tree. It began as a small seed. Spiritual life also begins with a seed—the seed of God's Word planted in the soil of our souls that eventually sprouts and becomes a new seedling as we are born again. But though we're saved, we aren't meant to remain spiritual seedlings, weak and vulnerable to every temptation or doubt or falsehood or fear. God's will is for us to grow strong in our faith and become mature, grounded in the truth of His Word and firmly committed to doing His will (1 Peter 2:2).

Giving your life to Christ is an essential first step—but it is only the first step. God's will is for you to become spiritually mature, growing stronger in your relationship to Christ and your service for Him. Conversion is the work of an instant; spiritual maturity is the work of a lifetime.

Is your faith like a seedling, a sprout, or a mature tree?

BELIEF IN THE RESURRECTION IS RATIONAL

For the word of the LORD is right, and all His work is done in truth.
PSALM 33:4

Many jurists of history became convinced that the resurrection of Jesus Christ is an attested fact of history. John Singleton Copley, Lord Lyndhurst, one of the greatest legal minds in nineteenth-century Britain, stated it this way: "I know pretty well what evidence is; and I tell you, such evidence as that for the Resurrection [of Christ] has never broken down yet."[6]

Simon Greenleaf of Harvard University was one of "the finest writers and best esteemed legal authorities in [the nineteenth] century."[7] In his book *Testimony of the Evangelists*, he concluded, "It was therefore impossible that [the gospel writers] could have persisted in affirming the truths they have narrated, had not Jesus actually rose from the dead."[8]

Look at the many statements from leading intellectuals who have studied the matter from the standpoint of valid evidence, and you'll see that the voice of the scholar harmonizes with that of the angels and the disciples to declare in certainty today: "Christ the Lord is risen today."[9]

Does it give you comfort knowing that some of the finest minds agree about the resurrection?

_____

_____

PROOF COMES BY FAITH

"I am the resurrection and the life. He who believes in Me, though he may die, he shall live. And whoever lives and believes in Me shall never die."

JOHN 11:25–26

Do you accept these words of Jesus? I do. Even His most avowed enemies never caught Him in a lie. He, who was truth itself, can be trusted implicitly. He said He would be in the grave three days—and He was. He said He would come forth from the grave—and He did. And we, also, will one day die and be resurrected. This is the great hope and certainty for those who follow Jesus.

Even without these proofs I would still know that Christ lives because He lives in me. I talk to Him every morning when I wake up. He walks with me, and even as I write these words, His presence is overwhelmingly known.

Are you looking for Jesus? He is near you today. Look at the cross, and you will see the evidence—His blood shed for you—but He is not there. Look at the tomb, and you will see the evidence—it is empty—for He lives! Look for Jesus—He is knocking at the door of your heart.

Is the Lord knocking at the door of your heart?

_____

_____

DID HE DIE FOR YOU?

"Do you believe this?"
JOHN 11:26

A little gypsy girl was sitting for a portrait in an artist's studio, and she noticed on the wall a half-finished portrait of Christ on the cross. The girl asked who it was. When told it was Jesus, she responded that He must have been a very wicked man to have been nailed to a cross. The painter told her that, on the contrary, "Christ was the best man that ever lived, and that He died on the cross that others might live." She looked at him with innocence and asked, "Did He die for you?" The question haunted the artist's conscience, for though he knew the truth about Christ, he had not accepted Him as his Savior. He found he was no longer satisfied with life until he answered the question that you must also answer: Did He die for you?[10]

Have you received the living Christ? I am not asking you to receive a Christ who is hanging dead on a cross. Take Christ into your life—the resurrected Christ, who walks with those He has transformed by His grace.

Did Jesus die for you?

_____

_____

SEPTEMBER

JESUS CHRIST, ITS HEAD

[God] put all things under His feet, and gave Him to be head over all things to the church, which is His body, the fullness of Him who fills all in all.
EPHESIANS 1:22–23

While there is only one universal church, there can be any number of local churches formed into various denominations. Some are divided along national and theological lines or according to the temperament of their members, yet we have only "one Lord."

Jesus Christ is the head of His church. From Him must spring all the activities and teachings of the church, for He is the fountainhead of all Christian experience.

In a railroad system there is always one central office from which orders governing the operations of all trains originate. In the army, one commanding general issues orders to the many groups under his jurisdiction. His various subordinates may interpret his orders in slightly different ways, but his orders still remain the basis for their conduct. Jesus Christ stands as the commanding general.

Is Jesus your commanding general?

_____

_____

Your Local Church

Not forsaking the assembling of ourselves together, as is the manner of some.

HEBREWS 10:25

As soon as you have accepted Christ as your Savior and put your trust and confidence in Him, you have already become a member of the great church invisible. You are a member of the household of faith. You are a part of the body of Christ. Now you are called upon to obey Christ, and if you obey Christ, you will follow His example of joining with others in the worship of God.

We are now talking about the local church, the one in your own community, of whose many imperfections and shortcomings you may be well aware. But we must remember that perfection does not exist among human beings, even in institutions created to the greater glory of God. Jesus is the only perfect Man who ever lived. The rest of us are, at best, but repentant sinners, try as we may to follow His magnificent example; and the church is turning a blind eye toward itself when it claims infallibility or perfection for itself or any of its members.

Do you give grace and forgiveness to people in your church?

_____

_____

ONE CHURCH

Now I plead with you, brethren, by the name of our Lord Jesus Christ, that you all speak the same thing, and that there be no divisions among you, but that you be perfectly joined together in the same mind and in the same judgment.
1 CORINTHIANS 1:10

In relation to the church, its very power comes directly from Jesus Christ, and it is up to every church group to follow His commands, abiding by His teachings to the fullest.

The church has been widely criticized for many internal squabbles, much hair-splitting, and apparent lack of unity. These, however, are superficial things; these are the conflicts that come from the slightly varying interpretations of the Word of God and in no way reflect upon the wisdom of Christ's absolute authority.

Study the underlying beliefs of the various denominations and you will find that basically and historically they are almost identical. Though they may differ in practice, fundamentally they all recognize Jesus Christ as God incarnate, who died upon the cross and rose again that man might have salvation—and that is the all-important fact to all humanity.

How can we encourage each other to grow in unity around God's truth?

_____

_____

FINDING THE RIGHT CHURCH FOR YOU

If we walk in the light as He is in the light, we have fellowship with one another, and the blood of Jesus Christ His Son cleanses us from all sin.

1 JOHN 1:7

Samuel Rutherford once advised some disgruntled church members that they were not responsible for the life of their pastor, but they were responsible to pray for him, and to remain in the church, and to work for the Lord. And that the Lord would honor and bless them for it.

Jesus intended His followers to remain faithful to His church. Today, you may feel overwhelmed at the choices available. You might have a natural tendency to return to the church of your childhood, or you may want to choose another based on your more spiritually mature judgment.

A church affiliation is not something to be entered into lightly, and if it is to give you the greatest possible opportunity to be of service to others, you must prayerfully select the one where you can be of the most service to God.

What criteria should be used when looking for a church home?

_____

_____

REMAIN TOGETHER

With all lowliness and gentleness, with longsuffering, bearing with one another in love, endeavoring to keep the unity of the Spirit in the bond of peace.
EPHESIANS 4:2–3

The true Christian goes to church not only for what he gets out of it but also for what he can put into it. He goes to add his prayers to those of others; he goes to add his voice to the other voices raised in praise of the Lord; he goes to add his strength in beseeching the Lord's blessing; he goes to add his weight of testimony to the power of salvation through the Lord Jesus Christ. He goes to join with others in the worship of God, in the contemplation of His boundless mercy and love. He also goes for the necessary companionship of fellow believers.

Christians who are not actively involved in the life of a local church are like a burning coal removed from the fire. The coal gradually cools, and its flame dies once it is removed from the bed of glowing coals. Don't let this happen to you. When the church remains strong, it burns brightly as a beacon of hope and peace.

Are you more tempted to go it alone or to join with other believers in worship?

_____

_____

TRUTH AND OPTIMISM

"He who endures to the end shall be saved."

MATTHEW 24:13

Admiral Jim Stockdale was one of the highest-ranking officers in the US Navy, served in Vietnam, and spent time as a prisoner of war in the infamous "Hanoi Hilton." He once was asked which men did not make it out of the war prison. His answer was surprising: "The optimists." He went on to explain. "You must never confuse faith that you will prevail in the end—which you can never afford to lose—with the discipline to confront the most brutal facts of your current reality."[1]

This is what Scripture teaches. We cannot take ourselves off the hook by hoping that we will escape God's judgment without confronting the brutal fact of sin and dealing with its reality. Sin is a killer, and sin will be massacred in the Day of Judgment.

Truth is not always pleasant, but truth is always absolute. When optimism ignores truth, the reality of hope dies. The truth about hope in God is found in His glorious Gospel, the Good News of salvation, motivated by the most magnificent four-letter word—*love.*

What is the difference between optimism and faith?

_____

_____

HOW TO BE SURE

These things have I written unto you.
1 JOHN 5:13 KJV

Some years ago a great preacher said, "We must so educate and train our youth in the Christian way of life that they will never know when they were not Christians." Much of the philosophy of religious education has been based upon this premise, and perhaps many have missed the essence of Christian experience because nothing more than religious training took its place. No change took place in the heart.

At the turn of the century, Professor Starbuck, a leading thinker in the field of psychology, observed that Christian workers generally were recruited from the ranks of those who had had a vital experience of conversion. He also observed that those who had a clear concept of what it means to be converted were mainly those who had come out of rural areas where in the early days they had had either little or no carefully planned religious training.

This is not a criticism of religious training, but it may be taken as a warning of the dangers involved in improper use of religious training that becomes a substitute for the experience of the new birth. You must be born again to be sure of salvation.

When were you saved?

_____

_____

A Peaceful Future and Present

For by grace are ye saved through faith; and that not of
yourselves: it is the gift of God: not of works.

EPHESIANS 2:8–9 KJV

The Bible promises that there will be a time when the whole world is going to have peace. It seems that the world is heading toward Armageddon. In Revelation 6:4 John, the beloved apostle, says there's a red horse, "and power was given to him that sat thereon to take peace from the earth" (KJV). We're not going to have peace—permanent peace—until the Prince of Peace comes.

And He is coming. One of these days the sky is going to break open and the Lord Jesus Christ will come back. He will set up His reign upon this planet, and we're going to have peace and social justice. What a wonderful time that's going to be!

Isaiah predicted, "The government shall be upon his shoulder: and his name shall be called Wonderful, Counsellor, the mighty God, the everlasting Father, the Prince of Peace. Of the increase of his government and peace there shall be no end" (Isaiah 9:6–7 KJV). Think of it: no fighting, no war, no hatred, no violence. It will all be peace.

Do you have peace in your heart?

_____

_____

Good Workmanship

"I have filled him with the Spirit of God, in wisdom, in understanding, in knowledge, and in all manner of workmanship, . . . to work in gold, in silver, in bronze, in cutting jewels for setting, in carving wood."
Exodus 31:3–5

Christians are given certain work to do and are taught to labor to the best of their ability.

The Bible speaks approvingly of Bezaleel as a worker in metals, stone, and wood. He was filled with the Holy Spirit for craftsmanship: Jacob and his sons were shepherds. Joseph was a prime minister. Daniel was a statesman. Both Joseph and Jesus were carpenters, and some of the disciples were fishermen.

The Christian ideal is that we seek God's guidance in performing our daily work in subordination to the Lord at all times. Let's not become so absorbed in the things of this life that we have no time for God, for He is the one who inspires us in our gifts, helps us in our work, and blesses us in our obedience.

What pleasures have you experienced from good work done well?

_____

_____

DAILY WITNESS

Whether you eat or drink, or whatever you do, do all to the glory of God.

1 CORINTHIANS 10:31

Daily fellowship with Christ should enable us to live realistically. My father-in-law, the late Dr. L. Nelson Bell, once wrote in the *Southern Presbyterian Journal*:

If you are in church on Sunday the people who see you there may presume that you are a Christian. But what about the people with whom you come in contact during the week? . . . Attendance at, and active participation in, the program and activities of the church are an inescapable part of Christian living. But we all know the business of making a living, the responsibilities of a home, the daily routine all combine to test the reality of our Christian experience and faith. In these daily contacts what do others see? Do acquaintances see anything in us to suggest that we are different from those who do not know Christ? Certainly one of the real tests of Christian character is to be found in the lives we live from day to day.

Do you bring glory to God and hope to others?

THE SYMBOL OF THE CROSS

God forbid that I should boast except in the cross of our Lord Jesus Christ.
GALATIANS 6:14

We thought the devil was here," said the firefighter, "but with this cross, we know God is here."[2] Among the rubble in the aftermath of 9/11, a twenty-foot steel-beam cross was uncovered. Though people from many walks of life watched in terror as the World Trade Center towers in New York collapsed, the sight of a cross brought hope to many—and terror to some. Atheists demanded that the cross, later displayed, be removed from the privately operated National September 11 Memorial and Museum. They claimed that many people were "injured" when they saw it.

To some the cross of Christ brings cheer; to others it incites fear. The cross can be of comfort to people's spirits, or it can reveal the corruption of the human heart and bring conviction of sin. When you see a cross, let it always remind you of the tremendous gift that Jesus gave us, but never forget that it was because of our sin that Christ had to die there.

What comes to mind when you see a cross?

_____

_____

PEACE ON EARTH

I take pleasure in infirmities, in reproaches, in needs, in persecutions, in distresses, for Christ's sake. For when I am weak, then I am strong.

2 CORINTHIANS 12:10

Every generation witnesses terrifying world events. The twenty-first century was inaugurated with the horrific 9/11 tragedy that set the whole world on edge. Today nations are in turmoil as governments struggle with how to defeat global terrorism. People are frantic, searching for solutions.

There is only one solution, and it is found in the righteous ruler; the Man of peace. Jesus holds the key to man's problems, which are bound up in one little word—*sin.*

I have talked with people from all walks of life about how they deal with their fears. Some turn to alcohol; others turn to mystic religions and amusement. I say to them, "Come to Christ; He will overcome your fears. He will strengthen you to stand strong in the face of trials and disappointments." In the midst of cataclysmic events, there is peace that passes understanding.

People think they want peace in the world, but what they really need is peace in their hearts. If that happened, there would be peace in the world as well.

What is the only hope for peace on earth?

_____

_____

THE CHRISTIAN EXPRESSION

"Let your light shine before others, that they may see your good deeds and glorify your Father in heaven."
MATTHEW 5:16 NIV

The reality of our Christian profession is shown in many ways: the things we say, as well as the things we do not say; the things we do, as well as the things we do not do. For while Christianity is not primarily a matter of externals, nevertheless it does find expression in conversation, habits, recreation, emphasis, and ambitions to be noted in our daily life. Does our conversation honor Christ? Are our habits those of which He approves? Are our sources of recreation those in which His presence can be a part? Do we bow our heads in a word of thanks when eating in a public place? Can people tell from the emphasis we attach to material things whether we have set our affection on things above, or whether we are primarily attached to this world? Do people see in us an ambition for place and position out of accord with that of a Christian? All of these are very real and practical questions that must be answered, interpreted, and lived before our fellow men.

Could a stranger tell you're a follower of Christ?

_____

_____

A GIFT TO THE WORLD

Let us hold fast the confession of our hope without
wavering, for He who promised is faithful.
HEBREWS 10:23

For decades the world has marveled at a once crown jewel—the Hope Diamond—the dazzling, blue 45-carat gem with an estimated value of $250 million.³ Its owner donated the historic treasure to the Smithsonian Museum as "a gift to the world."⁴ Solitary, it sits encased by thick bulletproof glass.

What hope does this rare stone bring to the peoples of the world? While it is grand in glory, it is untouchable; valuable but not priceless; a gift *to* the world but protected *from* the world, locked for safekeeping.

Is hope for you locked up, inaccessible, untouchable?

Maybe you are longing for hope and cannot find it. If so, dedicate yourself to the pursuit of hope that brings certainty if we embrace it. You see, it is not kept from you, locked away in a museum. It is made available and comes to you as hope from above. It is not a futuristic aspiration; it is a faith builder. Hope is an unseen commodity that pays dividends while we still live.

Do you feel hopeful or discouraged?

_____

_____

A NEW DOCUMENT

His compassions fail not. They are new every morning; great is Your faithfulness.
LAMENTATIONS 3:22–23

A contemporary philosopher, the late Richard Rorty, claimed that hope placed in the promise of Jesus Christ returning to earth has failed because He has not returned. This philosopher believed a new document of promise is needed for hope to exist again.[5]

My friend, there is a document of promise that has never grown old. It is new every morning.

The Bible says that Jesus Christ is the very hope that lies within. He is earth's only hope. He came to unlock the door of your soul to bring the light of salvation into your life. This is *the reason for my hope*, found in God's *salvation*.

Perhaps the greatest psychological, physical, and spiritual need all people have is the need for hope that builds our faith and points us beyond our problems.

We don't see the water in the rock, but nature proves it is there.

We don't see what is along our future's pathway, but we follow its lead.

Be filled with the dividends of joy and peace, bringing you into a living hope of salvation.

In whom is your hope never misplaced?

_____

_____

OPEN THE DOOR

"See, I have set before you an open door, and no one can shut it; for
you have . . . kept My word, and have not denied My name."

REVELATION 3:8

Today, we have extraordinary doors open to us for the Gospel.
Every nation has points of entry, just as the children of Israel did when they crossed the Jordan River into the promised land. God had delivered them out of slavery and persecution into a better country. As Jesus walked the Bible lands, He proclaimed, "I am the door. If anyone enters by Me, he will be saved" (John 10:9).

Every house and building has at least one entrance. The kingdom of God also has an entrance—only one—and it is Jesus Christ, the Door. The human heart has an entrance as well, but many have it bolted, defiantly refusing to let Christ come in. The Bible says, "Behold, I stand at the door and knock. If anyone hears My voice and opens the door, I will come in to him" (Revelation 3:20).

Think of how many doors Jesus probably built while He worked in Joseph's carpenter shop. He also formed our hearts and wants to dwell there. Won't you open the door of your heart to Him?

Has Christ entered your life?

_____

_____

A HOLY TRANSFUSION

For the life of the flesh is in the blood.
LEVITICUS 17:11

S ome say, "Christianity and Judaism are bloody religions! Why must they always be talking about blood?" The Bible tells us life is in the blood.

I recall seeing a placard while on a visit to the Mayo Clinic: "Give the Gift of Blood." If you or a loved one were in need of blood to sustain life, would you not feel tremendous relief to know that enough blood had been donated and banked for a life-saving transfusion? Physical life has been preserved through this procedure—people giving their own blood to save another.

The blood of Christ provides life and all that sustains life: redemption, remission, cleansing, justification, reconciliation, peace, access, fellowship, and protection from evil and the evil one.

Do you need a blood transfusion? You don't have to go through the process of finding the right match. The blood of Jesus is the right type of blood, and He offers it to you. The heart is the pump that keeps the blood flowing through the veins and arteries to cleanse the cells. Jesus' blood is infused with life forever.

What comes to mind when you realize God has given you a "blood transfusion," making you His child?

_____

_____

EXAMINE YOUR ACTIONS

By this we know that we know Him, if we keep His commandments.

1 JOHN 2:3

A man once told me, "Billy, last week I lost twenty-two thousand dollars on a deal because it was a little bit shady. Before my conversion I would have clinched the deal without a thought."

Salvation is free to us, but it cost Jesus His life. It will also cost you your sins if you choose to receive His gift. That does not mean you have to clean up your life before you can be saved. The Lord knows you don't have the power to do that. You must come to Him in repentance, and *then* His Holy Spirit will move in, take up residence in you, and empower you to walk away from sin. That's why Jesus paid for our sins with His blood—to set us on a new path with the Holy Spirit as our daily guide.

Do you show your love to Him when you cheat or lie or go against His commands? Live in obedience to the Lord, and seek to please Him in everything you do.

What empowers you to live a new life?

_____

_____

COMPASSIONATE JUDGE

"There is nothing covered that will not be revealed,
nor hidden that will not be known."
LUKE 12:2

Plato, the ancient Greek philosopher, said that the soul is always drawn to its judge. He reasoned that humans know instinctively that they will one day stand in resurrected form before God. People do not like to think of God in terms of judgment. But such an attitude is idolatry, an attempt to make God in our own image, as though we are the ones who are right.

These truths are hard, but they are necessary. We love to talk about God's Heaven but are reluctant to mention God's judgment seat. Yet the whole Gospel is not proclaimed until God's warning is given. The entire human race will stand before Him someday.

I don't want to be judged by an angel who never shed a tear or who never felt pain. I will be judged by the Lamb of God, who became flesh and dwelt among us. He is the only One worthy to judge our standing with Him.

No one deserves God's love, but He offers it anyway. His saving grace changes our course from eternal judgment to life eternal. Choose life.

Who judges the souls of mankind?

_____

_____

GOSPEL PLAN OF SALVATION

Jesus said to him, "I am the way, the truth, and the life.
No one comes to the Father except through Me."
JOHN 14:6

Today's technology has surpassed me. I am amazed to get into an automobile and see a moving map on the dashboard. Macular degeneration prevents my eyes from following the details, and my ears cannot distinctly hear the voice commands, but I know it works. This device informs the driver how long the trip will take, instructs when to turn, and even announces the arrival.

My friend, there is a heavenly GPS that will bring you safely to your eternal destination in Heaven. It is called the Gospel Plan of Salvation. It only has one direction—up—and the Navigator, the Lord Jesus Christ, is "the way." He appoints the time of arrival and has prepared all that is necessary to welcome us.

By nature, people are bent toward home. When we finish our day and evening activities, we generally head for our homes. Far better than any dream you can imagine is the supernatural transformation that will take place for all of God's people when He transports us to His heavenly home.

Are you following the heavenly GPS?

_____

_____

ETERNAL WORTH

The redemption of [the soul] is costly.
PSALM 49:8

The Scottish preacher John Harper was aboard the *Titanic* in 1912. When the ship went down, Harper drifted into a young man holding on to a plank. Harper said, "Young man, are you saved?"

The young man answered, "No."

A wave separated them. After a few minutes they were within speaking distance, and again Harper called out to him, "Has your soul made peace with God?"

The young man said, "Not yet."

A wave overwhelmed John Harper, and he was seen no more. But the words "Are you saved?" kept ringing in the young man's ears. Two weeks later the young man stood up in a youth meeting in New York, told his story, and said, "I am John Harper's last convert."

The soul is valuable because of the price paid for its redemption. John Harper knew the value of a soul almost lost at sea. As a result, a young man discovered that the worth of his soul was eternal. This is why Isaiah wrote, "Let him return to the LORD . . . for He will abundantly pardon" (55:7).

In this story, are you John Harper or the young man?

_____

_____

THE SOUL'S VALUE

The highway of the upright is to depart from evil;
He who keeps his way preserves his soul.

PROVERBS 16:17

The world's "worth" is staggering when you consider the wealth of governments, commerce, entertainment, technology, the arts, mineral deposits, and so forth. There is simply no way to calculate the treasure's sum. And yet one soul is worth more than all of this, and the devil knows it.

Voltaire gained the world of literature, but lost his soul.

Hitler gained a world of power, but lost his soul.

Mao Tse-tung once wrote, "It's not enough to have our people's allegiance; we must possess their very souls." This is what Satan wants—your soul.

Of all the possessions we hold dear, we must hold our souls closest, for they are God's treasure, the only thing we can take out of our earthly experience to Heaven. Your soul is traveling to an eternal destination. Are you following the caution signs along the way that God has posted throughout His Guidebook, the Bible? They are posted to keep you from trouble so that you can live life with joy, knowing that someday you will walk the streets of Heaven.

How can you guard your soul?

_____

_____

You Are Loved

By this we know love, because He laid down His life for us.
1 John 3:16

Many people go through life feeling unloved—and unlovable. Many feel unworthy of love. Sigmund Freud declared, "The communal life of human beings had, therefore, a two-fold foundation: the compulsion to work, which was created by external necessity, and the power of love."[6] "The supreme happiness of life," Victor Hugo said, "consists in the conviction that one is loved."[7] Even if you believe you are not loved, your feelings deceive you. The truth is Jesus loves you—the Bible tells you so.

I have heard about God's love my entire life, and I have seen it demonstrated. My sweet, godly mother taught me my first Bible verse, John 3:16: "For God so loved the world . . ." Not everyone grows up this way, I know. That's why I'm called to share this tremendous Good News—that you are indeed loved by God.

How does knowing you are loved affect your outlook on life?

_____

_____

EMERGENCY NUMBER

*"Call to Me, and I will answer you, and show you great
and mighty things, which you do not know."*

We have all memorized the emergency call number 9-1-1, but we also need to memorize the eternal call number: 33:3. "Call to Me, and I will answer you" (Jeremiah 33:3). This is a marvelous invitation from our Lord. But He didn't stop there. His invitation was followed by a list of great "I will" promises: I will bring health; I will heal; I will bring abundance of peace and truth; I will rebuild; I will cleanse; I will pardon (vv. 6–8).

Repentance of sin is all it takes to realize God's great love.

King David said, "The sacrifices of God are a broken spirit, a broken and a contrite heart—these, O God, You will not despise" (Psalm 51:17).

It is often into broken ground that the seeds of spring are planted; they germinate to grow into a bountiful harvest. And it is into broken hearts that God, in love, plants His Word to save and prepare His people for some great work. Call to Him; He is reaching out in everlasting love.

Has the Lord healed your broken heart?

_____

_____

THE LOVE OF GOD

*May our Lord Jesus Christ Himself, and our God and Father . . . comfort
your hearts and establish you in every good word and work.*
2 THESSALONIANS 2:16–17

Who can describe or measure the love of God? When we read of God's justice, it is justice tempered with love. When we read of God's righteousness, it is righteousness founded on love. When we read of God's atonement for sin, it is atonement necessitated because of His love, provided by His love, finished by His love.

When we read about the resurrection of Christ, we see the miracle of His love. When we read about the return of Christ, we long for the fulfillment of His love.

No matter how black, dirty, shameful, or terrible our sin, God will forgive. We may be at the very gate of Hell itself, but He will be reaching out in everlasting love. "The Mighty One, will save; He will rejoice over you with gladness, He will quiet you with His love, He will rejoice over you with singing" (Zephaniah 3:17). Even in the midst of misery, we find God's marvelous message calling us to salvation.

What is one way the Lord has demonstrated His love for you?

_____

_____

POWERFUL PRAYER

Peter put them all out, and knelt down and prayed.
ACTS 9:40

King Hezekiah prayed when his city was threatened by invading armies, and the nation was spared for another generation. The king had prayed and exalted the Almighty "that all the kingdoms of the earth may know that You are the LORD God, You alone" (2 Kings 19:19).

Daniel prayed three times a day for power to remain true to God (Daniel 6:13). Jesus prayed at the tomb of Lazarus so that the people would believe (John 11:41–42). Peter prayed, and Dorcas was raised to life (Acts 9:40).

John Wesley prayed, and revival came to England. Jonathan Edwards prayed, and revival came to America.

Who knows what amazing things the prayers of Christians today can do?

We must ask ourselves, "Why do we pray?" Do we really believe that we are speaking to almighty God? That He hears us? Do we really believe we are bowing before His throne in Heaven? Do we really believe He will answer us?

When you approach the throne of God, do so with faith, belief, and a heart that seeks to glorify Him.

When you pray, do you believe God hears you?

_____

_____

PRAY WITHOUT CEASING

Pray without ceasing, in everything give thanks.
1 THESSALONIANS 5:17

Jesus sits at the right hand of the Father in Heaven interceding in prayer for us (Hebrews 7:25). Through His prayers He empowers us to live for Him, all day, every day.

How quickly and carelessly, by contrast, we pray. Snatches of verses are hastily spoken in the morning, and then we say good-bye to God for the rest of the day until we rush through a few closing petitions at night. How little perseverance, persistence, praise, and pleading we show.

Some time ago I read about a man in Washington, DC, who had spent seventeen years securing favorable action on a claim of eighty-one thousand dollars against the government. Yet many people today will not pray seventeen minutes for the welfare of their immortal souls or for the salvation of other people.

"Pray without ceasing" (1 Thessalonians 5:17) should be the motto of every follower of Jesus Christ. Never stop, no matter how hopeless it may seem. Ask the Lord to help you pray that all you ask may be for the glory of the Lord Jesus Christ. This is the power of prayer.

What does it look like to pray without ceasing?

_____

_____

JESUS' GIFT OF PRAYER

"Father, I desire that they . . . may be with Me where
I am, that they may behold My glory."
JOHN 17:24

When we pray in adversity, we may not see the full answer until we come into the peace of Heaven. When we pray in the face of danger, we may not recognize the hand of protection until we are in His care. We often forget to pray when we are enjoying times of prosperity, security, and freedom. Yet this is the most critical time to pray so we do not become selfish, arrogant, and captivated by the world's charms.

We have learned to harness the power of the atom, but we have not—nor will we ever—learn how to harness the power of sin without God's help. People can be more powerful on their knees than behind the most powerful weapon made by man.

Prayer has eternal value. We will never know the full glory of our prayers until we are in the presence of the One who answers them. Jesus is praying for us today right where He is—in Heaven eternal—just as He prayed for us while on earth. We should thank Him every day for this wonderful and precious gift.

Do you pray when everything is going well?

_____

_____

TREASURES IN HEAVEN

"Do not lay up for yourselves treasures on earth, where moth and rust destroy . . . but lay up for yourselves treasures in heaven. . . . For where your treasure is, there your heart will be also."
MATTHEW 6:19–21

Two old friends were both dying. One was rich, the other poor. The rich man was not a Christian, but the poor man was a very strong believer in Christ. The rich man said to a visitor one day, "When I die, I shall have to leave my riches." Then he pointed to his dying friend and said, "And when he dies, he will go to his riches."

In a couple of sentences the rich man summed up a stark contrast between them. The man who possessed everything on earth in reality had nothing. The man with nothing on earth in reality had everything.

Does that mean that we must renounce everything we own? No—not unless God clearly commands us to do so. But it does mean we commit everything we have—including our lives—to Christ. Then we will have treasures in Heaven.

Is it easier to value the blessings we have on earth or those treasures we have in Heaven?

_____

_____

A SPIRIT OF SACRIFICE

"There is no one who has left house or brothers or sisters or father or mother or wife or children or lands, for My sake and the gospel's, who shall not receive a hundredfold now in this time . . . and in the age to come, eternal life."

MARK 10:29–30

There is a group of men in Scripture who also walked away from their life's work to follow Christ; many of them were fishermen from Galilee. The Gospels give us a wonderful glimpse into a conversation between Jesus and His disciples. Peter said, "See, we have left all and followed You" (Mark 10:28).

Jesus knows the motives, thoughts, and intents of the heart. "*I am* He who searches the minds and hearts. And I will give to each one of you according to your works" (Revelation 2:23). He was telling Peter—and us—that He would provide and that all the sacrifice would be worth it. The Lord is watching those who are faithful in giving themselves to the work of the Lord.

How do you think the disciples felt giving up everything to follow Jesus?

_____

_____

285

OCTOBER

THE SERVANT'S INHERITANCE

Whatever you do, do it heartily, as to the Lord and not to men, . . . for you serve the Lord Christ.

COLOSSIANS 3:23–24

Moses gave up all earthly glory and possessions to identify with God's people. He was the adopted child of an Egyptian princess, but he gave up the kingdom and crown of Egypt to be a child of God. Moses gave up the royal scepter to be rich in God's law. The prophet was known as a shepherd, a leader, a deliverer, a lawgiver, and a judge. But Moses said, "O my Lord, I am . . . Your servant" (Exodus 4:10); and when he died, God spoke of him as "Moses My servant" (Joshua 1:2).

When you reach Heaven, there will be no opportunity to brag of your exploits; but you will have eternity to rejoice in how you lived your life for Jesus because of His grace in you.

It may take a lifetime to accumulate wealth, but it can vanish in the blink of an eye. While the Bible teaches us to store up treasures in Heaven, the greatest treasure is in knowing that we will be rewarded by His very presence—forevermore.

Would you consider it an honor if the Lord called you His servant?

_____

_____

GOING HOME

They desire a better, that is, a heavenly country. . . .
[God] has prepared a city for them.

HEBREWS 11:16

A mother and son once lived in a miserable attic. Years before, she had married against her parents' wishes and had gone with her husband to live in a strange land. But her husband soon died, and she managed with great difficulty to secure the bare necessities. The boy's happiest times were when his mother told of her father's house in the old country, a place with grassy lawns, enormous trees, wide porches, and delicious meals. The child longed to live there.

One day the postman knocked at the door with a letter. The woman recognized her father's handwriting and with trembling fingers opened the envelope that held a check and a slip of paper with two words: "Come home."

A similar experience will come to all who know Christ. Someday you will receive this brief message: "The Father says come home."

The Bible teaches that we are strangers and pilgrims on earth seeking a homeland, a place prepared for us by God (Hebrews 11:16). Making your decision for Christ puts you on the road that leads to a heavenly home.

How is Heaven like coming home?

_____

_____

THE CHURCH'S FOUNDATION

He is the head of the body, the church, who is the beginning, the firstborn
from the dead, that in all things He may have the preeminence.
COLOSSIANS 1:18

What exactly is the church? Is it a building with a steeple or an abandoned sports arena that has been turned into a worship center? Is it an old sanctuary filled with wooden pews or a storefront stocked with folding chairs? Is church a place of prayer or community service?

What is the true church? One of the Greek words for church, *ekklésia*, means "the called-out ones"[1]—called out of the world, yet to be the light of Christ. This is troubling for many because as they strive to take God's Word to unbelievers, they are often more influenced by the ways of the world.

Most of all, the church belongs to Jesus Christ. He founded the church. The church does not belong to pastors or congregations but to Christ alone. It is His dwelling place on earth, through the lives of His followers. The world's sewage system threatens to contaminate the stream of Christian thought. The church must quickly recover the authoritative message of Christ.

Do you feel called out to be one of the Lord's people?

_____

_____

THE BRIDE OF CHRIST

Let us be glad and rejoice and give Him glory, for the marriage of
the Lamb has come, and His wife has made herself ready.

REVELATION 19:7

The church is the bride of Christ. This description may seem strange, but it is the relationship God had in mind in the beginning. When God took a rib from Adam's side and formed the woman, Adam's bride, this was a picture of what was to come—the church as the bride of Christ. When Christ finished His great work on the cross and gave up His Spirit, the blood that was shed gave birth to the church of the living God.

Not only is the church the bride of Christ, but the members of His body become "joint heirs with Christ" and the children of God (Romans 8:17).

That glorious day is coming when we will be caught up in the air with our Bridegroom, Jesus Christ. The bride of Christ is the triumphant and eternal church, which will be gathered to His side and reign with Him forever. The angels will sing, and instruments will resound; God's people will praise and worship the Redeemer. What a day that will be for the church eternal!

Are you excited about coming face-to-face with your Bridegroom?

FILLED WITH THE SPIRIT

"When the Helper comes, whom I shall send to you from the Father, the Spirit of truth who proceeds from the Father, He will testify of Me."
JOHN 15:26

The Holy Spirit gives liberty to the Christian, direction to the worker, discernment to the teacher, power to the Word, and fruit for faithful service.

If you know Christ, you don't need to beg for the Holy Spirit to come into your life. He is already there—whether you feel His presence or not. Don't confuse the Holy Spirit with an emotional feeling or a particular type of spiritual experience. It is never a question of how much you and I have of the Spirit, but of how much He has of us. Your body is the home of the Holy Spirit (1 Corinthians 6:19).

It is my belief that a person who is filled with the Spirit may not even be conscious of it. My friend, the late Roy Gustafson, once said, "The Holy Spirit didn't come to make us Holy Spirit-conscious but Christ-conscious." Are we?

Would you say you're more Holy Spirit-conscious or Christ-conscious?

_____

_____

SERVE AT HOME

Through love serve one another.
GALATIANS 5:13

An elderly couple had been praying for the Lord to show them how they could serve Him. Physically, they were unable to venture far from home. One day a young mother, their neighbor, knocked at their door and handed them some fresh bread she had baked. The couple, overwhelmed at her gift, invited her in. Looking into her pale face with dark circles under her eyes, they learned she was suffering from a serious disease and asked if they could pray with her. A tear fell on her cheek, and she said, "No one has ever prayed for me before." As the weeks and months passed, the couple came to know the woman and began looking after her children on occasion while the woman went for medical treatment. The couple baked cookies and taught the children Bible stories after school. In time the entire family came to know the Lord. This is service with eternal value.

Some believe that they can do God's work only on a mission field far away, but service begins right where you are.

How can you serve right where you are?

_____

_____

THE WORKING WORD

"You are already clean because of the word which I have spoken to you."
JOHN 15:3

There is no greater armor, no greater strength, no greater assurance than to be filled with the Word of God.

The Word of God convicts us. It cuts, pierces, pricks, smites, severs, carves, and shapes. "For the word of God is living and powerful, and sharper than any two-edged sword, piercing even to the division of soul and spirit, and of joints and marrow, and is a discerner of the thoughts and intents of the heart" (Hebrews 4:12).

The Word of God cleanses. Christ sanctifies and cleanses with the "washing of water by the word" (Ephesians 5:26).

The Word of God gives us new birth. First Peter 1:23 says we have been purified, "having been born again . . . through the word of God which lives and abides forever."

The Word of God is the Work of God. Oh, that we would hunger to be filled with the Word of God, for there is no greater armor, no greater strength, no greater assurance that He is with us and in us.

What has the Word of God done for you?

_____

_____

READ THE WORD

Forever, O LORD, Your word is settled in heaven.
PSALM 119:89

You may have heard the expression, "He (or she) is a walking Bible." It is a wonderful thing to hide the Word of God in our hearts; it helps us along the pathway of life. It is important, though, to back it up with our lives.

Read God's Word with reverence, for He is holy.

Read it with expectancy, believing God will speak to you.

Read it with dependence on the Holy Spirit, who will open your understanding.

Read it with conviction, to correct and encourage you.

Read it in obedience, so you can put it into action.

Read and then memorize as much as possible, so it will always be with you.

Read it in prayer, so its words will strengthen your faith.

Read and pass it on as a testimony to what God has done for you.

It is a joy to carry in our hands the blessed Scripture and to know where to find various passages. But one day He is coming soon to carry us into His everlasting light, where we will be in the very presence of the Word eternal.

Do you have reverence for the Bible?

_____

_____

FINDING THE TRUTH

The entirety of Your word is truth.
PSALM 119:160

The great quest for life has always been to find truth. Universities are filled with seekers who want to know the truth. But do they really? Often when they find truth, they reject it because sometimes the truth hurts. So they turn in another direction to find *a* truth that makes them feel better about their defiance of *the* truth.

Jesus did not say we would know *a* truth; He spoke of *the* truth. There may be some truth in various religions and philosophies, but Jesus is *all* truth and *the* Truth. In the same way, the Bible does not contain God's truth; the Bible *is* God's truth.

If our minds and hearts are not filled with God's truth, something else will take its place: cynicism, occultism, false religions, and philosophies. The list goes on. Where there is truth and error, there is always compromise.

There are those who seek freedom more than the truth. They are free to reject the truth, but the freedom they choose will not set them free. "You shall know the truth, and the truth shall make you free" (John 8:32).

What is more valuable to you: freedom or truth?

_____

_____

HARD TRUTHS

"For this cause I was born, and for this cause I have come into the world, that I should bear witness to the truth."

JOHN 18:37

Here is an honest statement: truth is not always pleasant. The reason God judges sin is because He is truth. Like a surgeon, He cuts out all that is false and wrong. His scalpel cuts across all that is dishonest, unfair, and unloving. Isaiah said, "Woe to those who call evil good, and good evil; who put darkness for light, and light for darkness; who put bitter for sweet, and sweet for bitter!" (5:20).

For this reason, Jesus plunged into the mire of our sin when He came into this world that He might save us from sin. Then He baptized us with the truth of His love that saves, disciplines, and will bring us to Heaven someday.

All of mankind should be bowing at the mention of His great name, thanking Him for these wonderful truths—someday all of creation will. "Only fear the LORD, and serve Him in truth with all your heart; for consider what great things He has done for you" (1 Samuel 12:24). What a wonderful reason to praise Him today.

What will it be like one day when all the world bows to the truth?

_____

_____

THE LIGHT OF THE WORLD

"I am the light of the world."
JOHN 8:12

Jesus provides for those who receive Him. Just as God provided daily manna to Israel on their wilderness journey, so Jesus provides for the soul-hunger of people today.

Jesus is also the everlasting Guide. The Lord led the Israelites through the Sinai Desert during the day with a pillar of cloud, and He provided light at night with a pillar of fire. He is the light of the world.

Scientists really don't know what light is, but we all know its many effects. We know that there could be no life upon the earth without light. What the sun is to the earth, Jesus Christ is to the spiritual world. What effect the sun has on nature is the effect Jesus has on our cold, lifeless, and sinful natures. Christ wants to turn His light on in our hearts. He wants us to be reflectors of His divine light.

I have traveled to every continent in the world and have been a witness to the difference God's light makes in the people who possess Him. We are His light in a dark world.

In what way are you a light in a dark world?

_____

_____

STANDING STRONG

"Blessed are those who are persecuted for righteousness'
sake, for theirs is the kingdom of heaven."
MATTHEW 5:10

Some years ago in a country where Christians were looked upon with suspicion and disfavor, a government leader said to me with an unscrupulous twinkle in his eye, "Christians seem to thrive under persecution. Perhaps we should prosper them, and they would disappear."

There is an underlying truth in this statement. Many rely on Christ when they have nothing to lean on except Him, but then they fall away when they climb the ladder of success. They think they can lean on their own power and authority, forgetting about Jesus. They just don't have time for Him anymore.

No one desires persecution, which can come in many forms, but may we be people empowered by the Lord to stand strong when those times come.

Throughout the world today there are people who are enduring cruelties because of their Christian faith. We must pray for them, and for ourselves, that in our own dying hour God will give us grace to endure until the end, anticipating the certainty of His glory to come.

How can we support persecuted Christians around the world?

_____

_____

THE ONE TRUE GOD

"I will shake all nations, and they shall come to the Desire of All Nations,
and I will fill this temple with glory," says the LORD *of hosts.*
HAGGAI 2:7

Blending religions is nothing new, but Christianity is not a religion—it is faith in the one true God. However, there is a great movement taking place involving people who call themselves Christians mixing with world religions. This practice is gaining acceptance—but not with God.

A famous Hollywood actress and Golden Globe winner considers herself a Buddhist while claiming an abiding belief in the traditional God. Others say, "I like the gentle Jesus, but I don't care for a judging God." The truth is they are one in the same. God is one, and faith in God cannot be blended or mixed with anything. People may believe that they can "mix it up," but God will one day "shake all nations," and all that does not glorify Him will become desolate.

The day is coming when every nation and all peoples will worship the one true God. So we must act now, seeking Him in spirit and truth. On that day, the Lord promises to gather the redeemed and bring them home, and "they shall trust in the name of the LORD" (Zephaniah 3:12).

Are you ready to be gathered home?

_____

_____

OPEN YOUR EARS

"Many nations shall be joined to the Lord in that day, and they shall become My people."

ZECHARIAH 2:11

A youth minister told a story as he stood before a large group of teenagers and taught the Scripture. One of the boys in the back of the room sat with his fingers in his ears and his eyes closed. At the end of the meeting, the minister asked him why. The young man said, "My parents made me come, but I don't have to listen."

It is hard for a believer in Christ to imagine such resistance, but the Lord told His people, and tells us today, "Call on My name, and I will answer" (Zechariah 13:9).

Ears that are shielded from God's voice have no hope. For those who do hear and respond according to His command, God grants His assurance that they belong to Him. If you haven't prepared to meet God in eternity, open up your ears and ask Him to engrave your heart with His wonderful name. And the Lord will be King over all the earth. "On that day there will be one Lord—his name alone will be worshiped" (14:9 NLT).

Is there anything blocking the sound of the Lord's voice in your life?

_____

_____

GOD HEARS YOUR PRAYERS

"In this manner, therefore, pray: . . .
For Yours is the kingdom and the power and the glory forever. Amen."
MATTHEW 6:9, 13

Only one power can redeem the course of events, and that is the power of prayer.

Prayer opens the gates of eternity to sinners saved by grace.

To whom shall we pray? To the Source of all power.

Dr. Donald Grey Barnhouse once said, "I am not so sure that I believe in the 'power of prayer,' but I do believe in the power of the Lord who answers prayer."[2]

The gods of this world will not answer prayer offered in their names because the gods are made by human hands. They cannot see, they cannot touch, they cannot hear, they cannot speak, they cannot comfort, they cannot deliver, and they cannot save. But from one end of the Bible to the other, and throughout history, we find the record of those who turned the tide of history through prayers offered in the mighty name of God. He hears. He answers. He saves.

Are your prayers mighty, or is it the Lord who is mighty to save?

_____

_____

HIS WILL BE DONE

Jesus spoke these words, lifted up His eyes to heaven, and said: "Father, the hour has come. Glorify Your Son, that Your Son also may glorify You."

JOHN 17:1

J esus said that His temple was a house of prayer (Matthew 21:13 NLT). I wonder what would happen in our churches and in our hearts if we were to begin each day praying as Jesus modeled in John 17.

We humans were fashioned in the beginning to live a life of prayer because prayer is fellowship with God. But sin erected a barrier between us and God. Our sin caused this great gap, but God provided His Son as our Mediator. We can know Him through reading His Word and praying to Him in His name and according to His will.

With God nothing is impossible. He knows what we cannot understand. So you must not put your will above God's will. Do not dictate to God. And do not expect an immediate answer, because He withholds His answers at times to grow our faith. Learn the difficult lesson of praying as the Son of God Himself prayed in Gethsemane: "Not my will, but thine, be done" (Luke 22:42 KJV).

Do you pray for the desires of your own heart or for the will of God?

_____

_____

BEHIND THE SCENES

For we are God's fellow workers; you are God's field, you are God's building.
1 CORINTHIANS 3:9

While much is said about Christian workers who are publicly visible, not much is said about the quiet works of God's servants. We will have to get to Heaven before we will fully realize the army of prayer warriors that made others' work possible. Just as the church is the body of Christ, the work is never accomplished by the act of just one, unless it is Christ's alone.

In our crusades over the years, we have watched the body of Christ operating in various ways—churches recruiting volunteers to help with parking, ushering, counseling, giving financially, and, most important, praying for the lost. All of these who have quietly and faithfully worked behind the scenes will be rewarded by the Lord Himself someday.

Then there are those who point people to the Savior by how they live, day in and day out. They are living examples who speak of Christ's virtues, instilling Christian character into the fabric of life so that when they are with others, no one can find fault in how they live. Christ will reward them.

What work has the Lord set aside for you to do behind the scenes?

_____

_____

INCOMPARABLE RICHES

[God] raised us up together, and made us sit together in the heavenly places in Christ Jesus, that in the ages to come He might show the exceeding riches of His grace in His kindness toward us in Christ Jesus.

EPHESIANS 2:6–7

God tells us to store up the right kind of riches in our lives. We often think of riches in a materialistic way, but God speaks of riches that don't fade away. When we live obediently for Him, He will deposit His riches in our hearts, creating an inward righteousness that produces the marks of a true believer in Christ (Ephesians 2:6–8).

When we possess the richness of salvation, our storehouse here will be full to overflowing with the fruit of the Spirit, unspeakable joy, peace that passes all understanding, wisdom, strength, and the love of Christ.

In Heaven there will be many believers who never received any acknowledgment while on earth, yet they faithfully prayed and humbly served Christ. I believe their crowns may sparkle with more jewels than the philanthropist who endowed the church and whose name is engraved on the plaque in the narthex.

Will you have a crown in Heaven?

_____

_____

A NEW HOPE AND A NEW HEART

"I will give you a new heart and put a new spirit within you; I will take the heart of stone out of your flesh and give you a heart of flesh."
EZEKIEL 36:26

Science is learning to control just about everything but man. More important than electricity, technology, and medicine are the issues of the heart. Solve the problems of hate, lust, greed, and prejudice—which produce social strife and ultimately war—and the world would be a different place. Our future is threatened by many dangers, but they all stem from the heart.

Greater than the enemy outside is the enemy within—sin. Every major civilization before us has collapsed from internal forces rather than military conquest. While ancient Rome's disintegration was hastened by foreign invasions, in the opinion of a well-known archaeologist, it collapsed "only after bribery and corruption had been rife for generations."

No matter how advanced its progress, any civilization that neglects its spiritual and moral life is going to disintegrate. This is the history of mankind, and it is our problem still today.

This is why Christ came—to give new hearts to the human race.

What is the condition of your heart today?

_____

_____

PROUD AMBASSADORS

*"Whoever confesses Me before men, him I will also
confess before My Father who is in heaven."*
MATTHEW 10:32

One day a student of a non-Christian faith came to me and said that he was convinced Jesus is the Son of God but that he couldn't confess Him publicly because in his home country the social cost would be too great.

I told him what the Bible says: "But whoever denies Me before men, him I will also deny before My Father who is in heaven" (Matthew 10:33).

Like the rich young ruler, that student went away sad. He had counted the cost and was not willing to pay it. He wasn't ready to put Christ first.

When ambassadors serve their countries, they cannot do so effectively if they are ashamed of whom they represent, even more so if one claims to serve the King of kings.

After Jesus ascended to Heaven, the apostles stood before their peers, their families, and their communities and governments unashamed of the Lord Jesus. They blazed a trail for all who would come after them. Now it is your turn.

Do you feel tentative about telling people you're a Christian?

PRAISE ETERNAL

[Christ] is God, the one who rules over everything and is worthy of eternal praise!
ROMANS 9:5 NLT

When we look back over the years at what God has done through our crusade ministry, we give Him praise for the privilege of preaching His Gospel. We give Him praise for answering the prayers of His people. We praise Him for souls won to the kingdom. But even more than this is our praise for Jesus Christ Himself and His great love that never fails.

Scripture speaks of praising the Lord continually and forever, in the past, present, and future. Praise should be on our lips and in our hearts. It should be demonstrated in our lives because this will be the grandeur of Heaven—praising Him eternally. It would serve us well to study passages that lift Him high.

The Bible urges the body of Christ—the church—to encourage one another in praise of the Savior. We must keep in mind that while it is difficult, He will be with us, and the trials we endure for His sake will strengthen us in faith and open doors so that we can speak boldly for Him.

Do you find it easy or difficult to praise the Lord during hard times?

GENUINE PRAISE

You are my God, and I will praise You;
You are my God, I will exalt You.
PSALM 118:28

P raise and worship" has become a cliché in many Christian circles. Do we really stop long enough to consider what it means and how it affects our daily lives? Praising the Lord is not something we are called to do on Sunday morning. It is a way of life—praising God no matter what we do or where we are. As believers we are to function by the power of God, who does all things well.

It is relatively easy to go to church and sing for an hour, but it is another matter entirely to live day in and day out praising the Lord with our obedience. When we are discouraged, "praise Him" (Psalm 42:5). Praise to God is the antidote for every trouble. When we praise Him, we are worshiping Him by keeping our eyes on Him.

Do not forsake the preparation of the heart when praising the Lord of Heaven, for He is worthy of genuine praise.

Do you praise God in all things?

_____

_____

A POSTURE OF PRAISE

In God we boast all day long,
And praise Your name forever.
PSALM 44:8

How should we praise? The psalmist tells us to praise Him with an upright heart (Psalm 32:11), to lift up our heads in praise (27:6), to use our tongues to praise His righteousness (35:28), to praise Him in conversation (50:23), to praise Him when we need to wait patiently (52:9), and to pray continually with praise (72:15).

Scripture tells us to direct our praise upward, not inward. Paul in particular tells us that a changed heart seeks praise from God, not from people (Romans 2:29). We all need to be reminded of this important truth: if we are seeking approval and praise from others, we do not have our minds on Christ and His glory.

In good times and troubled times, praise the Lord for His promise that He will never leave or forsake us. This is the key to enduring trials and temptations—with every breath, praise the Lord.

Are you directing your praise upward or inward?

_____

_____

ETERNAL PRAISE

Therefore by Him let us continually offer the sacrifice of praise to God.

HEBREWS 13:15

Peter referred to praise with eternity in mind: "praise ... at the revelation of Jesus Christ" (1 Peter 1:7), praise "of Him who called you out of darkness into His marvelous light" (2:9), and glorifying God "through Jesus Christ" with praise "forever" (4:11).

Throughout Scripture we see people of God who praised Him in the face of death, and unto death, as they each died as martyrs for the sake of and the eternal praise of Jesus Christ.

What will praise sound like in Heaven eternal? We will no longer sing praises in the midst of persecution, despair, or imprisonment, for "He has put a new song in my mouth," a song of praise to God (Psalm 40:3).

We will praise Him in His mighty expanse. We will sing praise to the Most High and praise His power. We will praise Him for His Word. And one day His holy name will be praised by everything that has breath. "The LORD shall reign forever ... praise the LORD!" (Psalm 146:10).

What will it be like when everything in the world praises the Lord?

_____

_____

WASHED CLEAN

Not having my own righteousness, which is from the law, but that which
is through faith in Christ, the righteousness which is from God by faith.
PHILIPPIANS 3:9

A local bank was robbed, and the thief demanded cash from the teller, but he didn't know that the bag she handed to him contained a dye bomb. It exploded, covering the money, the bag, and his hand. The law judged him because of the irrefutable evidence against him.

Because of sin, we have dye that has blackened our souls, and we can't wash it off. We're left with stains that will be revealed in the judgment. The only cleanser that will wash it pure as snow is the crimson blood of Jesus Christ, which gives believers a righteous standing before God.

When we accept Christ, the spiritual man is made new and given the Holy Spirit to change his nature, causing him to dwell on things that are righteous and holy. The spiritually minded become "partakers of the divine nature" (2 Peter 1:4). This doesn't mean believers never have temptations, but believers are given strength to turn away from them and live in the way that pleases God.

Do you relate to the bank robber with the stain of sin on you, or do you know you're forgiven?

_____

_____

JESUS' POWERFUL BLOOD

You who once were far off have been brought near by the blood of Christ.

EPHESIANS 2:13

The blood of Jesus Christ is the heart of the Gospel, and rightly so. What does the blood of Jesus do for you?

Blood cleanses. When you invite Christ into your life, His blood cleanses you and pumps through your spiritual veins with eternal life (1 John 1:7).

Blood justifies. Paul wrote that Christ "justified [us] by his blood" (Romans 5:8–9 KJV). We are justified—as though we had never sinned.

Blood reconciles. The Father takes pleasure in reconciling man to Himself and bringing "peace through the blood" of His Son's cross (Colossians 1:20).

Blood provides access. Christ's sacrifice replaced the animal sacrifice, no longer sufficient, giving us "full assurance of faith" in the blood that Jesus shed for us (Hebrews 10:19–22) so we now have full access to the Father's throne of grace.

As Jesus' blood flows through us, we are infused with life—forever (John 6:54).

What does the Bible say about the most important characteristic of the blood of Jesus?

_____

_____

THE GOSPEL OF OLD

We know that if our earthly house, this tent, is destroyed, we have a building from God, a house not made with hands, eternal in the heavens.

2 CORINTHIANS 5:1

My wife, Ruth, walked with me along the path of life for sixty-four years. She was the most godly woman I have ever known. She followed Christ along the pathway He marked out for her with grace and dignity, and she smiled through the journey—good or bad. When Ruth was separated from her pain-stricken body, and her earthly construction was complete, she found peace.

My wife loved old things; they represented character and survival. This love for the old made her treasure childhood memories from China. When Ruth died, the family had the Chinese character for righteousness engraved on a very old stone. She had looked forward to the day she would stand before the Lord, having awakened to righteousness.

As Christians we can look forward to standing in the righteousness of Christ because the Good News is the Gospel of old that is from the beginning and will forever endure.

"But the righteous has an everlasting foundation" (Proverbs 10:25).

What does Scripture say about *righteousness?*

SHED FOR ME

*With His own blood He entered the Most Holy Place once
for all, having obtained eternal redemption.*

HEBREWS 9:12

A great preacher by the name of César Malan met a young woman by the name of Charlotte Elliott. He told her that the greatest news he had ever heard was that the blood of Jesus Christ cleansed him from his sin.

Embittered because of ill health, she replied, "I cannot believe in the goodness of God, and I don't need the blood of Jesus Christ to forgive me for anything!"

Malan said, "I didn't mean to be offensive; I only meant to tell you that God loves you and that He has forgiven you at a great cost."

That night she could not sleep because of the preacher's words. She finally went to her knees and asked Christ into her heart. Years later she wrote, "Just as I am, without one plea, but that Thy blood was shed for me."[3]

Believers in Christ have a fabulous future ahead. Thank Jesus Christ now for the gift of His blood and what one eternal sacrifice would mean—eternal life.

Have you had a moment where you could not believe in the goodness of God?

REFLECTING CHRIST IN CHURCH

But you, beloved, building yourselves up on your most holy faith,
praying in the Holy Spirit, keep yourselves in the love of God.
JUDE VV. 20–21

Remembering that Jesus died for the body of Christ—the church—should cause us to examine church programs today and ask if Christ is preeminent. Believers should reflect Christ in every way. What a responsibility. What a privilege!

The church is to be built up on God's Word. Unless the church quickly recovers the authoritative biblical message, we may witness the spectacle of millions of Christians going outside the institutional church to find spiritual food. To some degree this is already happening, and the Bible gives warning (Hebrews 6:4–6).

Many churches now mold their programs around the community—not the Word of God. Church bulletins often reflect this by announcing grand programs and activities with little to no emphasis on God's Word. The Lord did not design the church to cater to people's wishes—the Lord breathed life into the church to learn, proclaim, and live out His truths.

In what ways does your church reflect Jesus?

_____

_____

OUR NEEDS ARE MET

"Do not worry about your life, what you will eat or what you will drink; nor about your body, what you will put on. Is not life more than food and the body more than clothing?"

MATTHEW 6:25

People have two great spiritual needs. The first is forgiveness, which God has made possible by sending His Son into the world to die for our sins. Our second need is goodness, which God also made possible by sending the Holy Spirit to dwell within us. We actually have the glory of the Lord with us in this life because His Spirit abides in us. Do we really comprehend that the Lord of all gives us a taste of His abundant attributes while we are still in these earthly bodies? Do our lives reflect this?

As needy people we ask the Lord for many things: food, clothing, jobs, homes, a spouse, children, and more. Our minds are focused on our physical needs. Instead, Paul prayed that the Holy Spirit will guide us in all truth and wisdom: "I pray that from his glorious, unlimited resources he will empower you with inner strength through his Spirit. Then Christ will make his home in your hearts as you trust in him" (Ephesians 3:16–17 NLT). This is a wonderful promise.

Do you pray for your spiritual needs, your physical needs, or both?

_____

_____

VICTORIOUS TRUTH

And we also bear witness, and you know that our testimony is true.
3 JOHN V. 12

The truth, the whole truth, and nothing but the truth, so help me God" is a familiar oath. It precedes a sworn testimony given by a witness who has made a commitment to speak truth no matter what, or risk the crime of perjury.

In recent years we have seen a great falling away from the truth, and often those who are found to be liars go unpunished. But I want to tell you about "The Truth." He is Jesus Christ, the Son of God and the Savior of the world.

"I tell you the truth" is one of the strongest and most frequently used phrases spoken by Jesus.

Jesus knows the lies of the devil. Listen—Satan always uses some of God's truth in his lies. This is his bait. But Jesus came to destroy the evil lies of Satan, and He patiently waits for His truth to take hold in people's hearts before He returns to strike the last blow on the devil's works. His truth will always win out.

What lies has the devil spoken to you?

_____

_____

November

GLORIFYING CHRIST

"Let your light so shine before men, that they may see your
good works and glorify your Father in heaven."
MATTHEW 5:16

Y ou may ask, "How can we glorify Christ?" By living for Him—trusting, loving, obeying, and serving Him, and relying on the Spirit's power to do it. We cannot glorify Him in the energy of the flesh. Only in the power of the Spirit can we live lives that glorify God, for it is through the Holy Spirit that Christ is glorified in us (Philippians 1:19–20).

Peter is a good example of this. He and John had been arrested for preaching and were brought before the religious leaders. When the leaders saw their boldness, "they marveled. And they realized that they had been with Jesus" (Acts 4:13). What could be more glorious than having "been with Jesus"?

The gospel accounts magnify the glory of Christ, which brings us hope and increases our anticipation of spending eternity with Him. If we do not yearn for God, we either do not possess Christ as our Savior, or we are not feeding our souls with spiritual truth from God's Word. Those who have followed Christ "will appear with Him in glory" (Colossians 3:4).

Do you yearn for God?

_____

_____

SERVING THE SERVANTS

As we have opportunity, let us do good to all, especially
to those who are of the household of faith.

GALATIANS 6:10

There is no more effective witness for Christ than for others to see believers dedicated to Jesus Christ in word and deed in all walks of life.

Believers are called to serve one another. While it is important to reach out to those who do not know the Lord, we must first reach out to those who love Him, encouraging and supporting them as they also serve Christ. Jesus commended those who supported believers and credited their service as though it was done for Him.

"For whoever gives you a cup of water to drink in My name, because you belong to Christ, assuredly, I say to you, he will by no means lose his reward" (Mark 9:41). Many people misunderstand this verse, so it is worth taking a closer look at what Jesus said. Many people believe that true service is only to the lost, but the verse makes it clear that Jesus was commending those who gave to His servants. The household of faith is close to the Lord's heart because it is His body on earth.

Do you give the gift of encouragement?

_____

_____

SERVE LIKE JESUS

"If anyone serves Me, let him follow Me; and where I am, there My servant will be also. If anyone serves Me, him My Father will honor."
JOHN 12:26

The Lord demonstrated the truest service when He willingly left the glories of Heaven to live among men, then die for them. Jesus entered into the arena of human troubles. He wept with people and rejoiced with them in their victories. We must do no less.

Jesus, by His own example, has shown us how to serve. It does not matter what titles or positions we hold. The Bible clearly teaches that we should be servants, and even more emphasis is given to those in leadership positions.

After Jesus washed the disciples' feet, He said, "If I then, your Lord and Teacher, have washed your feet, you also ought to wash one another's feet" (John 13:14). Start where you are. Do the few things in your pathway. Be faithful, and God will give the increase. Christian service, wherever we are, gives us the privilege of being intimately associated with Christ. And the faithful discharging of the responsibilities of true discipleship invokes the approval and favor of God Himself that will have eternal benefits.

What is it like to work for a servant leader?

_____

_____

THE GREAT PHYSICIAN

Today, if you will hear His voice,
Do not harden your hearts.

HEBREWS 3:15

A young man was in danger of losing his life to heart disease. The doctor told him that his only hope of survival was to have a heart transplant, which would require him to change some bad habits. The patient refused, saying that he didn't have the money. With great compassion, the doctor looked at him and said, "We have the donor organ, and I will pay the cost. Please don't refuse."

The young man grabbed hold of the doctor's arm and said, "Why would you do this when I have brought you so much grief and pain, Dad?"

And the physician-father answered, "Because I love you more than my own life."

To have a spiritual change of heart, you must accept what Jesus Christ has done and receive this gift offered in love and sacrifice so that you can live. The Great Physician, Jesus Christ, stepped out of Heaven and into our sin-sick world to perform heart surgery on mankind. This salvation is an act of God, initiated by God and sustained by God.

What does it mean to have a spiritual change of heart?

_____

_____

RECEIVING CHRIST

Whoever calls on the name of the LORD shall be saved.
ROMANS 10:13

A psychiatrist was interviewed and asked, "Why are there so many suicides?" He answered, "People will do just about anything to get rid of their guilt." I want to proclaim that you don't have to take such drastic measures. Jesus Christ has already died in your place to cover your guilt, shame, and sin of every kind. He already knows what is in your heart. He wants you to confess it, renounce it, and then live for Him.

If you will bring these burdens to Him, He will cleanse you, forgive you, and give you a new heart.

People have poured their hearts out with tears because their sins had been discovered. My friend, Jesus is waiting on you, but you have to do the turning. You do have to make a contribution to your salvation—you must receive it. Christ has done the hard part; you only have to make a conscious, deliberate decision to leave sin behind. The act of repentance does not make us worthy to be saved. It only conditions our hearts for receiving the wonderful grace of God.

Do you choose grace?

_____

_____

MADE NEW

"My salvation will be forever."
ISAIAH 51:6

Out of a Christian home came a young man who had no interest in Christ. One day his grandfather died unexpectedly. The boy was terribly shaken. He began to search out all the things his parents and grandparents had taught him, and the truth he found led him to salvation in Jesus Christ. People began to see an enormous change in the boy's behavior, even in his countenance. Someone asked him, "Was it your grandfather's death that changed you?"

"No," the boy said, "it was his life."

What a marvelous testimony to a life in Christ well-lived. The grandfather may have never traveled out of his neighborhood, but he lived the Gospel before those in his world.

We have a Father in Heaven who sent His Son to a rebellious and unbelieving world. It is not easy to bend our stubborn wills to receive His salvation. But once we do, instead of the stress and tension of a life out of harmony with God, the serenity of reconciliation will make you a new person.

Who can you be an example to?

_____

_____

THE STORM HAS PASSED

"Be faithful until death, and I will give you the crown of life."
REVELATION 2:10

Crossing the North Atlantic years ago, I looked out my porthole and saw the blackest cloud I had ever seen. Certain that we were in for a terrible storm, I asked the steward about it. He said, "Oh, we've already come through it. The storm is behind us."

When we receive salvation, we are forgiven—the storm is behind us. So why, then, does the Bible say believers will appear before the judgment seat of Christ? "We must all appear before the judgment seat of Christ, that each one may receive the things done in the body . . . whether good or bad" (2 Corinthians 5:10). The Lord will judge the living and the dead and will reward the redeemed for how we lived our lives in His name.

He will crown Old Testament saints and martyrs who died for His Word and His name, and He will crown the church for faithfulness to Him. When will this happen? When we stand before the Lord for His evaluation—not for condemnation of sin, for the storm of judgment has passed. This is a wonderful eternal promise for believers.

Are you assured or afraid to stand before the judgment seat of Christ?

_____

_____

HIS WORDS MATTER

In Him was life, and the life was the light of men.
JOHN 1:4

Dictators fear the Bible, and for good reason: it inspired Britain's Magna Carta and the United States' Declaration of Independence. While many nations disbelieve the Bible, it still remains the most powerful book ever written because it is the living Book.

There are those who argue this point, but the universe is sustained by the Word of God because it is the definitive Word of the Creator.

God and God's Word are inseparable. A man and his word may be two different things, but eternal God and the eternal Word are the same yesterday, today, and forever. The Bible is a miracle book because it comes from the Miracle Maker.

Most books live a few short years, are put on a shelf, and are often forgotten. But the Holy Bible has been ridiculed, burned, refuted, and trampled on, yet it still goes on forever because it is the living Word of God. "Heaven and earth will pass away, but My words will by no means pass away" (Matthew 24:35). His words matter!

Do you think the Bible will still be a powerful book a thousand years from now?

THE BLESSED WORD

Your word is a lamp to my feet
And a light to my path.
PSALM 119:105

Just as God breathed life into Adam, God breathed life into Scripture. His name and His Word are interchangeable (John 1:1–2).

The writer of Hebrews tells the progression of God's Word coming to the human race: God spoke at various times through the prophets; then God spoke to us by His Son, "upholding all things by the word of His power" (1:3).

God has not promised to bless my thoughts, but He has promised to bless His Word. Faith grows when it is planted in the fertile soil of Scripture. I always considered it a lost day if I did not spend time reading at least a passage in this sacred Book. When my eyesight failed, I was thankful to have committed much of God's Word to memory. The Bible is a mirror that helps us see our sin. As Christians, we have only one authority and one compass—the Word of God—and it will direct our every thought and step if we rely on Him.

What do you gain by daily studying the Word of God?

_____

_____

LIFE FROM THE WORD

"Have you not read in the book of Moses, in the burning bush passage, how God spoke to him, saying, 'I am the God of Abraham, the God of Isaac, and the God of Jacob'? He is not the God of the dead, but the God of the living."

MARK 12:26–27

God enables us to live a spiritual life by "every word that proceeds from the mouth of God" (Matthew 4:4). How does the Word help us?

The Word of God keeps us from sin. "Your word I have hidden in my heart, that I might not sin against You" (Psalm 119:11).

The Word of God guides our actions. "Blessed are all who hear the word of God and put it into practice" (Luke 11:28 NLT).

The Word of God brings rejoicing to our spirits. "God has spoken in His holiness: 'I will rejoice'" (Psalm 108:7).

The Word of God helps us discern the will of God. God the Spirit will never lead us contrary to the Word of God. God will always lead us to do everything that is right because He brought us forth by His own will and His own word (James 1:18).

Which one of the above characteristics of the Word resonates with you?

BLESSED BY THE WORD

I have treasured the words of His mouth
More than my necessary food.

JOB 23:12

The Word of God gives life to everything.

The Word of God nourishes our souls. We are told to desire the pure milk of the Word—it enables us to grow (1 Peter 2:2).

The Word of God is to be obeyed. "But those who obey God's word truly show how completely they love him. That is how we know we are living in him" (1 John 2:5 NLT).

The Word of God provides fellowship with Him. The story is told of a young lady who was given a new novel, but she thought it was the driest thing she'd ever read. Some months later she met a young man and fell in love. His name had seemed familiar to her, and when she picked up the novel again, she discovered that he had written the book. She began reading it again and couldn't put it down.

What made the difference? She had fallen in love with the author. When we fully realize who is speaking to us in the Word, we will look at it differently too.

Do you think of the Bible as a book written by someone you love?

_____

_____

TAUGHT BY THE WORD

Preach the word! Be ready in season and out of season. Convince, rebuke, exhort, with all longsuffering and teaching.

2 TIMOTHY 4:2

*T*he Word of God is the message we preach. The power of the preacher is not in his charisma, his popularity, or even his education; it is in faithfully declaring, "Thus saith the Lord." When I quote Scripture, I know I am quoting the very Word of God. This is why I have always used the phrase "The Bible says." The Spirit of God takes the Word of God and makes the child of God. Through the written Word we discover the living Word—Jesus Christ.

The Word of God brings encouragement. A little boy was silent for a long time, and his mother asked him what he was thinking about. With his head hovering over the pages of the Bible, he answered, "Oh, I'm watching Jesus raise Lazarus from the dead!" How we need to encourage our children to spend time in God's Word. The Bible tells us to "diligently" teach Scripture to our children, to sit and talk with them about it, and then live it in the home (Deuteronomy 6:6–9). This is so important.

How can you share the Bible with younger generations?

_____

_____

Hope from the Word

Lord, to whom shall we go? You have the words of eternal life.
JOHN 6:68

T o love the Word is to love God.
To receive the Word is to receive Jesus.
To believe the Word is to believe Christ.
To preach the Word is to proclaim the Gospel of His Word.

The Word of God gives us assurance for Heaven. I can remember as a young man having times of doubt as to my salvation because I compared my experience to others who had emotional conversions. After studying the Bible, however, I gained assurance of my commitment to Christ, "attaining to all riches of the full assurance of understanding" (Colossians 2:2), because His Word is certain.

The Word of God comforts us in death. "Write: 'Blessed are the dead who die in the Lord' . . . that they may rest from their labors, and their works follow them" (Revelation 14:13).

The Word of God brings hope for the future. "Now I saw heaven opened, and behold, a white horse. And He who sat on him was called Faithful and True. . . . His name is called The Word of God" (Revelation 19:11–13).

Do you love, receive, believe, and preach the Word daily?

_____

_____

TRUTH REVEALS

"He makes His sun rise on the evil and on the good,
and sends rain on the just and on the unjust."
MATTHEW 5:45

God has given every human being the very breath of life. He has given you the beauty of nature. He has given you talent and intelligence. He has given you opportunity. He has sustained you. And He has offered you His love.

All these good things come from Him. This is known as the common grace of God. He also gives you the right to reject Him, though in doing so He retains the right to judge and condemn you to a life forever separated from Him. When that happens, you will know the absolute truth. For the Bible says God's wrath will come to those "who suppress the truth in unrighteousness" (Romans 1:18). We are washed in Christ's blood.

God's courtroom will be arrayed in the light of the truth, just as it was when Jesus was brought to trial and given the opportunity to defend Himself. Pilate asked, "What is truth?" (John 18:38) after Jesus had told him, "Everyone who is of the truth hears My voice" (v. 37).

What is common grace?

_____

_____

TRUTH MATTERS

The truth of the LORD endures forever.
PSALM 117:2

Truth matters. Just because truth is unpopular doesn't mean that it should not be proclaimed.

It is Satan's purpose to steal the seed of truth from your heart by sending distracting and deceptive thoughts. The difference between a Christian and a non-Christian is that though both may have good and evil thoughts, Christ gives His followers discernment and the power to choose the right rather than the wrong. The Holy Spirit takes God's word of truth and ministers to our deepest needs. And the person who discovers truth has a serenity, peace, and certainty that others do not have (James 1:17–18).

Truth is timeless. It does not differ from one age to another, from one people to another, from one geographical location to another. The great all-prevailing Truth stands for time and eternity. And we will see Him in all His glory when He charges from eternity past into eternity present. His name is Faithful and True (Revelation 19:11), and He will reign from the City of Truth (Zechariah 8:3).

What truth do you feel is most under attack in our culture today?

_____

_____

A FRIEND'S ANSWER

He who turns a sinner from the error of his way will save a soul from death.

JAMES 5:20

Believers, take hold of someone who is a step away from the fire of the everlasting flame. People may resent you for caring about their eternal state, but warn them anyway.

So when some say, "It's none of your business," a friend will answer:

If you're drowning, I will not leave you alone. I have the Gospel lifeboat.

If you are starving, I will not leave you alone. I have the Bread of Life.

If you are lost in darkness, I will not leave you alone. I have the light of the Gospel.

If you are sick, I will not leave you alone. I will point you to the Great Physician.

If you are on the wrong road, I will not leave you alone. I will show you the Way.

We must use every opportunity to send out the powerful message of the Gospel.

Have you ever shared the Gospel with someone who is resistant?

OUR FAMILY TREE

Along the bank of the river, on this side and that, will grow all kinds of trees used for food; their leaves will not wither, and their fruit will not fail.
EZEKIEL 47:12

The Bible has a lot to say about trees. I can't help but wonder what went through the mind of Jesus as He worked in the carpenter's shop, filled with varied woods harvested from the forests. We certainly know that He spoke of trees to illustrate truth as He walked the valleys and hills with His disciples. Nearly every biblical writer wrote about the trees. Perhaps this is why Ezekiel described the coming kingdom as a place filled with thriving trees.

This is certainly a picture of the coming King: from the root of Jesse, from the seed of David, whose name is Branch. No wonder Jesus called Himself the true Vine—"I am the vine; you are the branches" (John 15:5 NLT)—for eternal life flows from the vine to the branches. This is Heaven's family tree. No wonder Jesus found strength as He kneeled among the olive trees in the Garden of Gethsemane and prayed.

What will you think of when you set your eyes on a tree today?

_____

_____

LIMITLESS GOD

[God] did this so all the nations of the earth might know that the LORD's hand is powerful, and so you might fear the LORD your God forever.

JOSHUA 4:24 NLT

Forever. That's another word for eternity—the never-ending state. Joshua reminded those in his command that God's power and might will save forever. As he reminded the Israelites, so must we remember that our reverence to almighty God will live forever in His sight, on earth and in Heaven.

The Lord has testified of His own promises to those who trust Him. What is your last will and testament to those whose lives you influence? What will you be remembered for when your days on earth end? If your heart has been captured by Christ and your lips declare that you believe in the Lord's powerful and mighty salvation, you will live in His everlasting presence.

There is no limit to God. There is no limit to God's wisdom. There is no limit to His power. There is no limit to His glory and love for mankind. He saves those who come to Him in their weakness. We don't have to lose in this life; we can choose to win and gain eternity in Heaven. He will empower us to live for Him.

Will you be remembered as someone who loved the Lord?

_____

_____

STAND FOR WHAT'S RIGHT

*In those days there was no king in Israel; everyone did what was right in
his own eyes. . . . The children of Israel did evil in the sight of the LORD.*
JUDGES 21:25; 2:11

Too many people today feel that the old moral standards are useless and
out of date. They believe they ought to be free to make up their own minds
about what is right and wrong, thus doing what is right in their own eyes.

That's where compromise slips in—that little voice that urges you to lighten
up, to give in, whispering that it's okay to go along in insignificant acts. But this
is the voice of temptation that comes from the devil.

You have heard the saying, "The devil is in the details." Well, Solomon wrote
that it is "the little foxes that spoil the vines" (Song of Solomon 2:15). If we do
not pay attention to the little things that distract us, we will find ourselves in
the midst of a big thing that will undo us. We convince ourselves that there is
no such thing as right or wrong, but the Bible tells us otherwise.

Don't settle for defeat when God has called us to victory.

Have you ever had a small distraction grow into something much larger?

_____

_____

MERCIFUL GOD

You are a God of forgiveness, gracious and merciful.
NEHEMIAH 9:17 NLT

We see the ever-present mercies of God demonstrated, even in the days of Queen Esther. Her uncle, Mordecai, had refused to bow to the wickedness of a man in authority over him (Esther 3:2). He and Esther both were willing to put their lives in jeopardy to protect their people. The Lord raised Mordecai up to a place of honor in the kingdom (9:4) for the purpose of keeping His eternal promise to Israel.

God places His people strategically—even in pagan societies—giving them opportunities to be obedient and stand up for the glory of His name. God's Word proves faithful, true, and forever merciful. "His mercy is on those who fear Him from generation to generation" (Luke 1:50).

While we remain earthbound, believers are the most privileged to spread God's message of mercy. Where have you been placed today? Don't be afraid, for God shows mercy to those who fear Him.

Do you feel you have been put in this place for such a time as this?

_____

_____

Living with Dying

Christ has indeed been raised from the dead.
1 Corinthians 15:20 NIV

When I was preaching in Memphis, Tennessee, in 1978, just months after Elvis Presley died, a number of articles were published about death. *Newsweek* even featured a cover story that May titled "Living with Dying."

Man's heart is consumed with the mystery and terror of continued life after death. It is a universal phenomenon. Yet few make the conscious choice of where they will spend eternity, even though it is their choice to make.

When Jesus died on the cross, He conquered death through His resurrection. There is no reason to fear eternity if you place your trust and faith wholly in the eternal One. The Bible tells us that before the beginning of time, God planned to show the grace of Jesus Christ through the Gospel that shows us the way to life and immortality. He holds the keys to death.

Throughout Scripture the Lord spoke through the patriarchs, prophets, and apostles and answered the ancient question from the book of Job: "If a man dies, shall he live again?" (14:14). Yes indeed. God sent His Son to rescue the human race, so we might live eternally with Him.

Where will you spend eternity?

_____

_____

HEIRS TO THE ESTATE

Since we are his children, we are his heirs. In fact, together
with Christ we are heirs of God's glory. But if we are to
share his glory, we must also share his suffering.

ROMANS 8:17 NLT

Kings are confined to living in palaces. Owners of vast properties live behind locked gates. God's Word, however, says that Christ will make us joint heirs in the kingdom of God. And just as God's habitation extends beyond the boundaries of creation, so will ours—without confinement.

He is the Landowner of Heaven, earth, and the whole universe; and He is going to share all of it with His people. No astute accountant could ever calculate the extent of God's estate, for it is priceless and without limit.

But what I do not want you to miss is the door to Heaven (Revelation 4:1). My friend, that door is the Lord Jesus Christ. If you do not open the door to your heart here on earth, you will never be able to walk through the door in Heaven.

Do not miss spending eternity in the "house of the LORD" (Psalm 23:6). The day we step through Heaven's gates, we will be free of the confinements of earth.

What does it mean to be joint heirs with Christ?

LOST AND FOUND

If you seek Him, He will be found by you; but if you
forsake Him, He will cast you off forever.
1 CHRONICLES 28:9

In the mountains of North Carolina, it is not unusual to hear of campers and hikers losing their way along trails that wind through the rugged forests, thick with brush and prone to rock slides. It doesn't take long for people to panic, wondering if they will ever be found.

If you found yourself wandering around in the forest with no food or water, no compass, and no communication device, would you be content to remain lost? If someone suddenly called out your name, would you remain hidden? It's doubtful. You would run toward the sound of the voice.

God is calling lost souls to come to Him. The world is filled with lost and wandering souls. What preparation have you made for your soul? If you stop and listen with your ears and your heart, you will hear God's voice.

Jesus has His hand outstretched, waiting for us. When we start down the road to repentance, He does not cast us off and forsake us. He is there to meet us and welcome us home.

Has the Lord called to you in the wilderness?

_____

_____

GUIDED THROUGH THE NIGHT

To this you were called, because Christ also suffered for us,
leaving us an example, that you should follow His steps.

1 PETER 2:21

There is a stretch of highway going up into the mountains of western North Carolina that has been under construction for many years. The North Carolina Department of Transportation has the monumental task of blasting through boulders and mangled tree roots to carve a smooth pathway into the high country. Vehicles have been caught in rockslides and temporary road closings. Signs flash through the night, "Proceed with Caution," guiding drivers through the winding, twisting maze.

When travelers get to the top of the mountain and see the welcomed sign, "End of Construction," they know they are nearing home.

Life, too, can be a bumpy journey. Detours get us off course, and signs warn us of danger ahead. The destination of the soul is of utmost importance to God, so He offers us daily guidance. He is there, watching every move we make. The question is, are we aware of Him? Can you see the flashing lights ahead? He is leading the way, and we are called to "follow His steps" (1 Peter 2:21).

What will you likely think of the next time you drive through construction?

_____

_____

EVERLASTING LOVE

"I have loved you with an everlasting love."
JEREMIAH 31:3

God's love did not begin at the cross, but in eternity past. Before the world was established, before the time clock of civilization began to move, God's love prevailed.

But not until the Good News of Jesus Christ burst onto the human scene was the word *love* understood on earth with such depth, as God coming down to us in human form, an expression of unmerited love.

If we truly love Christ in return, we will want to please and honor Him by the way we live. Even the thought of hurting Him or bringing disgrace to His name will be abhorrent to us.

The greatest act of love we can ever demonstrate is to tell others about God's love for them in Christ. When Christ's love fills our hearts, it puts selfishness on the run. "We love Him because He first loved us" (1 John 4:19).

The love of God that reaches man, however, can be entirely rejected. God will not force Himself upon anyone. It is our part to believe; it is our part to receive. Nobody else can do it for us.

Can you conceive of a love that existed before time?

_____

_____

RUN THE RIGHT WAY

Let us run with endurance the race that is set before us.

HEBREWS 12:1

The 1929 Rose Bowl had an incredibly talented football player named Roy Riegels, who picked up a fumble and ran sixty-four yards while seventy thousand people cheered him on. He was determined to win the game for the team. Instead, he ran the wrong way to a miserable defeat.

You have to know what you believe and why you believe it before you can know where you are going.

So you ask, "What must I do?" Say yes to Christ. It involves a choice of your intellect. It is a choice of your emotions. It is a choice of your will. It must be a choice of your total personality, yielded to Christ by faith in Him.

You may think because you've been in church all your life that you are on the right road. But that could be untrue if you are there for the wrong reason. Church membership does not save. Good deeds do not save. Only running toward Christ, repenting, and obeying His commands will ensure you're running in the right direction.

What are you running toward?

_____

_____

LOYALTY AND REDEMPTION

Wherever you go, I will go; and wherever you lodge.
RUTH 1:16

The Bible tells the story of Ruth and her mother-in-law, Naomi, who found herself widowed in the foreign land of Moab. Her sons had married Moabites but had both died young, leaving Naomi with two daughters-in-law, Orpah and Ruth. Naomi decided to return home to Israel and tried to persuade the young widows to remain in their homeland and remarry. Orpah did, but Ruth pleaded to go with Naomi, speaking some of the most beautiful words in Scripture: "Wherever you go, I will go."

No in-law story could be as precious as this. What Ruth saw in Naomi drew her to the Lord, and Ruth submitted herself and found security in Him.

I suppose I have always been drawn to this love story because my late wife's name was Ruth. But the story also pulls me in because it is a picture of God's great desire to be loved by His people. The Lord did something very wonderful in Ruth's life and the life of Boaz, Naomi's kinsman, who married Ruth and redeemed her heritage. He became a glorious picture of the eternal Redeemer who was to come.

How is the story of Ruth and Boaz like the picture of Christ and His people?

_____

_____

TRUTH WITHOUT COMPROMISE

O great and awesome God . . . Both my father's house and I
have sinned. We have acted very corruptly against You.

NEHEMIAH 1:5–7

The news came as a terrible shock. "The wall of Jerusalem is . . . broken down, and its gates are burned with fire" (Nehemiah 1:3). That was the report that came to Nehemiah in the land of Persia. He was devastated, and he wanted to return to Jerusalem. So Nehemiah prayed.

It is humbling to read the biblical prayers offered by God's servants, for when they prayed, they assumed responsibility for the people's sins. So Nehemiah rehearsed Israel's cycle of sin and remembered God's faithful mercy to them.

The Persian king, out of admiration for Nehemiah, granted his bold request to return to Jerusalem and rebuild the city wall. Here is an important lesson when we find ourselves among unbelievers, whether in school, at work, or even in the home: we must be a light for God's truth. We must pray that God will grant us favor with those who are watching our lives; that we will stand for the things of God without compromise, and perhaps the Lord will give us opportunities to demonstrate His power, love, and mercy.

When have you been the only Christian among unbelievers?

_____

_____

REMEMBRANCE

Remember the former things of old.
ISAIAH 46:9

S omeone once said, "The gift of old age is remembrance." While that may sound dreadful to some, reflection is biblical:

"Remember all the way which the LORD your God has led" (Deuteronomy 8:2 NASB).

"Remember and do all My commandments" (Numbers 15:40).

"Remember the word . . . of the LORD" (Joshua 1:13).

"Remember His marvelous works which He has done" (1 Chronicles 16:12).

These are remembrances worth recalling time and again. And there is great comfort available when we remember Him.

Not only does the Lord instruct us to remember, but the Bible reveals what the Lord Himself remembers—and what He chooses not to remember. "He remembers that we are dust" (Psalm 103:14); and to those who are repentant He says, "Their sin I will remember no more" (Jeremiah 31:34). I am so glad I can remember that promise. Because I have repented of my sin, God chooses to forget my sin. This is a glimpse into the heart of our Savior.

Can humans ever truly forget sin as the heavenly Father can?

_____

_____

EVERLASTING TRUTH

But know this, that in the last days perilous times will come:
For men will be lovers of themselves . . . always learning and
never able to come to the knowledge of the truth.

2 TIMOTHY 3:1–7

Buddha said, at the end of his life, "I am still searching for truth." This statement could be made by countless scientists, philosophers, and religious leaders throughout history. However, only Jesus Christ made the astonishing claim: "*I am . . . the truth*" (John 14:6).

Sir Isaac Newton wrote before his death, "I do not know what I may appear to the world, but to myself I seem to have been only like a little boy playing on the seashore, and diverting myself now and then in finding a smoother pebble or a prettier shell than ordinary, whilst the great ocean of truth lay all undiscovered before me."[1]

This "great ocean of truth" is the Word of God. It delivers up the human condition but does not leave us out in the waves to drown—unless we so choose. Seek God's truth, and you will find Him.

Do you identify with Sir Isaac Newton and his pretty shells?

_____

_____

December

JESUS, AGENT OF CHANGE

"Behold, I will do a new thing."
ISAIAH 43:19

Harvard graduate and Pulitzer Prize–winning columnist Walter Lippmann once stated: "For us all the world is disorderly and dangerous, ungoverned and apparently ungovernable."[1] Lippmann died in 1974, but his words still seem apt. Who alone can overcome the danger of evil and restore order? Who alone can govern the world?

The answer will come out of Heaven on the clouds of glory when the Holy One steps out from the throne room of Heaven and brings victorious change to this weary and wicked world. The God of hope will speak the Word, sending His Son once more from Heaven to earth; for this is the fulfillment of His whole Word to the whole world. He is the only Change Agent who transforms man's nature by changing his source of hope. But only those who have acknowledged this truth and accepted it will recognize Him on the great day that He comes again.

Who is this Man of hope? His name is Jesus Christ. Hope rests in God's Son alone, not in the affairs or the change agents of this world.

Are you confident that you will recognize Jesus when He comes again?

_____

_____

MORE THAN A SUPERHERO

"They will see the Son of Man coming in the clouds with great power and glory."
MARK 13:26

The Bible tells us that Jesus is coming back in great glory. Are you expecting Him?

He is not a caped crusader—He is the crucified Christ. He is not a legend—He is Lord. He isn't created by fantasy—He is favored by God. He is not an icon—He is the Intercessor. He is not a force—He is the Forgiver. He is not imaginary—He is infallible. He does not vanish into exile—He redeems to the end. He is not a virtual winner—He is the Victor. He does not resemble hope—He is the resurrection of Hope. He is not a revolutionary—He is the Righteous Ruler. He is not a knight in hiding—He is the coming King.

The Bible speaks the truth about the dark side of human nature and the dark future of those who refuse God's offer of salvation. I would not be honest with you if I just told you the happy ending. The truth is that there will be a glorious ending; but we must heed the Bible's warning of final judgment and prepare to meet God.

How can your life have a happy ending?

_____

_____

MEETING THE KING

Prepare to meet your God.
AMOS 4:12

If you were given the opportunity to meet a king, would you refuse the invitation out of fear? Or would you rush to put on your finest garment and wait patiently for an audience with royalty? The answer is found in whether you are received by the king as his ally or his rival. If you have obeyed the king, you will anticipate being in his presence. If you know that you have come against the king, you will be in terror of standing before him.

We see the world kicking God out of education, government, marriages, the home, and even church. Yet when terror strikes, people clasp their hands and bend their knees, calling on God to meet them in their time of distress, asking Him to lift their burden, begging for a different outcome.

Don't wait for tragedy to strike before you turn to Him. He is waiting for you to come to Him now. Don't wait for the day of doom—it will be too late. When you come to Him, you must remain with Him.

Those who have received Him should anticipate the moment of His return with thrilling wonder.

Have you turned to Jesus?

_____

_____

PREPARE FOR THE KING

Blessed are all those who wait for Him.
ISAIAH 30:18

The late Dr. S. M. Lockridge recorded a video tribute to Jesus Christ, the King of kings. It is worth seeing. This remarkable bit of preaching was combined with images, and the resulting video went viral on YouTube. It beautifully captures the enthusiasm of those who *know* Jesus is coming again. I love what he said. "Do you know Him? . . . You can't outlive Him, and you can't live without Him. . . . That's my King!"[2]

Christ's coming again is mentioned all through Scripture. We are told that the world will one day acknowledge that Jesus Christ is Lord (Philippians 2:10–11), that Jesus will sit on the throne (Luke 1:32), and that there will be universal joy among the redeemed (Isaiah 51:11).

What can we do to prepare for this great day? Believe in Him who makes your salvation sure. Rest in hope that He is purifying you (1 John 3:3). Desire His imminent return. Wait patiently for the promise to be fulfilled (Hebrews 11:9–10). Watch in faith for His coming again (Hebrews 11:13). Look for this blessed hope (Titus 2:13).

How patiently are you waiting for Christ's return?

READY FOR ETERNITY

Continue earnestly in prayer, being vigilant in it with thanksgiving.
COLOSSIANS 4:2

The Bible sounds the alarm and warns mankind to prepare for eternity. The Bible also predicts a fabulous future for those who trust in Him. The second coming of Christ will be so revolutionary that it will change every aspect of life on this planet. Christ will reign in righteousness. Disease will be eliminated. Death will be abolished. War will be eradicated. Nature will be transformed. Men, women, and children will live as life was originally designed, in fellowship with God and each other.

Does this give you hope for real change? If not, I urge you to examine where you stand before the God of judgment, but with the certain hope that He is the same God of peace.

Someone once observed that there are three days a week that we have no control over—yesterday, today, and tomorrow. We only have this moment in time to prepare for eternity. For those who delay, why do you wait? If you think you can clean up your past to make preparation feasible, your efforts are futile. You can't change your past, but you can change your future.

How often do you find yourself trying to clean up your past?

RESCUED

"I say these things that you may be saved."

JOHN 5:34

It was a privilege to know the late president Ronald Reagan. We talked many times about his brush with death in 1981 when he survived an assassination attempt. He considered himself forever indebted to those who took bullets for him. He was candid about his own mortality and told his son Michael, "I believe God spared me for a purpose. I want you to know that I've made a decision to recommit the rest of my life, and the rest of my presidency, to God."[3]

But even if we are saved from such experiences, we will eventually find ourselves facing other threats, whether an incurable disease, a fatal accident, or something as natural as growing old and wearing out from progression of the cycle of life.

No other human being, no matter how selfless or brave, can rescue us from the certainty of death. But that doesn't mean we can't be saved, that we have no hope of rescue. It just means we need to be clear about Who really saves us. Only Jesus can give us unwavering assurance of being saved for eternity.

Who is your ultimate rescuer in this life?

_____

_____

357

BELONG TO GOD

You are all sons of light and sons of the day. We are not of the night nor of darkness. . . . But let us who are of the day be sober, putting on the breastplate of faith and love, and as a helmet the hope of salvation.
1 THESSALONIANS 5:5, 8

Visiting with the president of Harvard University, I asked him, "What appears to be the thing that young people are looking for the most?"

Without hesitation he answered, "They want to belong."

How coincidental that Facebook, a twenty-first-century phenomenon, was conceived and given birth at Harvard. This social media networking website tapped into the deepest of human need—to belong. In October 2012, *Forbes* reported Facebook had topped a billion users—one out of every seven people on planet Earth.[4] One blogger stated that people's obsession with Facebook lies in the "innate human drive for social acceptance," which is "as old as human history."[5]

The human race has always been on a quest for truth and acceptance, yet men and women must accept the One who is the truth. Jesus Christ extends His long arm of salvation to all.

Should more time be spent daily on social media or with the Lord?

_____

_____

THE DEMANDS OF CHRIST

"If anyone loves Me, he will keep My word; and My Father will love him, and We will come to him and make Our home with him."

JOHN 14:23

A religion designed to reflect one's personal desire is contrary to having a personal relationship with God, who puts within His true follower His desires.

The Gospel of Jesus Christ has been watered down to a myth, causing young and old to doubt the authority of Scripture. Why is this? Society is doing a good job of convincing the world that Jesus has no power to judge sin.

Some believe that following His example of doing good to others is what empowers us to be good. Our world does not object to this kind of Christianity—content to have only a social Christ. But the world does object to a living Christ, a risen Christ who is all-knowing and all-powerful, because it doesn't want to meet the moral conditions that Jesus Christ demands. May we never try to rationalize away the fullness of Christ, which includes His resurrection and His demand that those who follow Him live in obedience to His Word.

What kind of world would there be if everyone believed in Christ?

BELONGING IN A DESIGNER WORLD

If we live, we live to the Lord; and if we die, we die to the Lord.
Therefore, whether we live or die, we are the Lord's.
ROMANS 14:8

Actor James Caan rightly pointed out that "a sense of belonging is a big thing today."[6] Yet we live in a cyberspace world, where many people feel more at ease staring into a screen than into human eyes, much less into "the eyes of the LORD [that] search the whole earth" (2 Chronicles 16:9 NLT).

Many are searching for God but in all the wrong places. Many are in distress, refusing to submit to God who created them, exchanging God's standard for alternative lifestyles and spiritualities of their own design that are not ordained by God, who is the very source of life.

One day we will meet God on His terms, on His turf, and in His way. We will behold the nail-scarred hands of God's Son that bear the marks of our sin, and only those who are His will be welcomed in. So we must turn from the designer world of futility and toward "the Way" of faith (Acts 24:14), the eternal world that God has designed for all who live according to His truth.

Is wanting to belong a good thing or a bad thing?

_____

_____

SOUL CARE

May the God of peace Himself sanctify you completely . . .
your whole spirit, soul, and body.
1 THESSALONIANS 5:23

The world would have us believe that we do not have souls or that we are our own gods. The *Huffington Post*'s article on "25 Ways to Feed Your Soul"[7] was really all about pampering self. Yet the world applauds the poets who have written about searching the soul and artists who have attempted to depict the depth of the soul.

Writer Douglas Coupland tapped into our cultural soul-confusion in a poignant line by a character in his novel *The Gum Thief*: "I don't deserve a soul, yet I still have one. I know because it hurts."[8] So many men, women, and children in our society know that ache. How I hope they hear the message that can bring comfort: God sanctifies the soul.

Tormented poet Sylvia Plath famously wrote that she was terrified by a "dark thing" inside her.[9] When the soul is separated from the God who made it, the soul is indeed dark. But Jesus said, "I am the light of the world. He who follows Me shall not walk in darkness, but have the light of life" (John 8:12).

Does your soul hurt?

_____

_____

A MATCH FOR THE SOUL

The eyes of all look expectantly to You, and You give them their food in due season. You open Your hand and satisfy the desire of every living thing.
PSALM 145:15–16

Matchmaking has become a booming business. Online services promise to bring light into your life by matching you up with someone just right for you.

Since the subject of the soul has a prominent place in our thinking, may I ask: Have you found the *sole* source of the real kind of love that can bring light into your life? Salvation in Jesus Christ is the only hope for your soul. Only He can illumine the dark corners of your life and give you soul satisfaction. You can continue searching for love, but your search will never come to a satisfying end. Or you can commit your life completely to the Lord, who brings true and lasting fulfillment to the human soul who sincerely seeks Him in truth.

You can belong to the Giver of life who saves souls from the weariness of manmade religion. You can have a personal relationship with Jesus Christ. That's what it means to be a Christian. Have you humbled yourself before Him?

Who is the only source of the love you need in your life?

PEACE FOR THE SOUL

"I will never leave you nor forsake you."
HEBREWS 13:5

You can belong to the Giver of life who saves souls from the weariness of manmade religion. You can have a personal relationship with Jesus Christ. That's what it means to be a Christian. Have you humbled yourself before Him?

Perhaps your answer is, "I think so." That answer will not bring peace to your soul. Nor will it enable you to walk in the power of knowing that Jesus Christ lives within you through His Holy Spirit, guiding you through the trials and tribulations of life that will surely come.

How does this happen? Christ indwells His followers by giving the gift of His Holy Spirit. He will not muscle His way in; you must invite Him in, accept His gift, knowing that He will never leave. The Holy Spirit then becomes your constant companion, a lifetime resident, One who will "never leave you nor forsake you" (Hebrews 13:5). He gives you the power to begin thinking new thoughts and behaving in ways that please Him—not yourself.

That is what it means to invite Jesus into your life.

What does it mean to humble yourself before the Lord?

_____

_____

BORN TO CRAWL, REBORN TO FLY

For you have been born again.
1 PETER 1:23 NIV

Who would ever look at a caterpillar inching on its belly in the dirt and think that within a short time it would be transformed into a flying wonder?

When it is time for the caterpillar to transform, it attaches itself firmly to a stem or branch and forms a chrysalis or spins a cocoon for protection. Then it waits—usually for months. From a slithering and destructive insect emerges a magnificent creature, feeding on the sweet nectar of the flowers. The beauty the butterfly adds to nature is intriguing as their wings absorb, reflect, and scatter light. The caterpillar is born to crawl, but it is reborn to fly. What a picture from God's creation.

The ancient Greek word for butterfly is *psyche*, meaning the very life of the soul. The caterpillar's transformation is a wonderfully symbolic picture of the miracle work of Christ in transforming a lost soul into a vibrant believer. The metamorphosis is a recurring miracle that He masterfully accomplishes in those who entrust their lives to the One who does His transforming work.

How has Jesus transformed you?

_____

_____

TAKING UP THE CROSS

"He who does not take his cross and follow after Me is not worthy of Me. He who finds his life will lose it, and he who loses his life for My sake will find it."

MATTHEW 10:38–39

Does someone become part of their country's military force by just saying they are? No, they join up, knowing that it may cost them their life. Before you ever put on a uniform, you must swear an oath, undergo extreme training, and submit yourself to superiors. The wonderful thing about Christianity is that when God's grace saves, God's Spirit moves in and makes the changes possible. Love for the world is replaced with love for God and the things that please Him.

You may listen to many voices that tell you what it means to be a Christian, but Jesus said, "He who loses his life for My sake will find it."

These are hard words, aren't they? The crowds who followed Jesus thought they were hard as well. But taking up His cross means to identify with the suffering of Jesus and accept His lordship. This is the glory of the cross.

What cross do you carry?

_____

_____

EVERYDAY FAITH

But we are not of those who draw back . . . but of
those who believe to the saving of the soul.
HEBREWS 10:39

B ecoming a Christian is more than making a decision to live a better life or to attend church more regularly. When we receive Jesus as Lord and Savior, something happens supernaturally. Christ comes to dwell in our hearts and gives us His own supernatural life—eternal life. But it is a mistake to imagine that from then on we are automatically and almost magically victorious over sin and doubt. Not so!

Each day we must have the same trust we experienced when we first came to know Christ. This is made possible by the fact that He becomes the predominant Person in our life and empowers us to think differently, to walk in truth, and to follow an upright path.

We cannot do this in our own power. It comes only when we receive Him as the Lord and Master of our lives. This is what it means to be a Christian—everyday faith, trusting Him every moment. Each day we renew our faith in God's assurance that He will give us the faith to follow Him.

Do you have everyday faith?

_____

_____

CHRIST CHANGES US

*If Christ is in you, the body is dead because of sin, but
the Spirit is life because of righteousness.*
ROMANS 8:10

Many people who think about becoming Christians ask, "What's in it for me? How can I benefit?" If the answer is only to keep you from Hell, you haven't considered the cost of living for Christ on earth.

The right question is not, "What's in it for me?" but rather, "Is Christ in me?" It means the Lord Jesus Christ will come into your life and reform, conform, and transform you into an obedient follower.

Most people are not willing to take their hands off their lives to that extent. But this is Christ's offer. When you acknowledge your sin and ask His forgiveness, He cleanses you from the sin that has entangled you and kept you estranged from Him. For Him to save you and then leave you to clean up your life would be impossible. So the Lord Jesus moves in and takes up residence in your life. God does not expect you to transform yourself before coming to Him in repentance. He calls you to Himself just as you are, but rest assured, things are going to change.

When you hear, "Things are going to change," does it make you afraid?

_____

_____

THE COMING KING

"Behold, the days are coming," says the LORD, *"that I will raise to David a Branch of righteousness; a King shall reign and prosper, and execute judgment and righteousness in the earth."*
JEREMIAH 23:5

David's life is a glimpse of the coming King. David was not only a shepherd boy; he was also a prophet and king. He knew that one day his descendant—and Savior—Jesus, born in the City of David, would ascend to the throne in the city of His God: Jerusalem. This is a tremendous vision of glory. It is not a dream or fantasy but the very reality of hope (Acts 2:25–31).

Jesus came as a prophet (Luke 4:24). Jesus is our Good Shepherd (John 10:11). And Jesus will come back as King (Revelation 17:14). The King of glory and the kingdom of God will rule the nations of the world. His kingdom is already being built up in the hearts of those who submit, surrender, and serve the King of kings in the kingdom of the ages, and we will worship Him on His everlasting throne. "Blessed be the LORD God of Israel from everlasting to everlasting!" (Psalm 41:13).

Do you think of Jesus more as your Shepherd or your King?

_____

_____

THE GREATEST MESSAGE

There is hope for a tree,
If it is cut down, that it will sprout again,
And that its tender shoots will not cease.

JOB 14:7

There is no greater sermon than what is found in Isaiah. He prophesied the tremendous life of the Lord Jesus Christ.

The Babe would be named Immanuel, God with us (Isaiah 7:14). Jesus was born among His very creation, and it isn't hard to imagine the animals bowing in reverence as they welcomed the Child who would be King into the world.

Isaiah wrote, "For He shall grow up . . . as a tender plant, and as a root out of dry ground. . . . He was wounded for our transgressions" (53:2–5).

And He died with a crown of thorns piercing His brow.

The world thought they had conquered the King of the Jews when they crucified Him, but Peter wrote that while Jesus bore our sins in His own body "on the tree" (1 Peter 2:24), the seed would live again—and He did.

The message of Christ's birth and coming return thrills the heart.

How can you know that God is with you?

_____

_____

HIS NAME IS THE BRANCH

There shall come forth a Rod from the stem of Jesse,
And a Branch shall grow out of his roots.

ISAIAH 11:1

No wonder He was a Carpenter. Cradled in a manger made of wood, He brought Christmas joy to the world at His birth. He is Jesus.

Nailed to an old rugged cross and lifted up to die for sin, He brought Easter glory to the world by His resurrection. He is the Savior.

Coming again as the Branch of righteousness, He will bring an everlasting kingdom and will reign in power. Behold! His name is the Branch.

Why Branch? At the time of Jesus' birth, the royal line of David—from which He came—had dried up in Israel. But He would still be King, for Branch is a title for Messiah and speaks of fruitfulness.

It is hard to grasp that a King would serve, but this is no ordinary king. This is Jesus, whose Father proclaimed, "I am bringing forth My Servant the Branch." He will be gloriously crowned. He will sit on His righteous throne and "from His place He shall branch out" (Zechariah 6:12)—to serve.

How will He serve? He will harvest His bounty—souls to fill Heaven.

Why is Jesus called "Branch"?

_____

_____

FUTURE PEACE

For unto us a Child is born, unto us a Son is given; and the government will be upon His shoulder. And His name will be called . . . Prince of Peace.

ISAIAH 9:6

A time is coming when the whole world will be at peace—it is a promise from God. But if we do not understand true peace, we open ourselves up to deceit. One day a deceiver will appear on the world's stage and proclaim that he will bring peace to the world. Those who follow him will go down with him.

An FBI agent once told my wife, "We spot counterfeits by studying the real thing." Likewise, how do we spot deceivers? By knowing the One who is real. Genuine truth will arrest the fraud.

Peace will not come to the earth until the Prince of Peace returns.

And He is coming. One of these days the sky is going to break open, and the Lord will come back and bring His wonderful peace.

Imagine! There has been no world peace since Cain murdered Abel. But God has not left us in hopeless despair. He sent the Lord Jesus, the Savior, who is the hope of peace.

Have you studied the real Christ enough to know a counterfeit?

GIFTS NEVER REDEEMED

Thanks be to God for His indescribable gift!
2 CORINTHIANS 9:15

You might be shocked to learn that Americans are sitting on thirty billion dollars in unused gift cards—gifts never redeemed![10] Numerous laws govern the booming gift-card business, and customers are often warned to check the issuer's redemption policy. Some cards must be redeemed by an expiration date. One online store specifies that to redeem a gift card for certain items, holders "must save the Gift Card . . . to [their] account."[11] Who would think that there would be so many strings attached to redeeming a gift? Yet the industry still seems to be flourishing.

Redemption is a word filled with hope and promise and involves a giver and a receiver. A gift is based on another's sacrifice and is rarely shunned by the one to whom it is offered. Would you say "no thanks" to someone who offered you a gift? Actually, some do. The choice is ours to receive it with thanks or turn our backs, rejecting the gift and the giver.

More valuable than any financial redemption is the hope of a redeemed life. Accept the Giver, Jesus Christ, who offers the great gift of salvation.

Have you redeemed the "gift card" of salvation?

_____

_____

HIS BIRTH WAS NOT THE BEGINNING

Who is the image of the invisible God, the firstborn of every creature: For by him were all things created, that are in heaven, and that are in earth.

COLOSSIANS 1:15–16 KJV

Who is God's Son, Jesus Christ? He is coequal with God the Father. He was not *a* Son of God but *the* Son of God. He is the Eternal Son of God—the Second Person of the Holy Trinity, God manifested in the flesh.

The Bible teaches that Jesus Christ had no beginning. He was never created. The Bible teaches that the heavens were created by Him (John 1:1–3). All the myriads of stars and flaming suns were created by Him. The earth was flung from His flaming fingertip. The birth of Jesus Christ that we celebrate at Christmastime was not His beginning. His origin is shrouded in the same mystery that baffles us when we inquire into the beginning of God. The Bible only tells us, "In the beginning was the Word, and the Word was with God, and the Word was God" (John 1:1).

The entire universe would smash into billions of atoms were it not for the cohesive power of Jesus Christ. Let us remember His great power when we celebrate His birth.

Why is it hard for us to comprehend Jesus was there in the beginning?

_____

_____

DEFINING HISTORY

Do not be afraid to take to you Mary your wife, for that which is conceived in her is of the Holy Spirit. And she will bring forth a Son, and you shall call His name JESUS, for He will save His people from their sins.
MATTHEW 1:20–21

Television and radio host Larry King was once asked what historical figure he would most want to interview. His answer? Jesus. "I would like to ask Him if He was indeed virgin-born. The answer to that question would define history for me."[12]

My response is always that Jesus *was* virgin born because the Bible says so. The angel appeared to Joseph and told him Mary would give birth to the Savior.

The virgin birth is a stumbling block for many because they refuse to believe God's Word—the Bible—as evidence. You cannot believe in someone if you do not believe their words.

Many people do not believe that Jesus ever existed, much less died and rose again, yet the calendar uses the birth of Jesus as the central point of time. Why? Because He came to earth, He died and rose again, and He is coming back. Jesus *has* defined history, giving hope for our tomorrows.

What would you ask Jesus if you were interviewing Him?

_____

_____

MAKE ROOM

She gave birth to her firstborn son; and she wrapped Him in cloths, and laid Him in a manger, because there was no room for them in the inn.

LUKE 2:7 NASB

Jesus is bigger than life, so when He comes into yours, there is no room for anything that does not glorify Him. When Jesus came to earth as a baby, there was no room in the inn. And people today still refuse to make room for Him in their hearts.

What about you? Will you make room for Him?

You cannot offer Him a stool in the corner of your heart. When He comes into your life, it is because you have set yourself aside as you stand in His presence. In doing so, He will sit on the throne of your life and teach you His truth, and His Spirit will transform your spirit. He becomes the center of life for the Christian, where the mind, heart, soul, and body are focused on the glory of Christ.

Are you willing? He seeks and saves those who are lost in sin (Luke 19:10). They exchange living in sin for living in Christ. Do you hear His voice?

Is there room at your inn for Jesus?

_____

_____

CHRIST HAS COME

*He is the image of the invisible God. . . . For in Him all
the fullness of Deity dwells in bodily form.*
COLOSSIANS 1:15; 2:9 NASB

Jesus Christ wasn't just a great religious teacher who walked on earth some two thousand years ago. The Bible says He was far more than that: He was God in human flesh. This is what we celebrate every Christmas—and this is what we should celebrate every day of our lives. The Bible tells us that on that first Christmas, God did something you and I can barely imagine: He came down from Heaven and became a man.

Do you want to know what God is like? Look at Jesus. The proof of His resurrection from the dead confirmed not only His victory over sin and death and Satan and Hell but also the truth of His divine nature. His teachings aren't just the musings of a profound philosopher or religious teacher; they are God's message to us. His deeds of mercy weren't just the actions of a particularly compassionate individual; they were a demonstration of God's love and concern for each one of us. Jesus gives us every reason to build our lives on Him.

Is it difficult to reconcile your images of God and Jesus?

_____

_____

GOD STEPPED DOWN

We are of good courage, I say, and prefer rather to be absent
from the body and to be at home with the Lord.

2 CORINTHIANS 5:8 NASB

During World War II, a mother took her son every day into the bedroom, where hung a large portrait of the boy's father. They would stand and gaze at the image of a man who was fighting for freedom. One day the boy looked up and said, "Mama, wouldn't it be great if Dad could just step down out of the frame?"

For centuries mankind has looked into the heavens to see if God would step out of the frame. At Bethlehem, two thousand years ago, He did. He is God incarnate. And in His coming, He changed everything we knew about death.

After Christ rose from the grave, the apostles began expressing the death of believers in the image frame of being "home with the Lord" (2 Corinthians 5:8 NASB). God would not have placed eternity in our hearts unless there was life beyond the grave. For the person who has turned from sin and received Christ as Lord and Savior, death is not the end. For the believer there is hope and future life.

What must it have been like for the Lord to step out of that frame?

_____

_____

THANKFULNESS AND LACK

"Finally," Paul told the Philippians, "whatever things are true . . . noble . . . just . . . pure . . . lovely, whatever things are of good report . . . meditate on these things."

PHILIPPIANS 4:8

When we are discouraged by what we lack, let's remember that many generations before us have been where we are today without the conveniences we enjoy. Most of us no longer have to grow our food, carry water every morning, or travel many miles just to talk to a friend. Instead of being frustrated by technologies, let's be thankful for the time they give us to concentrate on His blessings.

The apostle Paul wrote the marvelous words of hope in Philippians 4:8 to the church in Philippi while he was in prison. His living conditions were crude, yet he wrote a letter to his fellow believers in Christ to spur them on in the faith. He did not allow his imprisonment or his physical limitations to prevent him from encouraging and challenging others to persevere in doing what is right.

The Word of God should fill us with thankful hearts that God Himself has not forsaken us. Are you willing to be used by God regardless of any constraints?

How have you allowed God to use you?

_____

_____

HOPE AND CHANGE

Wait for His Son from heaven, whom He raised from the dead,
even Jesus who delivers us from the wrath to come.

1 THESSALONIANS 1:10

Are we ready for hope and change? Most would say yes. But how can anyone bring about change that will make this world better? I can tell you that no one belonging to the human race is capable. The flaw in human nature is too great. Humanity's lofty ideas at best fall short.

Hope and change according to the world's definitions are not the answers.

God is the source of real change coming to this world. No government can prevent it, no individual can escape it, and those who refuse to embrace its reality will never change its certainty. The end of the world as we know it will take place when Christ returns to earth. It is a doomsday prediction for scoffers who refuse to believe, but it is a glorious prospect for those who know He is coming again, for He alone holds the future in His hands.

Jesus Christ will one day come back in great glory—as King. Are you looking for Him?

> What kind of hope and change will Jesus bring as opposed to what politicians offer?
>
> _____
>
> _____

HEALED WITHIN

Those who are Christ's have crucified the flesh with its passions and desires.
GALATIANS 5:24

When doctors prescribe medication, its purpose is to begin healing the diseased organs and tissue deep inside of us. When Christ grants salvation, He begins a lifetime work deep within the heart. Change begins inwardly and comes to the surface.

It is human nature to desire a quick fix or a miracle pill. Christ's requirements were so demanding that many people refused to go with Him any further. They would go so far, and then they would turn away. That is why He made such a point of telling the crowds who followed Him, "Count the cost . . . count the cost . . . count the cost."

Jesus is saying to you as well: "If you follow Me, that means I become Lord and Master of your life. That means you become My learner, My disciple. And you must do My work by obeying My commands." Those truly seeking salvation surrender it all to Christ, who will forgive and grant the faith to believe in His power to move into their hearts and transform their lives. He will heal them and make them fit for eternal life with Him.

What does it cost you to follow Jesus?

NO REGRETS

"The Son of Man will come in the glory of His Father with His
angels, and then He will reward each according to his works."

MATTHEW 16:27

William Borden, heir to the Borden family fortune, was a young man burdened for lost souls in Asia. A friend wrote to Bill that he was throwing his life away to be a missionary. But Borden wrote in his Bible, "No reserves." Upon graduating from Yale in 1909, he turned down many lucrative job offers and wrote in his Bible, "No retreats." When he finished his graduate work at Princeton, he sailed to Egypt to study Arabic in hopes of working with Muslims. While there he contracted spinal meningitis. Within a month twenty-five-year-old Borden was dead. Many speculated that his death was a waste. In time it was discovered that Borden had written two more words in his Bible beneath his other entries: "No reserves. No retreats. No regrets."[13]

Borden had stored up treasure in Heaven that far exceeded the vast wealth he had given away on earth. Time revealed that his testimony had caused many others to serve God with their lives. Christ Himself "will reward each according to his works."

How can you live today so that you have no regrets at the end of your life?

_____

_____

MAKE PEACE WITH GOD

The day of the Lord will come as a thief in the night, in which the heavens will pass away with a great noise, and the elements will melt with fervent heat; both the earth and the works that are in it will be burned up.
2 PETER 3:10

A television network years ago aired a program called *The Day After*. At the end, it was as if the entire earth was a cemetery littered with corpses. For millions, this picture was a disturbing and traumatic experience.

If imagining such a possible nuclear winter experience caused millions to think of their future, how much more should the fact that however the end may come for them, the real "day after" for those who reject Christ is not this grim oblivion but even worse judgment and eternal Hell, which would make the TV portrayal seem like a picnic in comparison!

But your future does not hinge on the world situation, however grim it might become. It depends on what happened two thousand years ago at the cross and your acceptance or rejection of the Prince of Peace. Make your peace with God today.

Have you made your peace with God?

_____

_____

ABOUT THE AUTHOR

Billy Graham, world-renowned preacher, evangelist, and author, delivered the Gospel message to more people face-to-face than anyone in history and ministered on six continents in more than 185 countries. Millions have read his inspirational classics, including *Angels, Peace with God, The Holy Spirit, Hope for the Troubled Heart, How to Be Born Again, The Journey, Nearing Home,* and *The Reason for My Hope.*

January 1-31

1. Robert J. Morgan, *100 Bible Verses Everyone Should Know by Heart* (Nashville: Broadman & Holman, 2010), 42.
2. Ruth Bell Graham, *Clouds Are the Dust of His Feet* (Wheaton, IL: Crossway Books, 1992), 132.

February 1-29

1. Della McChain Warren, "Jesus Whispers Peace."

March 1-31

1. E. Stanley Jones, *Growing Spiritually* (Nashville: Abingdon, 1953), 313.
2. "Full Text of the Will of J. Pierpont Morgan: Will Executed Jan. 4, 1913—Codicil Executed Jan. 6, 1913—Died March 31, 1913," *New York Times*, April 20, 1913, http://query.nytimes.com/gst/abstract. html?res=FB0813F93A5D13738DDDA90A94DC405B838DF1D3 (accessed June 26, 2011).
3. "Introducing Root Cases," Root Cases LLC, accessed June 23, 2011, www. rootcases.com.

April 1-30

1. Henry F. Lyte, "Abide with Me" (1847).
2. Paul "Bear" Bryant, quoted in Pat Williams and Tommy Ford, *Bear Bryant on Leadership: Life Lessons from a Six-Time National Championship Coach* (Charleston, SC: Advantage, 2010), 147.
3. Illustration taken from conversation between Kristy Villa and Donna Lee Toney, during taping of segment on the Billy Graham Library, September 16, 2011, Lifetime TV, *Balancing Act*, cohost Kristy Villa (stage name) for Olga Villaverde, aired October 21, 2011. Used with permission.

July 1-31

1. Josephus, Jewish Antiquities, 18.3.3, quoted in Gerald Sigal, "Did Flavius Josephus Provide Corroborative Evidence for Christian Claims?" Jews for Judaism, http://www.jewsforjudaism.org/index.php?option=com_content&view=article&id=158:did-flavius-josephus-provides-corroborative-evidence-for-christian-claims&catid=49:trinity&Itemid=501.

2. "Why Are Atheists More Skeptical About Jesus Than They Are About Alexander the Great?," question posted on Ask the Atheists, October 25, 2007, www.asktheatheists.com/questions/114-why-are-atheists-more-skeptical-about-jesus.

August 1-31

1. Quoted in Ken Ham, "The Bible— It's Not Historical'" posted in AnswersinGenesis.org, April 1, 2003, www.answersingenesis.org /articles/au/bible-not-historical.

2. Kenneth Scott Latourette, *A History of Christianity,* vol. 1, *Beginnings to 1500,* rev. ed. (San Francisco: HarperSanFrancisco, 1975), 35, 44.

3. Pat Miller, "Death of a Genius," *Life,* May 2, 1955, 64.

4. Unnamed commenter on "Who Will Save Your Soul? by Jewel," Songfacts, http://www.songfacts.com/detail.php?id=1907.

5. "Who Will Save Your Soul? Lyrics by Jewel," Songfacts Lyrics, http://www.azlyrics.com/lyrics/jewel/whowillsaveyoursoul.html.

6. John Ankerberg and John Weldon, "The Evidence for the Resurrection of Jesus Christ" (PDF article), 5, *Philosophy and Religion,* www.philosophy-religion.org/faith/pdfs/resurrection.pdf.

7. *London Law Journal,* 1874, quoted in Irwin H. Linton, *A Lawyer Examines the Bible: A Defense of the Christian Faith* (San Diego: Creation Life Publishers, 1977), 36.

8. *Testimony of the Evangelists by Simon Greenleaf (1783–1853),* http://law2.umkc.edu/faculty/projects/ftrials/jesus/greenleaf/html, Douglas O. Linder, "The Trial of Jesus: Online Texts & Links," Famous Trials, UMKC School of Law, University of Missouri-Kansas City.

9. Charles Wesley, "Hymn for Easter Day" (1739), quoted in Collin Hansen, "Hymn for Easter Day," Christian History, http://www.christianitytoday.com/ch/news/2005/mar24.html.

10. James Hastings, ed., *The Great Texts of the Bible: Genesis to Numbers* (New York: Charles Scribner's Sons, 1911), 407–8.

September 1-30

1. Admiral Jim Stockdale, quoted in Jim Collins, *Good to Great: Why Some Companies Make the Leap . . . and Others Don't* (New York: Harper Business, 2001), 85.

2. Quoted in Michael Battle, *Practicing Reconciliation in a Violent World* (New York: Morehouse, 2005), 2.

3. "World's Most Expensive Colored Diamonds" (slideshow), *Elle*, November 18, 2011, http://www.elle.com/accessories/bags-shoes-jewelry/worlds-most-expensive-colored-diamonds-610199-10#slide-10.

4. The Hope Diamond, Harry Winston, http://www.harrywinston.com/our-story/hope-diamond.

5. Richard Rorty, *Philosophy and Social Hope* (London: Penguin Books, 1999), 204–8; http://www.answers.com/topic/hope#As_a_literary_concept.

6. Sigmund Freud, *Civilization and Its Discontents*, trans. and ed. James Strachey, Standard Edition (New York: W. W. Norton & Company, 1930), XXI.101.

7. Victor Hugo, *Les Misérables*, tr. Isabel F. Hapgood, chapter 4, on The Literature Network, www.online-literature.com/victor_hugo/les_miserables/43/.

October 1-31

1. HELPS Word-studies, s.v. Strong's NT 1577 (*ekklésia*); Bible Hub, http://biblehub.com/greek/1577.htm.

2. Donald Grey Barnhouse, in Charlie "Tremendous" Jones and Bob Kelly, *The Tremendous Power of Prayer* (West Monroe, LA: Howard, 2000), 66.

3. Charlotte Elliott, "Just As I Am" (music by William B. Bradbury), 1835; Cyberhymnal.org, http://cyberhymnal.org/htm/j/u/justasam.htm.

November 1-30

1. Sir Isaac Newton, quoted in G. W. Curtis, "Education and Local Patriotism," *Readings on American State Government*, ed. Paul Samuel Reinsh, (Boston: Ginn and Company, 1911), 330.

December 1-31

1. Quoted in BJ Penner, "BJ Penner: A Different World" (letter to the editor), *Merced Sun-Star*, http://www.mercedsunstar.com/2012/01/11/2187711/ bj-penner-a-different-world.html.
2. "That's My King," (transcript and video clips), Not Just Notes!, http://www. notjustnotes.ws/thatsmyking.htm; YouTube; Dr. S. M. Lockridge, "Do You Know Him? That's My King."
3. Michael Reagan, "Ronald Reagan at 100: The President, the Pope and the Medicine of Forgiveness," Opinion, Foxnews. com, February 6, 2011, www.foxnews.com/opinion/2011/02/06/ ronald-reagan-president-pope-medicine-forgiveness.
4. Dave Thier, "Facebook Has a Billion Users and a Revenue Question," *Forbes*, October 4, 2012, http://www.forbes.com/sites/davidthier/2012/10/04/ facebook-has-a-billion-users-and-a
       -revenue-question.
5. Jeremy Noonan, "The Quest for Belonging: The Social Network and 'The Inner Ring,'" *Musing and Motion*, March 1, 2011, http://musingandmotion.wordpress. com/2011/03/01/the-quest-for-belonging-the-social-network.
6. Alana Lee, "James Caan *Elf* Interview," BBC Home, November 2003, http:www. bbc.co.uk/films/2003/11/13/james_caan_elf_interview.shtml.
7. Janice Taylor, "25 Ways to Feed Your Soul: Stop the Insanity," The Blog, *Huffpost Healthy Living*, May 18, 2012, http://www.huffingtonpost.com/janice-taylor/ soul-tips_b_1512587.html.
8. Douglas Coupland, *The Gum Thief* (New York: Bloomsbury USA, 2007), 22.

9. Maria Theresa Ib, "Mind Over Myth?: The Divided Self in the Poetry of Sylvia Plath," www.sylviaplath.de/plath/dividedself.html.

10. Daniel Terdiman, "Study: Americans Sitting on $30 billion in Unused Gift Cards," *CNET News*, January 24, 2011, http://news.cnet.com/8301–13772_3–20029410–52.html.

11. "Redeeming a Barnes & Noble Gift Card or eGift Card at Barnes & Noble.com," Barnes & Noble, http://barnesandnoble.com/gc/gc_redeem.asp.

12. "The Virgin Birth of Jesus: Fact of Fable?," Religious Tolerance: Ontario Consultants on Religious Tolerance, www.religioustolerance.org/virgin_b.htm.

13. Howard Culbertson, "No Reserves. No Retreats. No Regrets," Christian Missions (Southern Nazarene University), http://home.snu.edu/~hculbert/regret.htm.